AQUINAS

IN THE

COURTROOM

AQUINAS
IN THE
COURTROOM

Lawyers, Judges, and Judicial Conduct

Charles P. Nemeth

Westport, Connecticut
London

The Library of Congress has cataloged the hardcover edition as follows:

Nemeth, Charles P., 1951–
    Aquinas in the courtroom : lawyers, judges, and judicial conduct / by Charles P. Nemeth.
      p.   cm.—(Contributions in philosophy, ISSN 0084–926X ; no. 82)
    Includes bibliographical references and index.
    ISBN 0-313-31929-4 (alk. paper)
    1. Thomas, Aquinas, Saint, 1225?–1274—Contributions in law. 2. Natural law. 3. Law
and ethics. 4. Law—Philosophy. I. Title. II. Series.
    K447.T45N46 2001
    340'.112—dc21   2001023332

British Library Cataloguing in Publication Data is available.

A hardcover edition of *Aquinas in the Courtroom* is available from
Greenwood Press, an imprint of Greenwood Publishing Group, Inc. (Contributions
in Philosophy, Number 82; ISBN 0-313-31929-4).

Library of Congress Catalog Card Number: 2001023332
ISBN 0-275-97290-9

First published in 2001

Praeger Publishers, 88 Post Road West, Westport, CT 06881
An imprint of Greenwood Publishing Group, Inc.
www.praeger.com

Printed in the United States of America

The paper used in this book complies with the
Permanent Paper Standard issued by the National
Information Standards Organization (Z39.48–1984).

10 9 8 7 6 5 4 3 2 1

To Mary Claire—my youngest daughter
rapidly unfolding—artistic, intellectual, and
pure at heart

To St. Thomas Aquinas—the Angelic Doctor—
timeless, unrivaled, and closest to God

To Justice Clarence Thomas—virtuous,
courageous, and unafraid of the natural law

Contents

Preface

Nothing seems to escape the incredible intellect and imagination of the Angelic Doctor. Whether it is law or limbo, St. Thomas issues a piercing assessment worth our attention. Paraphrasing an early mentor, the departed Dr. Ralph Masiello of Niagara University, St. Thomas just "gets to you, consumes you in such a way that he can only be divinely appointed and anointed." Later, in my studies at Duquesne University under Dr. Roland Ramirez, I witnessed a similar contagion. Whenever he would discuss St. Thomas, he did so gleefully, as if the material was as new as the first day he encountered it. Thomas never gets old or boring. For those willing to critically delve into his philosophy, he overtakes and overwhelms in ways not anticipated. Almost intoxicated by both his method and content, I find it nearly impossible to disregard Thomistic thought when considering any proposition, especially legal, ethical, and moral ones.

After two decades of practicing law and witnessing the decline of a once honorable profession, I became utterly disenchanted with the culture of litigation and legal advocacy. For the most part it had become an amoral wasteland of positive legal punditry where the morality of any particular legal conduct is deemed irrelevant to legal analysis. Aristotelian justice and Ciceronian honor were vanquished from the legal marketplace and replaced by a vapid language of rights, codes, and regulatory shields. The law, by its very existence, was and is legitimate, not because of the ends and goals of its subject matter, but because of its promulgation. Whether the law is right or good has become not a question of justice but of power base, authority, and opinion poll. The law, as traditionally defined, is now disenfranchised.

Being disenfranchised from the law is not a desirable situation for any practitioner or Catholic attempting the moral life. Here St. Thomas comes to the rescue again. His ruminations on law and jurisprudence are an impressive undertaking and quickly evident in most of his chief works. Readily discoverable in his magnificent opus are erudite discourses on every manner of substantive and procedural law, evidentiary analysis, testimonial delivery, matters of proof, burdens and presumptions, judicial and advocate conduct and character, criminal and civil practice standards, sentencing guidelines, and a captivating discussion of what it truly means to be a lawyer or judge. To be sure, Thomas's natural-law thought serves as the underpinning for any legal system worth its salt and delivers a permanency and universality that forges a more dependable jurisprudence than its utilitarian or positivist counterpart. In a way, St. Thomas provides a blueprint for the Catholic lawyer and judge by laying out the professional and ethical parameters that make the actor operate in accordance with reason and, therefore, act morally.

The fundamental purpose of this undertaking is to be a forum for these insights so that lawyers and judges of every ilk and persuasion will have no excuse for ignorance. Aside from this, Thomistic jurisprudence is the wellspring for renewal in a beleaguered justice system whose primary players, lawyers and judges, are in dramatic need of something over and above the status quo. The current state of affairs can no longer be tolerated. Greedy lawyers, corrupt judges, and advocacy tactics that care little for truth or justice promise a bleak future for these professions. The rest of us, especially members of the Bar, admitting our own inadequacies and frailties, cannot sit idly by. Our system is in a squalid state of affairs, and protestations about lawyer jokes from the American Bar Association or other petty umbrage do not cure a hobbled system that has lost its way.

If anything, this study will serve as a starting point for renewal and reexamination of the lawyer and the judge. Being Thomistic assuredly will elevate and improve the legal marketplace, and maybe, just maybe, prompt the type of questions that legal professionals have long avoided. When is a law just? Should the truth be denied to win the advocate's cause? Who is qualified to judge? What characteristics and traits are conducive to being a just lawyer? What is justice? Who is the virtuous person? Can a lawyer or judge perform his or her obligations without virtue? Is the soul of the lawyer and judge to be disregarded? From whence does the law come?

Chapter 1 introduces the legal heritage of Thomas Aquinas. While his thought and philosophy is original in many contexts, there is little question that Thomas listened intently to the lessons of history. Thomistic jurisprudence is an interesting blend of Aristotelian thought, Ciceronian honor, and the theological wisdom of the Church Fathers. Heavily dependent on historical traditions so evident in Western legal thought, Thomas's examination of law often refers to those who preceded him, the likes of Plato, Augustine, Isidore, Abelard, Anselm, Bonaventure, and Albert the Great. Thomas never disregards the importance of these thinkers, but delivers a legal vision bursting with rationality and the hierarchical schema that incorporates the eternal law of God. Thomas's natural-law philosophy is an advanced contribution to the legal dialogue, but the roots of this position are essential to any real understanding.

In Chapter 2, the reader is introduced to Thomas's legal philosophy in the most general sense. How Thomas constructs a series of interlocking and interdependent legal forms, namely the eternal, natural, divine, and human laws, is a brilliant enterprise. Thomistic jurisprudence does nothing in isolation but commences with the *eternal law* of the Creator, the architect of the universe. It then employs the revelatory messages entrenched in the New and Old Testaments and calls this instruction the *divine law*. As God creates, he impresses in creation, particularly the invention of man, a *natural law*, where dispositions, inclinations and rationality dictate the general course of human conduct. Natural law means that only certain ways of carrying out existence are acceptable, and while there may be some differences of opinion regarding the contingent determinations of living, the primary, primordial qualities of the human species operate in an environment of law. To procreate, to self-preserve, to sustain are not optional qualities but the law of our natures. In this way, law is the rule and measure of reason, because reason is the measure that crafts law. *Human law,* so often considered incidental in Thomistic thought, receives equal attention by Thomas. He fully appreciates the stability that human enactments bring to person and culture.

Chapter 3's emphasis on virtue and its relationship to law further reflects Thomas's vision of man. Since the Creator impresses natural qualities on the created, and since reason dictates a series of first principles, it is predictable that Thomas would conclude that the virtuous life is consistent with rationality. The virtuous life is the lawful and moral template for human existence. Hence,

Thomas's analysis of virtue and law, specifically in light of human operations and the common good of a nation, is an integral component of Thomistic jurisprudence.

The connection and commensurateness of law and justice is the central theme of Chapter 4. That a law, to be a law, should be just is indisputable in Thomistic jurisprudence. Defining justice is no easy undertaking, though Thomas's explanation is clear and succinct. Justice is giving each other what is due. Justice is proportionality and balance; justice is the equilibrium between people and their exchanges. As every other virtue, justice rationally represents what is normative for the human agent and the mean sought for interrelationships in an individual or collective sense. Justice is either *distributive*, whereby each earns or is owed what is due according to talents and circumstance, or justice is *commutative*, where the equality of exchange and result occurs. Commutative justice is the penalty for the crime, the price for the product, and the consequence for the action. No individual or nation, let alone a lawyer or judge, can function without justice. Another nuance in Thomas's justice is its legalistic quality, by which individual actions must be measured and adjudged in light of their effects on the common good.

Chapter 5's discussion of prudence continues Thomas's review of the interplay between law and virtue. Prudent actors know what to do and how to do it. It is the virtue of the skilled carpenter or judge and lawyer, who not only intellectualize the law but also put it to its proper effects. The prudent lawyer and judge conceptually master the law and then apply it appropriately.

Chapter 6's coverage is primarily concerned with the nature and definition of the *common good*. Any understanding of Thomistic jurisprudence evaluates collective impacts. Individual rights and adjudications are improper if separated from the communal conscience. Individuals live not as islands but as part of the larger community. Hence, any individualized judgment, even in the form of law or decision, cannot neglect the impact it would have on the commonwealth. Lawyers advocating and judges issuing rulings reference far more than the client or cause. Legal policy and practice demand attentiveness to the social health of the nation and the long-term ramifications of individual decision making. The common good is directed toward virtue, toward the good, and toward the God who fashions citizen and the nation state.

Legal judgments are rational exercises. Chapter 7 delves into the Thomistic concept of judgment. To judge rightly primarily requires an intellectual operation rather than an exclusive exercise of the will. Will poses alternative choices, while reason presents the correct choice to be made. To judge correctly, one must listen to reason's dictate: avoiding evil and doing good. Judgments are satisfactory only when consistent and compatible with reason and the virtuous disposition comportable with reason and the common good. It is *right reason* that manufactures intelligent judgments in law; it is right reason that signifies the sound legal mind.

Chapter 8 continues this bent with its coverage of the judgeship. Thomas's judge is the well-educated public official who insists on evidentiary rigor, demands truth in every context, and requires both case and advocate to adhere to the fundamental tenets of justice and the other virtuous dispositions. Reserved to public authority and separate from the ecclesiastical dimension, the Thomistic judge weighs evidence before legal proclamation, adheres to judicial processes that protect both the client and court, and affords a series of protections to those accused and confronted. Judges are obliged to follow jurisdictional requirements, afford counsel to the accused, and deliver punishment only after considering the individual circumstances of the case before the court.

In Chapter 9, the focus zeroes in on one of the two primary players in the justice system: the lawyer. Whether acting as advocate or counselor at law, Thomistic jurisprudence prescribes a series of professional competencies that are consistent with the moral life. The role of defense and prosecution do not escape Thomas's eye, though function can never replace truth over falsehood in the performance of legal task. Thomas's lawyer is a man or woman of virtue, who aggressively represents the client's interests, who rejects the unmeritorious case, who scoffs at causes of action that lack factual integrity, and who refuses to recognize any human law inconsistent with the eternal, divine, and natural law. Facts, not suspicion, are what guide the advocate; honesty toward client, opposing counsel, and the tribunal is a professional's code of honor.

Chapter 10 reviews the role and purpose of punishment in Thomistic thought. Driven by proportionality, a desire for just equilibrium, and a just version of vengeance, Thomas offers penology of pure consequence. Each form of punishment, no matter how small or draconian, is considered mandatory for a functional and efficacious justice system. Without it, the evil and wicked will multiply, as will their deeds. Of keen interest to many readers will be Thomas's glowing and unreserved support for the imposition of the death penalty. Imprisonment, term and time of incarceration, restitution and fines, and victim involvement in meting out the designated punishment receive close attention from Thomas's cutting mind.

The final chapter of this undertaking argues the relevancy of the Thomistic model. Chapter 11 sets a series of rationales as to why this jurisprudence is our last clear chance. Permanency and immutability characterize Thomas's jurisprudence. Instead of a legal system subject to whim and power, St. Thomas delivers a legal thought that is predictable and uniform in design, that anchors itself in the perennial truths of Western thought, and that delivers ethical and moral instruction to its participants. Thomas's legal ideology is contrasted with contemporary Codes of Judicial Conduct and ethical canons of the American Bar Association. Using the language of actual twentieth-century case law and examining the legal of reasoning of U.S. Supreme Court Justices Antonin Scalia and Clarence Thomas, the chapter shows how natural-law jurisprudence can never really be fully extinguished from the legal landscape. Present debate on abortion, same-sex marriage, sodomy, and reproductive rights surely are influenced by the world of St. Thomas. Our legal system is incapable of completely avoiding a philosophy that incorporates the nature of the human species.

That Thomas's legal philosophy is offered as an alternative to common wisdom is the chief reason for this project. These chapters urgently ask the philosopher and the practitioner to revisit a jurisprudence that stakes its heart and soul in the Divine Exemplar.

This project's existence depends on many worthy and admirable players. From the editorial end, it would have been an impossibility without Hope Haywood. Hope has been with me through thick and thin during many projects and undertakings, but this was her finest hour and achievement. There is simply no way to catalog all the details that make up this text. In some respects, its production was as rich and demanding as the text's subject matter. We are both glad we have reached the end of the road on this project.

At Greenwood Press, my heartfelt thanks go to Gillian Von Beebe former editor at Greenwood, and current editor Suzanne Staszak-Silva for the opportunity to work with such a prestigious press. A work of this type requires a publisher of serious sophistication and a vision to see the wisdom of the idea and plan. Greenwood and Praeger display these traits and more.

Dr. Roland E. Ramirez, a renowned Thomist scholar, was a perpetual source of encouragement during this work. Aside from being a true intellectual, Dr. Ramirez courageously withstands those who find Aquinas passé or irrelevant, and not only defends the brilliance of Thomistic thought but discerns its applicability in contemporary settings. To Dr. Michael Strasser goes similar plaudits. In Dr. Strasser one witnesses a lifetime dedication to the Thomist perspective and the full satisfaction that is derived from such an examination. Even after his retirement, Dr. Strasser yearned for the discussion and analysis Thomas generates. My heartfelt appreciation is delivered to Dr. Robert Madden, who along with his colleagues has committed his life to the search for philosophical truth and the role St. Thomas plays in exposing it. Thanks too are readily given to Dr. Eleanore Holveck whose aid will not be forgotten. At the State University of New York at Brockport, my ongoing gratitude to its president, Dr. Paul Yu; the academic vice president, Dr. Tim Flanagan; and dean, Dr. Joseph Mason. At California University of Pennsylvania, institutional support generously provided by its president, Angelo Armenti; the provost, Curtis Smith; and dean of Liberal Arts, Richard Helldobler. Each of these individuals makes scholarship a rational and rewarding activity.

Finally, family provides both impetus and comfort as I seek to carry out the role of lawyer and academic. My spouse of twenty-nine years, Jean Marie, and the children I have been blessed with, Eleanor, Stephen, Anne Marie, John, Joseph, Mary Claire, and Michael Augustine, provide meaning, actuality, and the "good" St. Thomas so passionately described.

CHAPTER 1

The Nature of Law in the Era of St. Thomas Aquinas

Any serious study and analysis of St. Thomas's jurisprudence cannot avoid his past and his predecessors. St. Thomas, though original and magnificently creative, was still shaped and sculpted by the beliefs of his era, and these same beliefs have their roots in tradition. The fullness of Thomistic thought exudes the brilliance of history, philosophy, and theology, the recognition that truth has been examined by others, and that the nature of law and its impact on person and politics is of universal interest. That Thomas owes a debt to the jurisprudential insights of his philosophical ancestry is without question. Many perceive Thomas's enterprise as a Christian continuation and modification of the Hellenic and Roman ideals. This view, while laudable, fails to capture the mettle of Thomas's intellect.

Going harder and faster than his predecessors, St. Thomas will engage the Augustinian precept on will and substitute reason as the rule and measure of all human activity, including law. Supreme rationality rather than the will of Anselm, Bonaventure, and Duns Scotus will be the shining hallmark of his legal thought.

Nature, in the tradition of Gratian, Isidore of Seville, and his mentor Albert the Great, will absorb Thomas, so much so that Thomas espouses that its Creator, the God of man and universe, by and through His eternal law, will burn into the human species an unchangeable, immutable instruction on how to live. This natural law falls from the Divine Exemplar and is transcribed into our hearts. The Old and New Testaments provide further guidance in the form of divine law. Finally, human law rounds out the Thomistic vision of law, an essential component in a just society.

Thomas's legal ideology draws heavily from the precedential value of his precursors and imparts to the philosophical world a jurisprudence of right. Before exposing the substance of Thomistic jurisprudence, a brief and admittedly general summary of his predecessors is presented.

ST. THOMAS'S LEGAL HERITAGE

Those entrusted with the enactment, enforcement, decision making, and advocacy of law in contemporary settings possess a conception, an idea, a meaning of what law is. Each judge and jurist, each scholar of jurisprudence, each lawyer, is laden with a foundational perception of the law's meaning. Judges and lawyers, by nature, ask hard questions about law, many of which extend far beyond the language of law or its precedent and principle. Where is the law rooted? From whence does the law derive its legitimacy and authority? What is the basis for the justness of any law? How can the law guarantee consistency, universality, or particularity? How is the law properly interpreted? On what theory rests the interpretation of the law? At the time of St. Thomas Aquinas (1225–1274), questions regarding the law's essence, its origin and enforceability, its tie to justice and injustice, were as commonly posed as today. Few would argue that the science and philosophy of jurisprudence, the interest in a foundational legal philosophy of right, good, and justice, is a perpetual enterprise. Legal thinkers, in the mold of St. Thomas, are really no different from the secular positivist, the utilitarian, or the relativist, because each camp is searching for the law's context. Each school of jurisprudence desires formal approval and legitimacy, a home to spring out of into the external world. In Thomas's case, the aim and ambition of any legal theory are essentially one of the *telos*, the teleologies of both man and his relationship with the Creator. Thomas's roots are cosmological and ontological, driven deep and unreservedly into the nature of man, his constitution, reason, intellect, and rationality. By contrast, the positivist, who solely grounds jurisprudence in a philosophy of enactment, constructs his or her legal edifice on the indemonstrable, sociological foundation that issues no definite philosophy of man. Utilitarians, in the tradition of Jeremy Bentham, manufacture a law's legitimacy from its inherent usefulness, a utility for the most part and for the most moments.[2] To the Hegelian, law is an expression, an unfolding of man as some historical form;[3] to the Marxian, law reflects the power base that wrenches both its authority and its corresponding materialism from the powerless and less influential.[4] In any backdrop of jurisprudence, from the extremely rational to the reactionary, legal philosophy yearns for a foundation. St. Thomas plants his feet in the soil of meaning, articulating a legal ideology that is consistent with his teleological approach, where law is a far more esoteric principle than simple enactment, where law draws in the comprehensive whole, the perfection of God and his creation, the natural, rational orders of the human species, and the ends and purposes of human existence.[5]

While Thomas can count on some support from the likes of Cajetan, Dominic Soto, Robert Bellarmine, Jacques Maritain, and Albert the Great, what unfolds in the pages that follow is not a majoritarian perspective in legal philosophy, but a distinct, unrivaled, and wholeheartedly independent portrait of law in the world of God and man.[6] Law for St. Thomas is an eclectic undertaking that is so unconcerned with what the majority demands that it refuses to recognize or acknowledge a promulgated law if contrary or incompatible with his definition.[7] Laws, for example, that are unjust are *nullities*: nonexistent attempts to be laws; they are futile, inoperative labels that oblige or bind no one. Laws contrary to the truth of God, inconsistent with justice, promotive of vice rather than virtue, are legal illusions unworthy of our respect. This capacity to disavow a promulgated, legislated, and/or enacted law is dramatic jurisprudence.

Minimally, Thomas's jurisprudence is courageous, standing tall against those who scoff at its metaphysical hierarchy of eternal, natural, divine, and human laws. Willing to unreservedly declare that a law, in order to be a law at all, must be true to this hierarchical framework, must never forget its origins, its authorship, Thomas is unafraid to link law to truth, justice, virtue, and goods. Assured that laws are formulated for the common good of a nation, rather than the mutterings of the individualist, the Thomist legislates for the whole, weighing communal impacts simultaneously with individual issues. The Thomist is incapable of bifurcating law from the operation of the human species, since law is the rule and measure of reason itself.[8] The essence of law resides in human intellectual operation. Law is a rational plan and rule of operation proper only to the rational being.[9]

St. Thomas viewed law as a juridical act, though amongst many other contexts. The bulk of present-day legal thinkers find it incomprehensible that law is looked at beyond its promulgated form. To be sure, laws are words, the stuff of enactments, legislative verbiage, and statutory interpretation. Promulgation, however, embraces not the essence of law, but a process, "a necessary condition that law be observed."[10] Western thought, since the time of the Hellenic world, takes for granted that law is a grander enterprise than only its making. For most of legal history, law had both transcendent and earthly qualities. The idea of law in a tiered sense, the higher over the lower, the superior over the inferior, the supernatural over the natural, is a long-standing theme in historical jurisprudence. To decipher these threads, St. Thomas carefully studied his legal heritage and those who authored jurisprudence leading up to his times.

THE SHAPING OF THOMAS'S JURISPRUDENCE

Before delving too deeply into St. Thomas's theory of law, an abbreviated overview of the historical and jurisprudential influence of his predecessors and contemporaries is a wise undertaking. The presentation offers no claim of comprehensiveness, only an introductory discourse on Thomas's major influences. To resist this type of inquiry would be at odds with Thomas's method. Throughout his incredible array of scholarship, Thomas anchors himself in the legal heritage so prevalent during his time. Thomas's endeavors, whether legal or theological, are replete with references to the giants of the Greek and Roman world, Church Fathers, and philosophers and schools of philosophy that posited a contrary ideal: Sophists, Epicureans, and other thinkers. The unparalleled richness of his philosophy, theology, and, yes, jurisprudence reflects an intellectual curiosity, an eagerness to compare perspectives in order to solidify his own thought. Thomas's legal philosophy is no exception to this policy of a wide expanse of authority, a generous dose of antagonistic beliefs, and a zeal to integrate the fullness of his Catholic, philosophic identity with intellectual history.

The Ancient Idea of Law

If anything is self-evident in Thomas's legal analysis, it is that law is, by its nature, far more than promulgation. Like ancient predecessors from Greece and Rome, Thomas defines law in graduated ways, with a higher law above and beyond the lower enactment, with a supremacy of goods and ends, and with an overall belief in law as the rule and measure of life and the universe itself.

How much exposure Thomas had to the political and legal philosophy of Plato is open to debate. Certain manuscripts were already translated into Latin during Thomas's time, including *Timaeus*, the *Phaedo*, and the *Meno*.[11] Hellenic thought—for example, Plato's theory of forms (the idea of perfection versus an imperfection)—testifies to this tendency.[12] Plato writes with regularity about law, the gods, divine and human justice, and a hierarchical perspective on morality, truth, and perfection. Plato accepts without much argument the existence of divine forces in human reality.[13] The "orderliness" of the universe recognizes that life, and by association, the law, depends upon or is subject to beings beyond the finite dimension. Heaven before earth, so to speak.

Early on, Plato portrays a reality twofold in design: one human, where the vagaries of day-to-day existence are grounded; another divine, where the divine god (or gods as the case may be) sets the example, provides, or detracts from human experience. In this sense, man makes or breaks his world by his adherence to law, but, as is typical in Greek theology, may be an unwitting recipient of a divinely generated justice or injustice. In Book I in the Laws this position is urged from the outset: "They are correct laws, laws that make those who use them happy. For they provide all the good things. Now the good things are two fold, some human, some divine. The former depend on the divine goods, and if a city receives the greater it will also acquire the lesser. If not, it will lack both."[14]

In Plato's world, human agents depend upon and pray to the gods for justice. Man alone is inadequate to assure a just society, for "if the gods are willing, the laws will succeed in making our city blessed and happy."[15] At the level of the divine, there is perfection, beauty, and justice that simply cannot be achieved in a changeable and terminal world. As with art, music, or a craft, perfection represents the acme of accomplishment. The divine provides the blueprint for what law is and should be, since the divine is encased without error, capable of self-movement and generation, and the cause of all else.

Nature also plays a pivotal role in Plato's perspective on law. That Plato has long been associated with some type of natural-law reasoning has been the subject of scholarly debate. This connection to nature further buttresses Plato's resistance to positivism and supports the loftier jurisprudence discussed thus far. To latch onto nature signifies Plato's comprehensive legal formula, a formula that readily accepts enactments and promulgations, though not in a metaphysical vacuum. Plato perceives nature as a grounding station, a panoply of norms and universal expectations. Nature is not exclusively a hodgepodge of occurrences without rhyme or design, but, more appropriately, is a rule and measure, an operation with not only means but proper ends, and an added entanglement with the divine.

Nature is not chance, but a divinely executed action. In Timaeus, Plato asserts that "all souls are said to have been made according to one formula, and the myth of the *Politicus* speaks of the whole human flock and of one divine shepherd."[16] In *The Phaedo*, Plato dwells intently upon how man's soul is guided by nature's prescription: "The subject of the Phaedo is not the soul of Greeks or Persians but the soul of man."[17]

Whether horses, eyes, or organic or inorganic matter, Plato discerns a natural law in every facet of existence. The order of things in general, according to Leo Strauss, "is established by nature."[18] In all facets of Plato's jurisprudence, nature stands neither alone nor in domination over man or the gods. For St. Thomas, the Platonic conceptions of divine law and nature's order will be central and undeniable tenets in his legal philosophy. Plato's laws of nations and the citizenry established a perennial perspective on law as enactment or law as reflection of the universe.

Aristotle's major contribution to the formulation of Thomas's jurisprudence dealt with the law's relationship to rationality and reason and how law, to be law at all, need not only to be consistent with reason, but to advance and promote the virtuous life. Reason is consistent with a good and virtuous existence and therefore a lawful life, while its contrary, vice, aligns itself with irrationality and illegality. Aristotelian thinking adopts an alternative to the forms, replacing this dualistic reality with a philosophy of being, actuality and potentiality, an ordering of life, means, ends, and goods, which Thomas vigorously agreed with.[19] When St. Thomas labels Aristotle "the Philosopher," he does so in awe. In short, St. Thomas's philosophy Christianizes Aristotle's. Throughout the *Treatise on Law*, repeated references to Aristotle's ideas of justice, reason, and law in a human and transcendent sense are evident.[20] In unity with Thomas, Aristotle discerns the habituating tendencies in law. Law and legislation are the means by which "all men become virtuous."[21] Aristotle poses the law's training propensity, especially for the young, who "must be regulated by laws."[22]

Aristotle's language of law is compatible with Thomas's, agreeing on goods, virtues, perfections, justice, ends and means, and a hierarchical vision that gazes far beyond promulgation. Aristotle exhorts the human agent "to become immortal as far as that is possible and do our utmost to live in accordance with what is highest in us," to live life "guided by reason," for such an existence "is the best and most pleasant for man," and to carry out existence in accordance with the "nature proper to each thing."[23] For Aristotle, the state and the law exist for happiness and the advancement of virtue and wisdom.[24] Individual virtue leads a collective of virtuous agents comprising the community and the communal good, Aristotle claims. Aristotle is incapable of differentiating individual conduct from its effect on the collective whole, for "it is evident that the same life is best for each individual, and for states and for mankind collectively."[25] That virtue is synonymous with law will be

Aristotle's legacy. Both Plato and Aristotle fix their eyes toward the heavens, knowing that any chance for temporary happiness in a mutable environment will depend on the celestial heights. This opinion of law is directly at odds with the positivist, whose only panorama is the here and now. Thomas, indebted to Plato and Aristotle, lifts the law up from the muck of daily living, ascending higher heights to the Olympian homestead where the gods reside.

Roman jurists, in the mold of Cicero, affirmed the connection between a higher and lower form of law. Cicero's masterpiece, *De Legibus* (On the Laws), expends considerable time laying out multiple levels in law, allowing for the necessity of positive human laws, then passionately reminding the reader not to forget the law's ultimate source. Thomas would be at home with Cicero's idea of *communion*, which ties together God and man: "Inasmuch as there is no attribute superior to reason, and it is present in both God and man, it must be the essential basis for communion between man and God."[26] When Cicero declares that God is the "supreme" law, by implication and explicit meaning he admits a continuum of laws, a series of law forms that stand atop one another, integrated yet simultaneously existing in separate or diverse domains.[27]

Cicero's legal dialogue anticipates the role of reason in jurisprudence. Cicero recognized that human beings are capable of reason and, as a result, are qualified to create laws. Reason, especially *recta ratio* (right reason), presumes a legal product in tune with the drafter's essential nature. Cicero describes how reason is the glue for both person and culture: "The essential justice that binds human society together and is maintained by one law is right reason, expressed in commands and prohibitions. Whoever disregards this law, whether written or unwritten, is unjust."[28]

Nature, Cicero declares, is our other dependable guide, and, in fact, justice itself is derived from nature. Cicero foretells the natural-law model proffered by St. Thomas, particularly the natural law's instructive powers, which are permanent fixtures and guideposts in moral activity: "Goodness is not just a matter of opinion—what idea is more absurd than that? Since then we distinguish good from evil by its nature, and since these qualities are fundamental in Nature, surely by a similar logic we may discriminate and judge between what is honorable and what is base according to Nature."[29]

Early Medieval Legal Thought

By the time of St. Augustine, the rudimentary, pagan conceptions of law donned a Stoic yet religious Christianized attitude, a sort of supreme cosmic rationality. The law's supremacy was not simply a perfection, a form without force, but the deliberation of a creating, perfect, and all-loving God. Augustine, throughout his brilliant inquiries, erects a multilevel edifice where law resides. According to St. Augustine, the eternal law of God, the *lex aeterna*, served as the starting point for human operations, since God is the author of the universe. Augustine declares God the primordial truth, where "truth is one and common to all, just as much as it is true."[30] Creation itself manifests this eternal perfection, the eternal law of the Supreme God who is its author. "And this physical and moral order, which in its sublime rationality and perfection is eternal and immutable, possesses all the characteristics of a law or norm which is also declaratory of an absolute and perfect universality, necessity, and rationality."[31]

In his *Confessions*, Augustine determines the futility of existence without reference to the perfection of God. "Wheresoever I found truth, there I found my God, truth itself, and since I first learned the truth I have not forgotten it. Therefore, ever since I learned about you, you abide in my memory, and I find you there when I recall you to mind and take delight in you."[32]

Augustine's *lex aeterna* is not a pantheistic ideal, where God is the universe itself. Instead, it is "the ineradicable and sublime administration of all things with proceeds from the Divine Providence."[33] The *lex aeterna* is a "divinely ordained orderliness" covering every aspect of human existence.[34] St. Augustine states, "To put in a few words, as best I can, the notion of eternal law that has been impressed upon our minds: it is that law by which it is just that everything be ordered in the highest degree [*ordinatissima*]."[35] Hovering over all levels of human existence, Augustine's *lex aeterna* perfectly represents law as the act of legislator, lawyer, and judge interpreting its content in submission to a divine plan and a divine will.[36]

In time, Thomas would avoid the Augustinian idea of the law being the product of *will*, divine or otherwise. Reason is the supreme measure for St. Thomas, and he is opposed to any conception of law that is fundamentally tied to the will of man or God. Thomas's *lex aeterna* is an expression of God's perfect, rational, creative essence, a universal, rational orderliness that accords with every being's ontological nature, rational freedom, and naturally selected ends. Augustine's *lex aeterna* is more Platonic, with humans being buffeted, directed by the divine will, while Thomas's person is a partner in moral determination. For Augustine, happiness and orderliness is a function of the self-will and of self-control, in tune with God's rational legal plan. Augustine portrays the happy life as choosing in sync with God's reason. "Or how does a man gain a happy life through his will, when although all want to be happy, there are so many unhappy men. . . . The eternal law, to which it is time now to turn our attention, established with immutable firmness the point that merit lies in the will, while happiness and unhappiness are a matter of reward and punishment."[37]

Participating more passively because our intellects are already infused and divinely ordered, Augustine places a higher value on will. From Thomas's perspective, reason, the intellect, discovers law first, then the will chooses to follow or disregard. To Augustine, choosing and willing comes first due to God's ordering process.[38]

Besides this, Augustine's contribution to the hierarchical ideal in law is quite evident in his discussion of the *lex naturalis*, the law of nature. Descending down from the apex of the eternal law is the imprint of the Creator on beings created. This imprint, this inherency, which Augustine terms the *lex naturalis*, is participatory in the *lex aeterna*. Transcribed, implanted in the soul of man, the *lex naturalis* is man's imperfect participation in the perfection of the eternal law. The natural law opens up a door to the eternal perfection of our Creator. Quoting Augustine, Thomas relates that the "law is written in the hearts of men, which iniquity itself effects not."[39]

Augustinian legal thought is essentially derivative in design, a plan certainly apparent in Thomas's model, extending to both the transcendental and temporal dimension. Augustine's natural law "is to be discovered in the divinely ordained ontological order. It is the observance of this infinite natural and moral order which forms the true substance of the Augustinian concept of law and right, justice and morality."[40] Human laws are not independent of this order, and are in fact partners to the natural and eternal laws. Human laws are crucial to individual and social operations and are, according to St. Augustine, "helpful to men living in this life."[41] Nations and states cannot exist without temporal laws.

When a human law is inconsistent with and contrary to the tenets of the eternal and natural law, it loses its force and identity as law. Augustine's maxim, "An unjust law is not a law at all," imparts the derivative quality of his jurisprudence.[42] He issues this provocative argument in *De Libero Arbitrio*: "We shall not, shall we, dare say that these laws are unjust—or rather, are not laws at all, for I think that a law that is not just is not a law."[43]

That Aquinas was touched by the Augustinian dynamic is not arguable. Most poignant, the Augustinian model of law prepares the way for Thomas's comprehensive schema, where law never stands in isolation, but instead integrates itself into the exquisite fullness of human existence.

During the centuries following Augustine's contribution, various insights were added to this metaphysical conception of law. Thomas himself depends upon, at select queries in the *Summa Theologica*, the writings of Isidore of Seville, whose seventh-century analysis of the natural law struck a chord in Thomas's legal reasoning.[44] In Thomas's *Treatise on Law*, two questions are posed that expressly mention Isidore:

Whether Isidore appropriately described the quality of positive law? [Utrum Isidorus convenienter qualitatem legis positivae describat?][45]

Whether Isidore's division of human laws is appropriate? [Utrum Isidorus convenienter ponat divisionnem humanarum legum?][46]

Each inquiry represents a continuation of this hierarchical tendency, for human laws are not severable from the higher laws that justify their enactment. Isidore's "natural law is a law common to all peoples (nations), and is held to be not something established by man himself, but rather a common natural instinct."[47] Of import to Thomas will be Isidore's willingness to author a series of particular determinations that represent the content of the natural law, most of which is instinctual, including marriage (*viri et feminae coniunctio*), procreation and education of offspring (*liberorum susceptio et educatio*), and other prescriptions.[48]

Quite evident in Isidore's work is the recognition of how authority, legal or otherwise, descends from God. Government and individual both function because of it. Kings as well as subjects were bound by the law identically. These same characters compel king and citizen to obey the law so that justice might be nurtured. Truth is the ruler's guide.[49] Isidore's prevailing imperative was to demand and search for certitude, because each thing tends "one end of truth" (*ad unum veritatis finem*).[50]

Isidore perceived his jurisprudential endeavor as one terminating in questions of salvation, a persistent theme in Thomas's thought. Even when human activities are not defined criminally, Thomas, inheriting Isidore's tendency, still labeled the conduct "sin." When dealing with heretics, Isidore employs the language of both truth and law in his analysis of heretical behavior. In his letter to General Claudius, the flavor is obvious:

Thus beware, beloved son, lest because God has made you victorious with triumphal victories and strength of arms over fallen enemies, you succumb, conquered ignominiously by heretical persuasions; for while you labor to rescue them from the error of death, they themselves stay awake to submerge you in the abyss of error; from their conversation or solace I advise every Christian to abstain under the threat of divine judgment, as if from lethal poison, unless he is proven in divine precepts by experience of works and is erudite in the Holy Scriptures.[51]

Other questions posed by Isidore reflect a prophetic legal thinker, examples being the interplay between law and custom, the relationship and contrast between military and civilian law, and civil law with criminal law.[52] Laws also must be enacted without private gain, but common purpose.[53]

Legal Thought in the Later Middle Ages

Between the time of Isidore and the eleventh century, the contributions to legal theory are scant, with most authors remaining true to the Augustinian model. By this time a vigorous debate on the nature of law reemerged, and St. Thomas was directly influenced by these profound examinations. St. Anselm of Canterbury showed little hesitation in calling for a higher form of law. Anselm's *Cur Deus Homo* advanced numerous themes compatible with the Thomistic ideal. God is "the supreme good, is justice himself and is the perfection all beings seek."[54] Law can only be law when compatible with justice, God being its highest and greatest good. Anselm's *De Conceptu Virginalia et de Originali Peccato* also affords insight into how God is enthroned above any theory of law and justice. Nothing in God is injustice or unjust (*a quo nihil est injustum*).[55] At the pinnacle of justice is truth itself, and justice instructs the human person on how to live with self and others.[56] In this truth (*summa veritas*), God subsists and nothing else can corrupt (*per se subsistens nullius rei est*).[57]

For Anselm, justice is a rectitude of will, in contrast to Thomas's intellectual thesis. Rectitude seeks the mean between extremes. Rectitude is only possible when a man orders and directs "his life according to the rules of divine or eternal law."[58]

Peter Abelard's philosophic approach lent further support to Thomas's jurisprudence. Abelard made notable contributions to a theory of jurisprudence by his threefold categories of law: God-given law, natural law, and the law of the Old and New Testaments.[59] Mixing the transient reality of man with divine revelation bespeaks a commitment to teleology. Replaying St. Paul's message that there is a law inscribed or written in the hearts of men, "which enables them naturally to do the things which the written law commands," attests to Abelard's multidimensional perspective.[60]

Abelard's conceptual approach accepts the dominant position divine law assumes. Not only is man, by committing crimes, displeasing his nature, he is displeasing his Creator. Abelard summarizes in his *Ethics*:

If perhaps someone asks whence we can infer that the transgression of adultery displeases God more than overeating, I think divine law can teach us, which has not instituted any satisfaction of punishment to penalize the latter, but it has decreed that the former be damned not with any penalty but with the supreme affliction of death. For where the love of our neighbour, which the Apostle says is "the fulfilling of the Law," is more fully damaged, more is done against it and sin is greater.[61]

The significance of Abelard's thought rests in his emphasis on particular legal and moral situations. Abelard builds a more complex series of rules that were derived not only from the Testaments, but from the natural law impressed in the psyche of the human species. Abelard's ethical theory stresses the universality and immutability of our natural-law imprint. The natural law, impressed on Christian, Jew, and Pagan, is simultaneously revealed in Scripture and encapsulates "the basic moral prohibitions of murder, stealing and so on."[62]

Abelard also comments on the relationship of justice, the ethical life of the individual, and the common good, a deeply ingrained Thomistic component. Justice is not exclusively what is due another, since any theory of reciprocity and equality is impossible without reference to the collective whole. Abelard clearly delivers this principle:

For it often happens that, when we give someone what is his due on account of his merits, what we do for one individual brings common harm. Therefore, in order to prevent the part being put before the whole, the individual before the community, to the definition [of justice] there is added "provided that the common utility is preserved." We should do all things so that we each seek not our own, but the common good, and provide for the public welfare rather than that of our families and live not for ourselves but our fatherland.[63]

Finally, Abelard's message clearly includes the formative nature of law in its most general sense, for human beings who sin or are in error are corrected by the compulsion of the law.[64] By the twelfth century it would be difficult to find a legal thinker who did not share the basic sentiments outlined to this point. The law, structured in tiers and escalating dimensions, anchored its legitimacy in a higher–lower continuum. The legal thought of Gratian, particularly his Decretals, and more specifically his Treatise on Laws at DD (distinctions) 1–20, provides a glimpse of the St. Thomas to come. Though law consists of "ordinance and usage," the term imputes justice.[65] In Gratian, virtue is presented as essential to any definition of law, and the overall purpose of the law is to lead men to virtue so that "human temerity can be controlled, innocence can be protected in the midst of wicked people, and the capacity of the wicked to harm others can be restrained by fear of punishment."[66] These same human laws prodding man to virtue are legitimate only to the extent compatible with a natural law, infused by the Creator. Gratian further comments, "Now natural law similarly prevails by dignity over custom and enactments. So whatever has been either received in usages or set down in writing is to be held null and void if it is contrary to natural law."[67]

Gratian's natural law is what is contained in the law and the Gospel. Further, Gratian's natural law, just as Abelard attempts, delivers a series of general precepts, "common to all nations" and to all peoples.[68] These primary tenets of the natural law are, by way of example,

The union of men and women, the succession and rearing of children, the common possession of all things, the identical liberty of all, or the acquisition of things that are taken from the heavens, earth, or sea, as well as the return of a thing deposited or of money entrusted to one, and the repelling of violence by force. This, and anything similar, is never regarded as unjust but is held to be natural and equitable.[69]

At this stage definite signs of the natural law's participatory qualities, its binding and obligatory power, and its resistance and condemnation of human laws enacted contrarily to its content are evident. As a rule, Gratian argues, "dispensation" from its content is not permitted.[70]

Alexander of Hales, one of Thomas's closest contemporaries, dwelled upon similar subject matter in his *Summa Universae Theologiae*. A hierarchy of laws underscores Alexander's legal formula for every law, even the positive variety, is bound to the eternal law of God.[71] This eternal law is impressed and imprinted in the souls of rational creatures (*animae rationali imprimatur*).[72] Alexander's legal thinking is undeniably derivative, maintaining that every law, human or divine, derives its force from the *lege aeterna* assuming that the law is just and good.[73] The *legis aeternae* is immutable and absolute.[74] An unjust law (*lex iniqua*) is not derived from the eternal law. Such a law is described by Alexander as "*malitiam*" or "*devective debito ordine*."[75]

Both human law and natural law are derived from eternal law as well. At the lower part of the legal continuum, human laws are integrated into his hierarchical plan (*tractae sunt a lege aeterna*).[76] The same conclusion is obvious for the natural law, since every good is undeniably and universally from the eternal good just as the natural law is derived from the eternal law.[77]

Alexander's natural-law inquiry strikingly sets the tone for Thomas to pursue the subject of law. Alexander, in unity with Thomas,

[margin note: positive law]

is reverential about the natural law, its immutability, its rationality, its mandatory connection to the *ius postivum* and, finally, its
intensive leadership in helping the human agent to do what is right
and to forever journey to the God who implants its directives.[78]
Alexander's natural-law reasoning is an intensely intimate participation with the eternal law of God. Its precepts ordinate us toward God and assure that we love God over all things (*quod
diligamus deum super omnia*).[79] Alexander's analysis of law in all
its contexts foretells Thomas's masterful inquiry. Law, to be law at
all, concerns itself with justice, the blessed, the beautiful, and the
sacred.[80]

[margin note: St. Bonaventure]

Closer in time to St. Thomas are the life and works of Johannes
Fidenza, more commonly known as St. Bonaventure. Plainly,
Bonaventure concurs on the historical generalities so obvious in
Medieval jurisprudence. Bonaventure's natural law is a blend of
imprints, scriptural instruction, and universal truths. He sums up
the idea as "lex naturalis est impressio facta in anima a lege
aeterna."[81] The dictates of the natural law reflect "the eternal law,
which is the ultimate rule of all human action and the principal
source of the order of human life."[82] The dictates include, but are
not limited to, a natural knowledge of God, an instant realization
of His perfection, and that good is to be done and evil to be avoided.

[margin note: stress habit of the intel. leads t. deciding rightly]

In this stratosphere above the positivists, Bonaventure foretells
Thomas's other positions, including the role of practical reason in
decision making, habits, virtues, and the idea of *synderesis*, by which
men choose the good not by compulsion, but from desire.
Bonaventure confidently appreciates how the intellect is subject to
habituation in the form of right reason, a *recta ratio* by which it
deliberates and counsels rightly without coercion or enticement.

[margin note: Intel → over will]

Bonaventure's portrayal of the human player concludes that will
moves the intellect, while Thomas proffers the intellect in primacy
over the will. The natural law naturally binds the will.[83]

Taken as a whole, Bonaventure's thought posits practical reason
as "infallibly connected with volition," but this interaction never
detracts from the primacy and celebration of will.[84] Similar to Augustine, Bonaventure's man needs some form of illumination, a divine gravitational pull, so to speak. The Aquinian man, whose will
chooses, can only do so because it is "impregnated by reason."[85] In
Bonaventure the imprint is in the human constitution, starting with
Adam and Eve.[86] The intellect "exercises final causality in moving
the will, i.e., the intellect's judgment presents some good which as
a goal moves the will to act."[87] The arguments made, though contrary to one another, still assume a teleological vision of law. In

either case, whether intellectualized or willed, the law is more noble than the positivist's ambition.

Thomas's mentor, St. Albert the Great, devised a philosophical approach that merges the temporality of the human agent, his or her astounding freedom of intellect, and a theory of law that encompasses the Thomistic perspective.[88] Thomas's relationship with Albert was one of student–professor, with Thomas studying "under Albert for four full years at Cologne."[89] By most accounts, the mutual experience was one of respect and admiration, and throughout both their respective lives their intellectual interests largely were in concurrence.[90] "There can be little doubt now that Thomas kept himself well-informed of Albert's views, even those with which he had to disagree."[91]

Albert perceives law in both a personal and political sense: to control the masses, to maintain order, and to compel nations and states to unite. Law is a sanction, an authoritative reminder, as well as a tool for human advancement and virtue, making both individual citizen and the nation good (*voluntas omnis legislatoris est, ut bonos secundum virtutem cives faciat*).[92] As in Thomistic thought, it is evident in Albert's work that the law would possess both individual and collective qualitites. Individual goods would be identical to communal goods (*bonum gentis est divinius quam bonum unius hominis*).[93]

Albert's definition of the natural law exhibits exceptional unity with Thomistic thought, since it is universal in design and principle, instinctually and inherently known and understood, and "scripta in homine per hoc quod accipit rationem."[94] This instinctual, inherent character, while comprehended differently by differing players, is universally experienced. While positive human law differs across the world's stage, the natural law is the same for all (*sit idem apud omnes*).[95] The natural law, strictly defined, is innate, universal, and the dictate of reason.[96] Such a law cannot be banished from memory, but its extent and quality may diminish or differ in the consideration of particular dilemmas. No dispensation from its content is possible, nor can it be altered or eliminated, Albert holds, for *natura est ratio*.[97] Of considerable importance to Albert and of subsequent influence on St. Thomas is how the natural law intersects with the divine law, the law of salvation. The Grace of Christ can only be compatible with the natural law (*et ipsa gratia in nullo naturae contrariatur*).[98]

Albert confirmed that the intellect is the central basis for law, both in deliberative and command capacity, that law is an obligatory act, not because a law is willed, but because reason and the intellect have ends and goods that cannot be avoided. Only intellect can discern truth, objective reality—the essence of obligation. Only reason binds the human action and, as a result, nothing but reason can provide the underpinning for law. Albert connects reason to the obligatoriness of the natural law (*obligatio iuris naturalis*).[99] Only intellect is capable of discerning reality and Albert recognized that reason was the link, the conduit between the will and objective reality. Obligation emerges not from choice but from truth itself. The intellect alone discovers prima facie truth. The will must choose among this reality. It is in the contemplative life, not the active life, that man reaches the fullness of his being. Contemplation is the province of reason, not will. Reason is what makes the man and the law. Albert characterizes the essence of man as reason, not will:

This makes it evident that the contemplation of wonderful truths is the highest delight and the most natural occupation, in which people's whole human nature, precisely as such, blossoms, particularly in the contemplation of the things of God, because it is particularly in these that the intellect discovers itself in its proper nature, because human beings, precisely as human, are essentially intellect.[100]

Albert resists those "who maintained not only the superiority of the will and affection over intellect and knowledge, but also on the divine illumination of the created intellect, plurality of substantial forms, universal hylomorphism, *rationes seminales*, and the identity of the human soul with its faculties."[101] Reason is therefore nobler than the will and serves as the legitimate anchor for law and legal thinking. When adopting Albert's rational model, Thomas abandons a long line of thinkers who expressed a preference for will. The implications for Thomistic legal philosophy are many. Reason is the "*mensura*" that insures a lawful person and community.[102] In this way reason is law (*Ratio autem ordinis in civilibus iudiciis est mensura et regula politici, et haec est lex*).[103]

Albert is equally dedicated to a perpetual dialogue on justice and injustice, a tendency similar to his student Thomas. Justice, as well as other virtues, are intimately part of Albert's jurisprudence. Law's consistent interdependency with reason can only prompt discussion of final ends, goods, and the virtuous life. Albert's law, the *regula vivendi*, to be law at all, inevitably advances virtue.[104] Justice, in its most general sense, is giving one another that debitum, what is due.[105] Justice is rectitude, ordination of people and things; legal justice is communal relationships in balance; and justice is always toward another. Justice is concerned with every act of virtue (*justitia concernit actus virtutum*).[106]

AN OVERVIEW OF ST. THOMAS'S LEGAL THOUGHT

Building on the depth and breadth of those preceding him, St. Thomas would author a legal theory that incorporates all that makes us human and that law, whether eternal, natural, divine, or human, can rationally expect from us. Thomas's insight into the nature of law, as will be displayed in the chapters that follow, is erudite and profound. Law is an ordinance of reason, since every human agent is endowed with rational faculties. In a similar way, God's eternal law is His own intellect, the divine exemplar, the blueprint for existence. Incredibly, God and man share rationality, although man's version is imperfect. St. Thomas indicates that this rational force in the human person is his or her chance to participate in the eternal law of the divine intellect, in divine reason. God's reason embraces, by its perfect nature, incalculable goodness, purity, and perfection. Man's nature, which is identified by its rationality, will essentially apprehend these same ends. It will have no other choice. It is will that corrodes this settled order. It is intellect that knows worthy goods. St. Thomas states in the *Summa Contra Gentiles*, "But all things are known to flee from evil; in fact, intelligent agents avoid a thing for this reason: they recognize it as an evil thing. Now, all natural agents resist corruption, which is an evil for each individual, to the full extent of their power. Therefore, all things act for the sake of a good."[107]

The will of man, contrasted with reason, can and does what it wills. The will's willing can be about bad, evil ends, while reason is powerless to identify destructive purposes. Early on, St. Thomas poses this inevitable and unstoppable path reason takes. Reason does not elect as will does; it commands (*imperium*), it moves the will, but cannot force the will. In will, the beauty and tragedy of human freedom unfolds. The complete human act has both qualities, intellect and will, with intellect reigning supreme.[108] In choosing intellect and rationality as his foundation, St. Thomas speaks loudly of his preference for the permanent, the dependable, and the certain. Thomas's law is not subject to the whims of individual wills, but planted in the firm earth of reason. Even if *Deus est rationalissime et ordinatissime volens*, a premise central to Duns Scotus's theory of morality, will man, as author and promulgator of law, merely be willed in order to will?[109] Is the law nothing more than "an effect of God's paternal solicitude for man?"[110]

Suffice it to say, Thomistic jurisprudence is planted in the mind of man, forged and burned into the intellect and delivering predictable and reliable messages about what our ends are. The messages are unambiguous and universal. Whether their content is understood is not in dispute; whether the instructions are adopted and adhered to is a matter of will. Reason is law, for it ordains the actor toward those ends the intellect unequivocally prescribes. As such, law is, for St. Thomas, admittedly promulgated and enacted, but its wings spread throughout the human horizon. Law is virtue. Law is justice. Law is prudence. Law is judgment. Law is the common good. Law is happiness. Law is the ultimate end of the rational creature, God.

What is so reassuring about Thomistic jurisprudence is its teleological permanence. Anton-Herman Chroust describes Thomas's enterprise, where the intellect of God is the *lex aeterna*, as the "measure of every corner of being."[111] Thomas's picture of human operations is psychologically complicated yet beautifully accurate. Man engages the universe in greater ways than the appetitive, the sensual, or the pleasurable. Man, like the laws enacted, mirrors the wholeness of human life. In *Love and Friendship*, Thomas uses a broad brush to describe man: "The good man wishes and performs good because of himself, i.e., because of his intellectual nature, which is principal in man. (That seems most important which is principal in a being.) Thus the virtuous man always strives to act according to reason. Therefore it is plain that in so doing he also always wishes that which is good for himself."[112]

Man is never alone, nor are his laws. Law is seen not simply as the act of the legislator, but a product intended toward a specific end of happiness and the virtuous life. So much of contemporary philosophy, including its jurisprudence with its unbridled emphasis on "I," as Alasdair MacIntyre puts it, is hopelessly tied to a theory of individual jurisprudence.[113] The human agent searches for "right" and statutory protections, all in the context of self rather than the telos so firmly suggested by Thomas. Thomistic thought, legal or otherwise, is not only a personal inquiry but a teleological excursion. It is within the "social, moral and intellectual context" that the human species moves "towards the end of a perfected science, in which a finally adequate comprehension of first principles has been achieved, that the Aristotelean and Thomistic conceptions of truth and rational justification find their place."[114] Laws unsupportive of these goals will not train or educate the young or old. Good laws, by friendly coercion, make the actor "accustomed to good things which will not be distasteful but pleasant after the habit has been formed."[115] Throughout his analysis, St. Thomas discerns the interplay and the compatibility of law and virtue. Virtue is the ordered disposition of the soul, the proper habituation and inclination to acceptable goods, and, thus, a suitable exercise of reason. As such, virtue experiences the effect of law, and by implication is within its general definition. St. Thomas repeatedly refers to virtue in the *Treatise on Law*, for to be a law it must make the subject good.[116]

From Aristotle to Albert, Thomas draws from the wellspring of learned insight, envisioning the law in its proper setting: magnificently more than any juridical act, as both human instrument and an ordination toward the perfect, and as the perfect itself.

NOTES

1. The classic treatise, Thomas E. Davitt, *The Nature of Law* (St. Louis: B. Herder, 1951), assesses the comparative foundations of positivism and Thomism.

2. See Gerald J. Postema, *Bentham and the Common Law Tradition* (Oxford: Clarendon Press, 1986).

3. See G.W.F. Hegel, *Science of Logic*, trans. Miller (London: Allen, 1969).

4. See Heinrich A. Rommen, *The Natural Law*, trans. T. Hanley (St. Louis: B. Herder, 1948), 91, 125.

5. Vernon J. Bourke characterizes Thomas's legal school as a "workable philosophy of law" that "requires acceptance of the view that the human mind knows universal meanings." Vernon J. Bourke, "The Ethical Justification of Legal Punishment," *American Journal of Jurisprudence* 22 (1977): 14.

6. Roberti Bellarmini, *Opera Omnia, De Summo Pontefice, Tomus Primus* (Naples, 1872); Albert the Great, *Opera omnia*, Borgnet edition (Paris: Apud Ludovicum Vives, 1890–1899); Cajetan (Thomas de Vio), *Commentaria in Summam Theologicam S. Thomae* (Antwerp, 1568), Leonine edition (Rome 1888–1906); Dominic Soto, *De justitia et jure* (Venice, 1602); Jacques Maritain, *The Rights of Man and Natural Law*, trans. Doris C. Anson (New York: Charles Scribner's Sons, 1943).

7. St. Thomas Aquinas, *Summa Theologica*, trans. English Dominican Friars, vol. 1 (New York: Benziger, 1947), bk. pt. I–II, Q. 95, a. 2.

8. Ibid., I–II Q. 90, a. 1.

9. St. Thomas Aquinas, *Summa Contra Gentiles*, vol. 4, 2d ed., trans. Vernon J. Bourke (Notre Dame: University of Notre Dame Press, 1975), bk. III, pt. II, ch. 114, 3.

10. George Quentin Friel, *Punishment in Philosophy of Saint Thomas Aquinas and among Some Primitive Peoples* (Washington, D.C.: Catholic University of America Press, 1939), 121.

11. Raymond Klibansky, *The Continuity of the Platonic Tradition during the Middle Ages* (London: The Warburg Institute, 1939), 29–31. Klibansky deduces that the mere might of Platonic thought through the ages would alone cause Thomas to be aware of its basic underpinnings. The Middle Ages, as today, saw Platonism "as a force continuously stimulating scientific thought, aesthetic feeling, and religious consciousness" (p. 37).

12. Plato's theory of forms is apparent in a multiplicity of his works, including *Symposium, Phaedo, Republic*, and *Phaedrus*.

13. An example being, "First, there's the earth, the sun, the stars, and all things, and this beautiful orderliness of the seasons, divided into years and months. Then there's the fact that all Greeks and barbarians believe the gods exist." Plato, *The Laws of Plato*, ed. Thomas L. Pangle (New York: Basic Books, 1980), b X 886a.

14. Ibid., b I 631b–c.

15. Ibid., b IV 718b.

16. John Wild, *Plato's Modern Enemies and the Theory of Natural Law* (London: University of Chicago Press, 1953), portrays nature's underpinnings in Platonic thought: "The unwritten laws of nature hold universally and underlie the written positive laws of every genuinely human community" (p. 153).

17. Ibid.

18. Leo Strauss, *The Argument and the Action of Plato's Laws* (Chicago: University of Chicago Press, 1975), 8. See also Jerome Hall, "Plato's Legal Philosophy," *Indiana Law Journal* 31 (1955–1956): 204.

19. Aristotle's rejection of forms is in "Metaphysics," in *The Basic Works of Aristotle*, ed. Richard McKeon (New York: Random House, 1941), 1040 b-27-30.

20. Aquinas, *Theologica*, vol. 1, I–II, Q. 90, a. 1, ad 2, referring to Aristotle's *Ethics*.

21. Aristotle, *Nicomachean Ethics*, trans. Martin Ostwald (New York: Bobbs-Merrill, 1962), X, 9, 1180a.

22. Ibid.

23. Ibid., X, 8, 1178a.

24. Aristotle, "Politics," in *The Basic Works of Aristotle*, ed. Richard McKeon (New York: Random House, 1941), VII, 3, 11325b.

25. Ibid.

26. Cicero, "On the Laws: Book One," in *Selected Works of Cicero*, trans. Harry M. Hubbett (New York: Walter J. Black, 1948), 228.

27. Ibid., 228–229.

28. Ibid., 237.

29. Ibid., 239. See also Cicero, *De Republica*, ed. Clinton Walker Keys (London: William Heinemann, 1927).

30. St. Augustine, *On Free Choice of the Will*, trans. Anna S. Benjamin and L. H. Hackstaff (New York: Macmillan, 1964), bk. 2, 10, 115.

31. Anton-Hermann Chroust, "The Philosophy of Law of St. Thomas Aquinas: His Fundamental Ideas and Some of His Historical Precursors," *American Journal of Jurisprudence* 19 (1974): 3.

32. St. Augustine, *The Confessions of St. Augustine*, trans. John K. Ryan (New York: Doubleday, 1960), bk. 10, ch. 24, sec. 35.

33. Augustine, *Free Choice*, bk. 1, 6.

34. Chroust, "Philosophy of Aquinas," 2, n. 6.

35. Augustine, *Free Choice*, bk. 1, 6, 51.

36. Anton-Herman Chroust's, "Philosophy of Aquinas," 3, precise inquiry into legal thought preceding St. Thomas captures the Augustinian way:

The *lex aeterna*, according to St. Augustine, defines and determines man's relations to God, to the universe, and to his fellow men. In brief, it constitutes the surest road to God. At the same time the *lex aeterna* is the most concise as well as the most sublime manifestation of God's infinite wisdom, perfect intellect, and boundless love. In this it is a deliberate act of God and as such, the ultimate and absolute justification and, at the same time, encompasses everything created.

37. Augustine, *Free Choice*, bk. 1, 14, 100–101.

38. Davitt, *Nature of Law*, 134–135.

39. Aquinas, *Theologica*, vol. 1, I–II, Q. 94, a. 6, sed contra.

40. Anton-Hermann Chroust, "The Philosophy of Law from St. Augustine to St. Thomas Aquinas," *New Scholasticism* 20 (1946): 27.

41. Augustine, *Free Choice*, bk. 1, 6.

42. Ibid., bk. 1, 5, 33.

43. Ibid.

44. St. Thomas references Isidore twenty-five times in *Theologica*, vol. 1, I–II, Q. 90–97 and seven times in I–II, Q. 98–108. See Jean Tonneau, "The Teaching of the Thomist Tract on Law," *The Thomist* 34 (1970): 31.

45. Aquinas, *Theologica*, vol. 1, I–II, Q. 95, a. 3. See also Aquinas, *Theologica*, vol. 3, 386.

46. Aquinas, *Theologica*, vol. 1, I–II, Q. 95, a. 4. See also Aquinas, *Theologica*, vol. 3, 387.

47. St. Isidore of Seville, *Isidori Hispalensis Episcopi Etymologiarum sive Originum Libri*, ed. W. Lindsay (London: Oxford University Press, 1962), bk. V, 4–6.

48. Ibid., 2.

49. Marie R. Madden, *Political Theory and Law in Medieval Spain* (New York: Fordham University Press, 1930), 26.

50. Isidore of Seville, *The Letters of St. Isidore of Seville*, trans. Gordon B. Ford, Jr., 2d ed. (Amsterdam: Adolf M. Hakkert, 1970), Letter VI, 32, 33.

51. Ibid., Letter VI, 35, 37.

Cave igitur, dilectissime fili, ut quia Deus triumphalibus trophaeis armorum strenuitate prostratis inimicis te fecit victoriosum, haereticis suasionibus ignominiose ne victus succumbas; te enim laborante eos ab errore mortis eruere, ipsi invigilant te in praecipitium erroris demergere, a quorum confabulatione vel solatio quemlibet Christicolam, tanquam a lethifero veneno, sub obtestatione divini judicii praecipimus abstinere, nisi fuerit in divinis praeceptis experientia operum probatus, et sacris eruditus Scripturis.

52. See Isidore, *Hispalensis Episcopi*, bk. V.

53. Ibid., bk. V, XXI, 5. "Nullo privato commodo, sed pro communi civium utilate conscripta."

54. St. Anselm, *Cur Deus Homo*, in *Opera Omnia*, vol. II, trans. Franciscus Salesius Schmitt (Rome: Ex Officina San Saini et Soc., 1940), Capit I, pp. 98, 3–5. "Quapropter rationalis natura justa facta est, ut summo bono, id est deo, fruendo beata esset. Homo ergo qui rationalis natura est, factus est iustus ad hoc, ut deo fruendo beatus esset."

55. Anselm, *De Conceptu Virginali et de Originali Peccato*, in *Opera Omnia*, vol. II, trans. Franciscus Salesius Schmitt (Rome: Ex Officina San Saini et Soc., 1940), Capit. IV, pp. 145, 30–31.

56. Anselm, *De Veritate*, in *Opera Omnia*, vol. I, trans. Franciscus Salesius Schmitt (Stuttgart: Friedrich, Frommann, Verlag, 1984), Capit. XII, pp. 191, 27–29. "Omnem veritatem esse rectitudinem, et rectitudo mihi videtur idem esse quod justitia: justitiam quoque me doce quid esse intelligam."

57. Ibid., Capit. XIII, pp. 199, 27–28.

58. John F. Quinn, "The Moral Philosophy of St. Bonaventure," in *Bonaventure and Aquinas: Enduring Philosophers*, ed. Robert W. Shahan and Francis J. Kovach (Norman: University of Oklahoma Press, 1976), 28.

59. See E. M. Buytaert, ed., *Peter Abelard: Proceedings of the International Conference, Louvain, May 10–12, 1971* (Louvain: Leuven University Press, 1974).

60. John Marenbon, *The Philosophy of Peter Abelard* (Cambridge: Cambridge University Press, 1997), 267.

61. Peter Abelard, *Ethics*, trans. D. E. Luscombe (Oxford: Clarendon Press, 1971), 75.

Quod siquis forte requirat unde conicere possimus Deo magis displicere transgressionem adulterii quam superfluitatem cibi, lex diuina, ut arbitror, docere nos potest quae ad aliud puniendum nullam penae satisfactionem instituit, hoc ucro non qualibet pena, sed summa mortis afflictione dampnari decreuit. Quo enim caritas proximi quam Apostolus "plenitudinem legis" dicit amplius leditur, magis contra eam agitur et amplius peccatur.

62. Marenbon, *Philosophy*, 270.

63. Peter Abelard, *Collationes*, 118: 2068; 119: 2075.

64. Abelard, *Ethics*, 41.

65. Gratian, *The Treatise on Laws (Decretum DD. 1–20)*, trans. James Gordley (Washington, D.C.: Catholic University of America Press, 1993), D. 1, C. 2.

66. Ibid., D. 4, C. 1.

67. Ibid., D. 8, pt. 2.

68. Ibid., D. 1, C. 6 § 2.

69. Ibid., D. 1, C.7 § 3.

70. Ibid., D. 13, pt. 1.

71. Alexander of Hales, *Summa Universae Theologicae*, (Florence: Ex Typographia Collegii S. Bonaventurae, 1948), IV, pars II, Inq 1, Q Unica, Caput VII, Article IV, solutio.

72. Ibid., IV, pars II, Inq. I, Q. I, Caput I, ad obiecta 3.

73. Ibid., IV, pars II, Inq. I, Q. I, Caput VII.

74. Ibid., IV, pars II, Inq. I, Q. I, Caput V, Ad oppositum, a; Caput VI.

75. Ibid., IV, pars II, Inq. I, Q. I, Caput VII, articulus I.

76. Ibid., IV, pars II, Inq. I, Q. I, Caput VII, art. III, solutio.

77. Ibid., IV, pars II, Inq. I, Q. I, Caput VII, art. IV, Ad oppositum. "Omnis bonitas est universaliter a bonitate aeterna; ergo monis lex naturalis, cum sit bona, est universaliter a lege aeterna."

78. Ibid., IV, pars II, Inq. II, Q. III, Caput II; Q. I, Caput I; Q. IV, Membrum II, Caput II.

79. Ibid., IV, pars II, Inq. II, Q. IV, Membrum II, Caput I; Caput III.

80. Ibid., IV, pars II, Inq. I, Q. I, Caput VIII, art. 5–6.

81. St. Bonaventure, *Quaestio disputata, De perfectione evangelica*, V, 117–198. See also Bonaventure's intricate discussion of God, grace, and nature in *Breviloquium* (Venetiis, 1894); "Sentiarum," in *Opera Omnia*, ed. Ludovicus Vivies (Paris: 1865), Book II, dist. XXXIX, art. i.

82. Quinn, "Moral Philosophy," 33. See also Matthew M. Benedictis, *The Social Thought of St. Bonaventure* (Westport, Conn.: Greenwood Press, 1972); Etienne Gilson, *The Philosophy of St. Bonaventure* (New York: Sheed & Ward, 1938).

83. Quinn, "Moral Philosophy," 39, summarizes the debate:

Reason and will have free choice rather than free judgment, Bonaventure maintains, for choice regulates reason by a command of the will, but judgment regulates it by the rule of truth, or the eternal law. A judge is one who decides a case according to law, but an arbiter is one who decides it by his own will. The faculty of freedom, therefore, is named properly from choice, because the decisions of free choice, properly considered, are made more according to will than according to precept of law.

84. Lawrence David Roberts, *John Duns Scotus and the Concept of Human Freedom* (Ann Arbor, Mich.: Xerox University Microfilms, 1969), 23.

85. Ibid.

86. St. Bonaventure, *Breviloquim* (Venetiis, 1894), V. I, pt. III, 6.

87. Roberts, *John Duns Scotus*, 27.

88. George Reilly deems Albert a remarkable pathfinder: "Now there is nothing remarkable about this nor is it difficult to explain. St. Albert the Great was a pioneer in the use of the entire Aristotelian philosophy for the service of Christian truth; this he was by his own efforts." George C. Reilly, *The Psychology of St. Albert the Great Compared with That of Saint Thomas* (Washington, D.C.: Catholic University of America Press, 1934), 75.

89. James A. Weisheipl, *Thomas d'Aquino and Albert His Teacher* (Toronto: Pontifical Institute of Mediaeval Studies, 1980), 7.

90. Simon Tugwell, ed. and trans., *Albert and Thomas: Selected Writings* (New York: Paulist Press, 1988), 11.

91. Weisheipl, *Thomas d'Aquino*, 14.

92. Alberti Magni, *De Bono* (Aedibus Aschendorff: Monasterii Westfalorum, 1951), t 5, Q. 2, art. 1, solutio.

93. Albertus Magnus, *Opera Omnia, Super Ethica* (Aedibus Aschendorff: Monasterii Westfalorum, 1987), Liber X, Lectio XIX, Contra (3).

94. Alberti, *De Bono*, t 5, Q. 1, art. 1, solutio.

95. Ibid., t 5, Q. 1, art. 1 (23).

96. Ibid., t 5, Q. 1, art. 1, solutio (16). "Innata vis inseruit, . . . et nihil est de illo iure naturali nisi universalia morum, quae dictat conscientia ex ipsa ratione boni."

97. Ibid., t 5, Q. 1, art. 4 (3). "Natura autem nulla de causa potest mutari vel etiam destructa recompensari; ergo non recipit dispensationem; ergo nec ius eius, quia stante natura hominis, inquantum homo est, stabit ius ipsius."

98. Ibid., t 5, Q. 2, art. 2, solutio (4).

99. Ibid., t 5, Q. 1, art. 1, solutio (2).

100. Albertus Magnus, *De Intellectu et Intelligibili* (Aedibus Aschendorff: Monasterii Westfalorum, 1951), II 6–9 (B 9, p. 515).

101. Weisheipl, *Thomas d'Aquino*, 17.

102. Alberti, *Opera Omnia, Super Ethica*, XIV, pars I, Liber V, Lectio XI.

103. Alberti, *Super Ethica*, XIV, Pars I, Liber V, Lectio XI, Octavo videtur, solutio (1). Stanley B. Cunningham, "Albertus Magnus and the Problem of Moral Virtue," *Vivarium* 2 (1969): 102, describes the views advanced by Albert as trail breaking yet evolutionary. Albert, says Cunningham, does "validate and emphasize, to a greater extent than any of his predecessors, the purely rational and natural factors in the morality of acts. Every *naturally* virtuous act is a morally good act. Every *rational* act is a moral act (with the added stipulation that futile or idle acts are evil). In relation to his predecessors and contemporaries, Albert's position represents an advance."

104. Alberti, *Super Ethica*, XIV, Pars II, Liber X, Lectio XVIII, Quinto videtur. "Sed lex est praeceptum quoddam; ergo est tantum de actibus virtutis; et sic omnis lex videtur esse bona."

105. Alberti, *De Bono*, t 5, Q. 3, art. 1.

106. Ibid., t 5, Q. 4, art. 2, respondeo.

107. Thomas Aquinas, *Summa Contra Gentiles*, trans. Vernon J. Bourke, vol. 3 (Notre Dame: University of Notre Dame Press: 1975), bk. 3, ch. 3, 8.

108. Aquinas, *Theologica*, vol. 1, I–II, Q. 90, a. 1. See Charles D. Skok, *Prudent Civil Legislation According to St. Thomas and Some Controversial American Law* (Rome: Catholic Book Agency, 1967), 31.

109. Efrem Bettoni, *Duns Scotus: The Basic Principles of His Philosophy*, trans. Bernardine Bonansea (Washington, D.C.: Catholic University of America Press, 1961), 161, n. 132.

110. Ibid., 181.

111. Chroust, "Philosophy of Aquinas," 25.

112. Thomas Aquinas, *On Aristotle's Love and Friendship*, trans. Pierre Conway (Providence: Providence College Press, 1951), bk. 9, ch. 4.

113. Alasdair MacIntyre, *First Principles, Final Ends and Contemporary Philosophical Issues: The Aquinas Lecture 1990* (Milwaukee: Marquette University Press, 1990), 12.

114. Ibid., 43.

115. Thomas Aquinas, *Commentary on the Nicomachean Ethics*, trans. C. I. Litzinger (Chicago: Henry Regnery, 1964), X. L.XIV:C 2149.

116. Thomas Aquinas, *The Basic Writings of St. Thomas Aquinas*, ed. Anton C. Pegis (New York: Random House, 1944), I–II, Q. 92, a. 1, c.

CHAPTER 2

St. Thomas on Law

In God, Imprinted in His creatures

How it is known

A survey of St. Thomas's four-part hierarchy of laws is indispensable to understanding any subsequent advice for legal practitioners. Judges and lawyers need to cast aside any traditional and
exclusive reliance on the promulgative school. Law, for St. Thomas, leaps far beyond the text. Its essence is formulated in God
Himself, by and through the eternal law. The *lex aeterna* is the
divine exemplar and the perfection that is the supreme rationality
of the Creator. The law that is God gradually finds its imprint in
His creatures, especially the rational ones, by and through the imprints of the natural law. St. Thomas determines that the natural
law is burned, impressed into our very essence. Doing good and
avoiding evil is naturally known to all rational beings. With a little
more reflection, the human agent easily discovers the secondary
precepts of the natural law: self-preservation, procreation, communal living, and so on. Other conclusions are discoverable in particularized settings.

Knowing our general inadequacy, God's message in the Old and
New Testaments is sent as the divine law, that revelatory guidance to the people of God. Recognizing our political and social inclinations, St. Thomas accepts both the value and the necessity of
human law. Without human enactments, order in local community
or the sovereign state would be impossible. Human law, to be just,
must be consistent with the entire hierarchy of laws, or lack the
status or nature of law.

w/out positive law + order in local communities

THE THOMISTIC IDEA OF LAW

When contemporary thinkers employ the term "law," they yearn for definition, an anchor, a foundation of meaning. Exactly what a law means depends on perspective. A common conception of law is that of a rule, regulation, statute, or ordinance; a case issued by judicial authority; or some other concretization of a particular legal idea or principle. Laws are as numerous and meaningful as the scope of their coverage, and are, without much argument, *juridical* instruments: law's content commands, prohibits, enhances, advances, or restricts a good or end. As comprehended by St. Thomas, law is juridical, but only partially.[1] Thomas paints the broadest picture of law possible. First, law is synonymous with God, with rationality, and with a rational plan of creation and operations. Even the irrational creature, as directed by God through natural inclination, has a legalistic quality. Law pertains to the species. Modern-day legal thinkers would be confused by the comprehensiveness of his definition:

Just as the acts of irrational creatures are directed by God through a rational plan which pertains to their species, so are the acts of men directed by God inasmuch as they pertain to the individual, as we have shown. But the acts of irrational creatures, as pertaining to the species, are directed by God through natural inclination, which goes along with the nature of the species. Therefore, over and above this, something must be given to men whereby they may be directed in their own personal acts. And this we call law.[2]

Therefore, Thomistic law defines itself in a more profound sense beyond promulgation, for the law's essence mirrors the fullness of God's creation, the nature of his creatures, and the unfolding of species and their corresponding operations. Law is supreme, divine legislation in addition to its positive codification or ordinance; it is the plan for a life consistent with this divine rationality—a life of virtue—and it is the order "whereby man clings to God."[3]

Law as the Rule and Measure of Reason

In Thomas's view, law is a "certain rational plan and rule of operation," and especially proper "to rational creatures only."[4] St. Thomas confidently asserts that "law is something pertaining to reason" and a measure of human activity (*Ergo lex est aliquid rationis*).[5] If it is a measure of human action, one must presuppose there is a connection to human reason, since only the human species analyzes, deliberates, and counsels about activity and movement. Law is entwined with being itself. Some have argued that St. Thomas's perspective on law is almost cosmic, a reflection of how all movement occurs, whether of the heavenly body, the animal or plant, or the laws of physics. Anton-Hermann Chroust discovers a ("universal cosmic orderliness" in Thomistic jurisprudence:

First, the ontological order in which being as such tends towards the preservation of its own being in accordance with its ontological nature. In the case of man this inclination manifests itself in the preservation of life and in all of man's actions conducive to this preservation. Secondly, the vitalistic order in which being tends towards positive action. In the case of man this tendency becomes an inclination to act appropriately and in accordance with his own being and purpose. And, thirdly, the order of the rational and social animal which is also the domain of free moral self-determination.[6]

In a way, each of Chroust's assertions is valid, because St. Thomas perceives law as an ordination, an impetus, an activity seeking proper ends, a fulfillment of essence and perfection of operation. Etienne Gilson eloquently corroborates:

The first, and the most vast of all, is the universe. All beings created by God and maintained in existence by His will, can be regarded as one huge society in which all of us are members, along with animals, and even with things. There is not a single creature, animate or inanimate, which does not act in conformity with certain ends. Animals and things are subject to these rules and tend toward their ends without knowing them. Man, on the contrary, is conscious of them, and his moral justice consists in accepting them voluntarily. All the laws of nature, all the laws of morality or of society ought to be considered as so many particular cases of one single law, divine law. Now, God's rule for the government of the universe is, like God Himself, necessarily eternal. Thus the name *eternal law* is given to this first law, sole source of all others.[7]

Stated concisely, the law represents rationality, an orderliness in individual and rational existence. Law, aside from its enactment, is the handmaiden of reason itself. When dealing with the law's essence, St. Thomas imparts primary stature to reason:

Law is a rule and measure of acts, whereby man is induced to act or is restrained from acting; for lex [law] is derived from *ligare* [to bind], because it binds one to act. Now the rule and measure of human acts is the reason, which is the first principle of human acts, as is evident from what has been stated above. For it belongs to the reason to direct to the end, which is the first principle in all matters of action, according to the Philosopher.[8]

By contrast, human activities and movements contrary to reason's operations will lack the stature of law and legality. Thomas's perennial affection is for the word, *ordo*, as evidenced in St. Thomas's grand jurisprudence.

At one
of will
Boy of
intellect.

The model St. Thomas provides is not one of will, but of intellect, of reason in the human person. A host of Thomas's interpreters have compared a jurisprudence based on intellect compared to one based on will.[9] Thomas indicates that law is a dictate, an ordination of reason, standing in a superior position to human will. Reason mirrors the law of our being, our consistent and compatible dispositions toward particular goods and ends. Every agent intends an end.[10] Reason tells the human actor not simply what law is in form, but what should be done to be consistent with the laws of our nature. (Reason instructs and guides us.)

Law as an Instrument of the Common Good

Since man is a social animal, any legitimate theory of law extends to a culture, a community, a civilization. St. Thomas is well aware that the ordinating influence of law does not terminate with individual activity, because it just as pertinently applies to the common good of a nation as it applies to the common good of its individual citizenry. In response to whether a law should be crafted for the individual or common case, St. Thomas indicates that every human law derives legitimacy from its relationship to the common interest. Laws consist of far more than individual applications, and are germane to the life of a nation: "Hence human laws should be proportioned to the common good. Now the common good comprises many things. Therefore law should take account of many things, as to persons, as to matters, and as to times."[11]

With keen insight, Thomas discerns the futility of a law that applies in the individual scenario alone. Laws are implemented not for the single person or the one-time circumstance, but instead law is a common precept applicable to a community of men.[12] It is for the multitude that laws exist, because laws for the community are nothing more than the social sum of its members. Law, particularly the human variety, "is framed for the multitude of beings."[13] Law is equated with happiness in both individual and culture. If lacking a communal component, the enactment would be "devoid of the nature of law" (*opere non habeat rationem legis*).[14]

Law as Good and End

Any Thomistic understanding of law considers the concept of the good, whether temporal or the ultimate good, the penultimate end of man: God. Holistic in style, universal in approach, Thomistic law pulls in all that is good, beautiful, and perfect and finds final solace only in the beatific vision. Thomistic jurisprudence embraces more than the functionality of utilitarianism, the artificiality of Marxism, and tranformative humanism.[15] A theory of law, says St. Thomas, is loftier, rising above "prejudice and passion," and fixing "upon eternal reasons to reaffirm a forgotten truth, formulate a new principle, or overturn an established error."[16]

To be consistent with reason, a person seeks perfection in every category of life. He or she can will otherwise, but in the intricate and incomprehensible act of creation itself, God could not fashion a being who would command his or her own destruction. Since the Creator is all good, so too are the creatures molded in God's image. These ideas will be more easily understood in the context of Aquinas's various kinds of law, specifically the eternal, natural, divine, and human laws. Man's reason, the artifice of law itself, can readily discover these ends. Perfect, unreserved happiness resides only in the splendor of divine perfection. "Perfect orderliness," as Chroust terms it, is "declaratory of the *summum bonum*, that is, of God."[17]

At every level of Thomistic thinking, legal or otherwise, God is the ultimate end of the reasoning, intellectual creature. St. Thomas urges us, "Now, from what has been seen earlier, it is established that God is the ultimate end of the whole of things; that an intellectual nature alone attains to Him in Himself, that is by knowing and loving Him, as is evident from what has been said."[18]

THE VARIOUS KINDS OF LAW

To fathom Thomistic jurisprudence one dwells upon more than the law as an instrument or mechanism. Positivism, the present penchant of jurisprudence, the idea that laws are laws because they are promulgated, is patently insufficient to a Thomistic thinker. St. Thomas, impressed with the power of human law, though aware of its limitations, designs a multitiered construct, a hierarchical architectetonic of laws in four categories: the eternal, the natural, the divine, and the human. These four types exist independently yet dependently, distinct yet unified and integrated. Succinctly put, the hierarchy implies unity, but is dedicated to a priority of one type of law over the others. An elementary depiction would be as shown at Figure 2.1.

In the plan of God, the higher law descends to the lower law. Thomas sees lower forms of the law as derived from the higher form. This derivative quality commences with the eternal law, the divine exemplar that is the blueprint for the universe and its law.[19] Divine revelation, centrally exposed in biblical instruction, gives clarification to the people of God. Creation, especially the rational variety, participates in the eternal law by and through the natural

Figure 2.1
Hierarchy of Laws

Eternal Law → *Divine Law* → *Natural Law* → *Human Law*

law. Positive laws, the promulgations of man, are a necessary component for a civil society. Unified and interdependent in design, Thomistic law is complicated yet elementary. At its peak, God's eternal law watches over the other categories. "The exemplar of divine Wisdom is the eternal law" [Ratio autem divinae sapientiae est lex aeterna], Thomas relates, and as a result "all laws proceed from the eternal law" [Omnes leges a lege aeterna procedunt].[20]

At the human level, each derives its legitimacy from its superior counterpart. A judge, jurist, lawmaker, and lawyer cannot differentiate or chop up their legal inquiry; for example, forgetting man's natural inclination in a case of sodomy; proclaiming a humanistic notion of individual rights at the expense of common welfare; enacting a statute, interpreting a case, or applying a principle without regard for spiritual, moral, or revelatory considerations. Pure functionalism, legal emotivism, or subjectivism lack the larger framework advanced by St. Thomas. Within the *Treatise on Law*, St. Thomas offers a series of interlocking and interdependent categories of law, each form gauged in its relationship to the others before legal action will have legitimacy. The clamor of the crowd and weeping and gnashing of the individual will not suffice. St. Thomas asserts that law is a rational exercise:

Since law is a kind of rule and measure, it may be in something in two ways. First, as in that which measures and rules and since this is proper to reason, it follows that, in this way, law is in the reason alone. Secondly, as in that which is ruled and measured. In this way, law is in all those things that are inclined to something by reason of some law, so that any inclination arising from a law may be called a law.[21]

The Eternal Law

At the pinnacle in Thomistic jurisprudence is the eternal law of God, the rational architect of the universe and its creatures. God, as author and architect, expresses perfection, omniscience, and pure rationality. God, by and through the eternal law, fashions an exemplar for man and the universe. The eternal law, as Gilson urges, is that which "makes us what we are."[22] The *lex aeterna* is the blueprint for an ordered existence, the benchmark for perfection in every facet of existence. It is "the objective and absolute *a priori* of everything that may properly be called a rule and a measure."[23]

In calling God's law the "supreme exemplar," Aquinas foundationally sets the basis for all legal practice and theory in this perennial, permanent, and immutable dimension.[24] God, the artist and the craftsman, makes only good things, and as a result, molds creatures with lawful inclinations and components. Aquinas characterizes objects or beings by the "emanation" from God's being containing or being the law itself, and the "extensiveness" of God's influence on reality itself.[25] The perfection of God is not an unbridgeable valley, due to God's creative relationship with His authorship of the world. Creation possesses an artistic or demonstrative quality that inevitably and intimately bonds the Creator with the created. The divine God moves "all things to their due end," and "bears the character of law" [Moventis omnia ad debitum finem obtinet rationem legis].[26]

The perfect God naturally has a perfect legal constitution, though His complete content and subject matter are unknowable to temporal species like man. The eternal law is incapable of promulgation, since such promulgation is meaningless.[27] Thomas recognizes the human inadequacy of knowing directly and primarily what the eternal actually is, since the law is God Himself. What is irrefutable is that only God knows His own eternal law in its fullness. As imperfect beings, we can struggle only to know the effects of the eternal law. Thomas holds that we "cannot know the things that are of God as they are in themselves; but they are made known to us in their effects, according to *Rom. i. 20: The invisible things of God . . . are clearly seen, being understood by the things that are made.*"[28]

Later on man will get closer to knowing these effects by nature's instructions on the norms for human activity. St. Thomas is wise enough to equate the eternal law of God with that of God Himself. All that is created by God, "whether contingent or necessary, is subject to the eternal law."[29] God's law is the supreme norm for all living beings and creation. Governance of the universe by God imputes a law of operations. Thomas simultaneously uses the term "government" when God is described as "the ruler of the universe" [principe universitatis].[30] This rule has the quality of and the "nature of a law" [legis habet rationem].[31]

When St. Thomas queries whether all human affairs are subject to the eternal law, only an answer in the affirmative is possible. Even the wicked and the perverse are subject to the eternal law.

Even the "blessed and the damned are under the eternal law."[32] Even the ignorant cannot disavow some knowledge of the eternal law, since their being still reflects the Creator by its effects. Even the lustful and the slaves of flesh cannot "dominate" and destroy the good of one's nature, for "there remains in man the inclination to do the things which belong to the eternal law."[33] Nothing and no one can evade the eternal law. The eternal law, residing within, or more accurately inherently within, the God of creation, is the measure of all activity. Thomas does not hesitate calling God's law truth itself. At Question 93, Article 1, he summarizes that "the divine intellect is true in itself, and its exemplar is truth itself."[34]

St. Thomas's evaluation of law cannot and does not end here; practical and pragmatic reality would not allow it. As creatures, as living agents of God's creation simultaneously recognizing our own inadequacies to comprehend the eternal law, we need a legal benchmark that can be understood, the natural law.

The Natural Law

Since the human species is powerless to fully learn the mind of God and His eternal law, St. Thomas recommends a look at our very natures. Nature, in a scientific, physical sense has an order, a series of operational rules. Nature "in its purity . . . is rather like the word life."[35] Man is a creature of nature and thereby subsists of rules and operational qualities. C. S. Lewis's critical mind poses the foundational meaning of nature: "By far the commonest native meaning of *natura* is something like sort, kind, quality, or character. When you ask, in our modern idiom, what something 'is like', you are asking for its *natura*. When you want to tell a man the *natura* of anything you describe the thing."[36] Thomas gets to the core of nature in his work *On Kingship*, for "whatever is in accord with nature is best, for in all things nature does what is best."[37]

As author of nature, God could not and would not forge a creation of disorder and anarchy, but more predictably, infuses and imprints an orderly, lawful, natural sequence in each of his creatures: "The manifold and beautiful order of nature is the work of a designing mind of vast intelligence; and must be ultimately explained by the existence of a personal God."[38] Undoubtedly, human beings, like other beings, display natural inclinations, preferences, propensities, and dispositions that mirror the wisdom of the author. Gilson artfully offers this analysis: "Granted this, it is clear that the precepts of natural law correspond exactly with our natural inclinations and that their order is the same. Man is, to begin with, a being like all others. More particularly, he is a living being, like all other animals. Finally, by the privilege of this nature, he is a rational being. Thus it is that three great natural laws bind him, each in its own way."[39]

The term, "natural law" references two critical Thomistic ideas: (1) the nature of a being itself and (2) law as an operation of that nature. To say someone or something has a nature is to typify its very existence. Then, apply law to that nature and that nature unfolds before us: Doing what it must and should do to preserve its existence signifies nature as well.[40] Nor is the natural law some changeable phenomena deposited in the creature for the moment. St. Thomas resists the effort to call the natural law an habituation, because habits increase or decrease while natures are fixed.[41] Habits increase, decrease, and tend toward good things or malevolent ones. Natures are poured during a being's construction phase. A loose and impressive comparison might be this: As the eternal law is God Himself, the natural law is a mirror of really what we are as beings, because this is the eternal plan. The natural law is imprinted on a person, infused into his or her nature, "written" in his or her heart. How could it be otherwise when the creature reflects the Maker? Regularly found within the body of St. Thomas's work is the term "imprint," which represents the mark of the maker. The human person partakes and participates in the eternal law of God. Human beings "derive their respective inclinations to their proper acts and ends" [inquantum scilicet ex impressione ejus habent inclinationes in proprios actus et fines].[42] Rational creatures among all others participate most generally, Thomas remarks, "The rational creature is subject to divine providence in a more excellent way, in so far as it itself partakes of a share of providence, by being provident both for itself and for others. Therefore it has a share of the eternal reason, whereby it has a natural inclination to its proper act and end; and this participation of the eternal law in the rational creature is called the natural law."[43]

One should not think that St. Thomas's natural law is one of strict biology—it is much more comprehensive, more ambitious. A biological phenomenon would act out of necessity or pure function, while Thomas's natural being moves primarily due to its rational form. Thomistic natural law fully expects reason to be the receiver of God's design. Nor is it a series of legal annotations, codifications, and enactments. More apt, the natural law is a reflection of the whole. Ignatius Eschmann cogently defines the natural law as "not a statute enacted by the divine Legislator, but is the self-same act by which the Creator brought into being our rational nature."[44] Inclinations, tendencies, and propensities are not blank, intellectual exercises, especially since the natural-law theory of St. Thomas centrally depends upon reason for its discernment. Natural law for St. Thomas is more than Newtonian physics or evolutionary development. Natural law for St. Thomas is in service to the human condition, and is easily gleaned from human operation.

That water travels to its lowest point, or that bears propagate their species is not natural law activity as St. Thomas defines it. "It is nature itself that is, more precisely, rational nature; it is reason understood as the power of reasoning."[45] Only rational creatures possess the natural law. Natural law is about inclinations and imprints, how human creatures live in accordance with their overall constitution. The human player living compatibly with these natural impressions lives as the Creator intended. Natural law cannot be removed—"blotted out"—moreover, it cannot be forgotten nor can its content be denied on the basis of ignorance.[46] Natural law is the human person's participation in the eternal law of God: "Thus man has a natural inclination to know the truth about God, and to live in society; and in this respect, whatever pertains to this inclination belongs to the natural law: *e.g.*, to shun ignorance, to avoid offending those among whom one has to live, and other such things regarding the above inclination."[47]

From the Thomistic view, man is forged so tightly with the natural law that we cannot extricate ourselves from its influence. We can't even intend contrary to what we are, though we can will the difference, choosing evil that "is a result apart from intention."[48] Wickedness or unlawfulness does not reside in reason or our constitution, for "such a thing is not the necessary result of what is intended; rather, it is repugnant to what is intended."[49] St. Thomas does not compartmentalize the natural law's influence on human operations but recognizes its determinative power. Every inclination in the human actor, particularly those touched or controlled by reason, deals with our natural-law imprint.[50]

Those who argue its relativity, inapplicability, and selectivity as to person or precept would be at odds with Thomistic doctrine. Natural-law reasoning is scathingly critiqued by those who allege its intractability and absolutist tendencies,[51] a situation arising from language like this:

It is therefore evident that, as regards the common principles whether of speculative or of practical reason, truth or rectitude is the same for all, and is equally known by all. But as to the proper conclusions of the speculative reason, the truth is the same for all, but it is not equally known to all. Thus, it is true for all that the three angles of a triangle are together equal to two right angles, although it is not known to all. But as to the proper conclusions of the practical reason, neither is the truth or rectitude the same for all, nor where it is the same, is it equally known by all.[52]

Critics, however, cannot fathom that natural-law reasoning only insists that a person act in conformity with what reason instructs. That there is one type of human person—the rational one—is indisputable. Reason commands as natural inclinations enunciate. In this sense, it would be ludicrous to fashion another species endowed with another version of reason. Therefore, in human conduct reason rules and commands the other powers, and this universal condition labels permanently the natural law.[53] This unchangeable, immutable reflection of the eternal law; this participation, albeit imperfect, by man in the eternal law; this imprint, messaging inclinations and ends for the human person, is the essence of the natural law. Quoting Gratian's *Decretals*, St. Thomas summarizes the permanency of the natural law as follows: "It is said in the *Decretals: The natural law dates from the creation of the rational creature. It does not vary according to time, but remains unchangeable.*"[54]

The Content of the Natural Law

Any reasoned analysis of the natural law inspects the sum and substance of its content. Thus far, descriptive terms, like inclinations and imprints, have been employed to describe the natural law, but this is inadequate. What is it that we are inclined about? Since law is reason's rule and measure, and since all human beings seek the good, the natural law must be rooted in one, basic tenet. Invariably, St. Thomas calls this fundamental inclination, to do good and avoid evil, the "primary precept" or the "first principle" of the natural law. This initial principle that "good is to be done and promoted, and evil is to be avoided" [quod bonum est faciendum et prosequendum, et malum vitandum] serves as the cog in Thomas's natural-law philosophy.[55] Practical reason naturally identifies the good to be pursued and the evils to be shunned. Of course, this position is consistent with St. Thomas's view of man's end or purpose in existence, and is particularly logical as to previous definitions of what a law is. This primary and common precept is part of our very fabric of being, Gilson argues: "To say that we must do good and avoid evil is not arbitrarily to decree a moral law; it is merely to read a natural law which is written in the very substance of beings and to bring to light the hidden spring of all their operations. We have to do it, because it is our nature to do it. Such a precept is but a verification of fact."[56]

This doing good and avoiding evil provides, at best, a generalized prescription for life, and at worst gives fodder to those who challenge or debate the content or ingredients of its recipe. In the first instance, this primary precept is only a call that the human actor "act in accordance with reason . . . with the created pattern of our nature and species."[57] While only rational creatures intellectualize natural-law precepts, every being moves toward its proper end or goal.[58]

Few would contest that St. Thomas knows that human beings already know its content, because the natural law is the dictate of reason.[59] Admittedly, some persons may know its content better than others, but only in particular applications or specifications. This fundamental precept, doing good and avoiding evil, is known equally by all. St. Thomas exhibits an understanding of human differences in discerning not truth or the primary precept of the natural law, but the determinations of practical rectitude that are "not equally known to all" [non est aequaliter omnibus nota].[60] This "golden rule of the natural law" is effortlessly understood "without investigation . . . known and approved by all humans."[61]

The matter of the natural law's instruction does not end with this common precept. Rather, Thomas turns his attention to human operations, those predictable, commonly observed, universally conducted types of behavior apparent in all people and all civilizations. In the average case, and for the average person, moral guideposts and legal parameters are crucial. Early in his work, St. Thomas grounded his natural-law reasoning in nature itself. That which is compatible with nature will be lawful; that contrary to it, unlawful. In the *Commentary on the Sentences*, he distinguishes activity according to the ends nature mandates for "whatever renders an action improportionate [*inconvenientem*] to the end which nature intends to obtain by a certain work is said to be contrary to natural law."[62] Similarly, his *Summa Contra Gentiles* paints a picture of this legal barometer: "The operation appropriate to a given being is a consequent of that nature. Now it is obvious that there is a determinate kind of nature for man. Therefore there must be some operations that are in themselves appropriate for man."[63]

In this way, one determines the lawfulness of conduct by its relationship to the actor's nature. From this point on, St. Thomas expands the primary precept to an *ad seriatim* listing of what he terms "self-evident principles." Nature, as a biological phenomenon, doesn't act, but the human person, by the use of reason, exhibits certain inclinations, and these inclinations are based on various goods. Thomas's theory of the natural law catalogues these inclinations as essentially self-evident, discoverable by all who engage in "slight reflection."[64] At Question 94, Article 2, a list of these first principles is announced:

For there is in man, first of all, an inclination to good in accordance with the nature which he has in common with all substances, inasmuch, namely, as every substance seeks the preservation of its own being, according to its nature; and by reason of this inclination, whatever is a means of preserving human life, and of warding off its obstacles, belongs to the natural law. Secondly, there is in man an inclination to things that pertain to him more specially, according to that nature which he has in common with other animals; and in virtue of this inclination, those things are said to belong to the natural law *which nature has taught to all animals*, such as sexual intercourse, the education of offspring and so forth.[65]

These inclinations of social existence, propagation of the species, self-preservation, and the inherent desire to know truth and God are universally true in all rational beings.[66] They are unavoidably consistent with human experience and are "propositiones per se notae quoad se et quoad nos."[67] Unnatural activities are deductively inconsistent with nature. C. S. Lewis reminds us that when inconsistency lends to unnatural vice, "it is a departure for the worse."[68]

Being self-evident propositions, the actor has no choice but to make decisions compatible with their subject matter. This is why a natural-law theorist has little or no quandary reconciling the current debates over abortion, homosexuality, or assisted suicide. These first principles of the natural law set out a formula, a series of criteria that forbid each of these activities. While the doing of good and avoiding of evil is known in and of itself, these *prima principia legis naturae* may be conditionally self-evident.

Ethicists, moralists, and jurists on a hunt for a more substantive list of do's and don'ts in the first indemonstrable principle of the natural law are surely to be disappointed. At this stage, all Thomas has argued is that every rational creature seeks its proper end: the good of temporal existence and the ultimate end of God. Reason is the rule and measure of human action and thus the conduit of law. Reason, as the eternal law and divine exemplar infused in it, drives toward the good. This is its natural law, which is man's participation in the eternal law. Another way of characterizing the process is to do good and avoid evil. In order to do so, one must examine our natural tendencies, our propensities, and our inclinations. After completing this speculative task, a series of self-evident, indemonstrable primary principles of the natural law emerge (e.g., self-preservation, procreation, etc.). There are "certain things which the natural reason of every man, of its own accord and at once, judges to be done or not to be done."[69] Writing in theological terms, St. Thomas labels acts contrary to our nature "special sins," for such conduct is contrary to what is proper for man, or against a "nature which is common to man and other animals, and in this sense, certain special sins are said to be against nature: *e.g.,* contrary to sexual intercourse, which is natural to all animals, is unisexual lust, which has received the special name of the unnatural crime."[70] These self-evident principles of the natural law are so easily discerned and universally understood that promulgation is not warranted.

Secondary Precepts of the Natural Law

One unfailing attribute found in Thomistic jurisprudence is its hierarchical structure, from God to man and then to all beings in Creation. As a result, St. Thomas is doggedly determined that laws be instructional to man, laying out parameters of conduct and serving as an instrument in moral valuation. Throughout his articulation, St. Thomas never falls prey to the general moral norm being the particular moral resolution, nor the particular being the general. Already reviewed is the need for law to be applicable in the common or general case and to be instituted and applied for the purpose of the common good. Each case may have a general rule of operation, but particular circumstances may alter the applicability of the general rule. This is true in every legal scenario, including the principles that emanate from the natural law. St. Thomas is fond of the expression "light of reason" when discussing the effects of the natural law, and sapient enough to realize that light will vary in the human intellect. While no man "can have an erroneous judgment about" the first principles of the natural law, those emanating further down the continuum are not as expeditiously discovered.[71]

These other principles are labeled secondary, or, by some, tertiary, derivations of fundamental natural-law principles.[72] The clear-cut, undeniable tenets of first principles lose their punch, or at least their ease of discovery, as one moves to more particular cases. Despite this growing remoteness, many secondary conclusions are entangled with the primary precepts. St. Thomas even says that our legal reasoning "will be found to fail the more, according as we descend further towards the particular."[73]

Found within this arena of secondary principles will be more particularized moral and legal issues. For example, is it self-evident, or readily understood, that adultery is opposed to the natural law, or divorce, masturbation, polygamy, contraception, and so on? These questions can be reconciled using natural-law reasoning, but their solution calls for more scrutiny than questions regarding suicide or abortion. Thomas labels these secondary questions "proximate" to the first principles, derivable therefrom, and even allows for a greater flexibility in the resolution of said cases.[74] There may even be times when following the natural law would create an ironic injustice; for example, the maintenance of life of fetus over life of mother, or the condemnation of a soldier who, by giving up his life for comrade, fails to preserve himself. In these and other special cases, "observance of such precepts" [observantiam talium praeceptorum] will not be possible.[75]

Secondary precepts are so designated because of their intimate relationship to the ends and goods suitable for man. Conduct, in the most particularized categories, can be evaluated for moral legitimacy and legality by the ends promoted. If the ends are contrary to human perfection, the conduct or law would be contrary to the natural law. Thomas writes splendidly about this interplay between lawfulness, natural law, and ends in the *Summa Contra Gentiles*: "Now, it is good for each person to attain his end, whereas it is bad for him to swerve away from his proper end. Now, this should be considered applicable to the parts, just as it is to the whole being; for instance, each and every part of man, and every one of his acts, should attain the proper end."[76] More exactingly, Thomas zeros in on the moral dilemmas associated with propagation and procreation to illuminate his idea:

Now, though the male semen is superfluous in regard to the preservation of the individual, it is nevertheless necessary in regard to the propagation of the species. Other superfluous things, such as excrement, urine, sweat, and such things, are not at all necessary; hence, their emission contributes to man's good. Now this is not what is sought in the case of semen, but, rather, to emit it for the purpose of generation, to which purpose the sexual act is directed.[77]

Furthermore, a series of predictable ethical dilemmas can be speedily reconciled by adhering to these basic propositions. Polygamy is contrary to the natural law because "one female is for one male is a consequence of natural instinct."[78] Incestuous marriage is inconsistent with natural-law precepts, since "it is unfitting for one to be conjugally united with persons to whom one should naturally be subject."[79] Promiscuity, inordinate affections, and gluttony are distortions of the ends man normally seeks and to engage in such vices is a departure from "the order of reason."[80]

Within this scenario, we are attuned to the difficulties of secondary or tertiary natural-law problems. Licitness can evolve into illicitness because the initial goodness of the conduct, an example being sexual intercourse, evolves or degenerates into excessive or compulsive behaviors, or because the conduct is undertaken contrary to its inherent ends. Thomas's distinction is fully developed in the *Summa Contra Gentiles*:

Now, since the use of food and sexual capacities is not illicit in itself, but can only be illicit when it departs from the order of reason, and since external possessions are necessary for the taking of food, for the upbringing of offspring and the support of a family, and for other needs of the body, it follows also that the possession of wealth is not in itself illicit, provided the order of reason be respected. That is to say, a man must justly possess what he has; he must not set the end of his will in these things, and he must use them in a fitting way for his own and others' benefit.[81]

Despite this apparent flexibility, inclusion in the circle of secondary principles is selective. Remember

two very important questions in St. Thomas's teaching, the question concerning the "closeness," *propinquus*, of the secondary precepts, and that involving the distinction between the procedure of *determinatio* and that of *demonstratio*. In a sense these two matters were complimentary. The idea of secondary precepts being *propinquus*, or closely related to the self-evident principles of natural law, seems to indicate that for a precept to belong to the class of secondary ones it is necessary that it be very closely linked with the primary precepts.[82]

Attacked by a host of critics for pontificating a rigid formula of ethical choice, St. Thomas's work is assuredly at odds with those espousing any theory of relativity. The relativists, after angrily reviewing the natural law's dictates and conclusions, cannot accept restrictions in human activity. These restrictions are invariably labeled the enemies of freedom. Freedom for St. Thomas is more than the will to act, to do what one chooses, since activity, like law, must be measured and evaluated in light of reason's instruction. All the natural law does is guarantee the freedom of the human person to be exactly who he or she is. Characterizing Thomas as a moral dictator is an absurd caricature.

The Divine Law

Thomas's recognition of the divine exemplar, the divine intellect giving rationality to the universe, and the view that God's very being is the eternal law itself, is often considered the thesis of divine law. Divine law, while having the qualities of God's rationality and plan, is not the same as eternal law. Divine law, in the most elementary framework, is the Old and New Testaments, which comprise the Bible. It is easy to interchangeably term the eternal law the divine, and the divine the eternal, for common parlance often does so. Instead, one finds St. Thomas fully cognizant of the role and purpose of Scripture in the life of the Christian, and that this same Scripture has revelatory qualities. Scripture explains the mind and particular commands of a transcendent, perfect God. In addition, the eternal, natural, and human laws, while interdependent and unified in a teleological sense, do not, according to St. Thomas, directly address the law of salvation. Thomas suggests divine law serves this end:

> The end of the divine law is to bring man to that end which is everlasting happiness; and this end is hindered by any sin, not only of external action, but also of internal action. Consequently, that which suffices for the perfection of human law, viz., the prohibition and punishment of sin, does not suffice for the perfection of the divine law; but it is requisite that it should make man altogether fit to partake of everlasting happiness.[83]

It is obvious that St. Thomas is not just paying lip service as to the divine law's value in his jurisprudence. Heavily and regularly seen throughout his works is a litany of citations to Scripture passages. Jean Tonneau's essential study, *Teaching of the Thomistic Tract on Law*, mathematically computes the number of times St. Thomas utilizes scriptural references in the *Treatise on Law* at Questions 90 through 108. The results present a scholar who integrates the sum and substance of divine instruction and simultaneously depends upon secular giants like Aristotle and Cicero (see Table 2.1).[84]

It is nearly impossible to find a topic where he does not reference a scriptural authority. For most contemporary legal practitioners, reliance on biblical rules and authority in legal decision making would border on the bizarre, but such a practice is perfectly compatible with a Thomistic vision incapable of segregating a life of religious experience from human activity. Without question, St. Thomas is strongly dependent on the instruction, the divinely inspired education and guidance, that the Old and New Testaments provide. Man and man alone is simply incapable of operating without divine instruction, for "human reason is not infallible and with the best will in the world people fall into subjective error in working out the details of right and wrong."[85]

On the other hand, it is quite apparent that St. Thomas's hierarchical coverage of law, the eternal to human legal continuum, spends less time on the divine law that its temporal counterpart, human law. Henle describes this portion of the *Treatise on Law* as "strictly a religious or theological one," and this emphasis is not as frequently confronted in St. Thomas's jurisprudence.[86] In fact, earlier works, like the *Summa Contra Gentiles*, appear to inaccurately distinguish between these categories of divine and eternal. In Book 3, on provi-

Table 2.1
St. Thomas's Use of Scripture
The quotations will be distributed in three columns: A. Citations borrowed from questions 90–97; B. Citations borrowed from questions 98–108; C. The total of the two predceding columns reflecting the entire text . . .

	A	B	C
Bible	64	660	724
Aristotle	48	48	96
Augustine	35	52	87
Biblical glosses	5	28	33
Isidore	25	7	32
"Jura" (Digest, juricons. Etc.)	12	0	12
Maimonides	0	9	9
Gratian and Gregory IX	8	0	8
Cicero	3	5	8
Denys	0	5	5
Jerome	0	5	5
Chrysostom	0	4	4
Damascene	2	0	2
Ambrose	0	2	2
Gregory the Great	0	2	2
Josephus	0	2	2

dence, St. Thomas elevates the divine law more than usual, for its word is God's and its source the highest and most perfect good. The end of every law, Thomas declares, including the divine law, is to "make men good."[87] At this stage of his legal analysis, he appears to liberally interchange eternal and divine law terms. Missing within the *Summa Contra Gentiles* is the natural law's participatory role in God's eternal law, and the distinction between the revelation of God's Testaments and the law of God, the *lex aeterna*. As Thomas's thought matures, the distinction between eternal and divine will be clarified. In the *Treatise on Law*, St. Thomas unassailably depends on God's word and its integral, central role in the life of the Christian player.

It is just this quality of "directing human conduct" that makes divine law central to St. Thomas.[88] Accepting the condition of hu-

Table 2.1 (*continued*)

	A	B	C
Boethius	1	1	2
Hilary	1	1	2
Peter Lombard	1	0	1
Basil	1	0	1
Julius Caesar	1	0	1
Ausonius	1	0	1
Ambrosiaster	0	1	1
Bede the Venerable	0	1	1
Cassiodorus	0	1	1
Hesychius	0	1	1
Pelagius	0	1	1
Pseudo-Chrysostom	0	1	1
Theodore of Mopsuestia	0	1	1
Origen	0	1	1
Plato	0	1	1
Valerianus Maximus	0	1	1
	208	841	1049

Source: Jean Tonneau, "The Teaching of the Thomist Tract on Law," *The Thomist* 34 (1970): 31. Used by permission.

man frailty and imperfection and realizing the historical evidence for both success and failure on the part of God's people, St. Thomas looks to scriptural instruction as a guide in a world of competing moral claims. When in doubt, God's word can and does resolve dilemmas, legal or otherwise. To assure salvation, God's divine instruction helps man "know without any doubt what he ought to do and what he ought to avoid" [homo absque omni dubitatione scire possit quid ei sit agendum et quid vitandum].[89]

In man's incompetency to do what is right and God's unbridled generosity in His revealing, through Scripture, the plan for human operations, the divine law anchors humankind in God's great scheme.[90] Comprehensively, Thomas inserts the divine promulgations of both the Old Law and the New, so that even though the "benefits of nature" are not forfeited, the "benefits of grace" are not lost through sin.[91]

Even more persuasive is St. Thomas's argument of need as it relates to man's final end of happiness and God. Some might claim that God has equipped the human agent and instilled and imprinted in his or her nature the blueprint for the happy life. Since we cannot comprehend the eternal law of God, understanding its effects alone, and since nature, the natural law of our operations, is for the most part nontheological in design, St. Thomas expresses an urgency about this theological dimension. Aquinas himself argues that the principles of the natural law were "contained in the Old Law."[92] It is clear what he means: "By the natural law the eternal law is participated proportionately to the capacity of human nature. But to his supernatural end man needs to be directed in a yet higher way. Hence the additional law given by God, whereby man shares more perfectly in the eternal law."[93]

This supernatural end is just as compatible with the perception of St. Thomas on the natural end. Theologically, the divine law is a revealed message on how to achieve the end God intends for His creatures, and the end is not exclusively about function, machination, or bodily perfection, "because it is by law that man is directed how to perform his proper acts in view of his last end" [quia per legem dirigitur homo ad actus proprios in ordine ad ultimum finem].[94] Eternal happiness is an end that "exceeds man's natural ability," and the divine law fills the void.[95] St. Thomas agrees with this relational quality of the divine law, since its prime aim is leading man to God, "either in this life or in the life to come" [vel in praesenti, vel in futura vita], for the foremost purpose of the law "is for man to cling to God."[96]

At other points in Thomas's work we decipher the instructional and educational role served by the divine law. Biblical history more than adequately manifests the need for divine scriptural reminders. The people of God have abbreviated memories of God's promises and God's law, so much so that "the natural law began to be obscured because of the exuberance of sin.[97]

In short, the divine law directly enunciates the faith, since human reason alone cannot fully discern the things of God.[98] In both the Old and New Testaments, St. Thomas declares the plan of salvation as proclaimed by the Creator. Whether by the Old Testament's stern deterrent mentality, or the New Testament's all-encompassing charity, both scriptural domains lay out a map for salvation. The *Decalogue*, as an illustration, represents the divine law's capacity to guide, to instruct, and to lead man to proper ends, on the way giving one another their due.[99] Divine law continually serves as a reminder to the Christian citizen and moral agent, transmitting its luminous beacon of moral truth to those "habituated to sin" and "darkened as to what ought to be done in particular."[100]

Much more could be said about this component of St. Thomas's legal philosophy, but suffice it to say, the divine law is yet another reflection of God's love for His creation. Like a father to his family, St. Thomas declares the critical function of divine law in the life of the human person: "As the father of a family issues different commands to the children and to the adults, so also the one King, God, in His one kingdom, gave one law to men while they were yet imperfect, and another more perfect law when, by the preceding law, they had been led to a greater capacity for divine things."[101]

Human Law

Those less learned about Aquinas often assume that human law is either incidental or deficient when compared to the eternal, natural, and divine law. The things of the earth are by no means as lofty or principled as the perfections of God. Nor are the legal musings of man as legislator, lawyer, and judge possibly on par with the divine or eternal promulgations. Despite the imperfection, human laws are essential to Thomas's theory of law, since their content aims "at the ordering of human life . . . under the precepts of a life we have to lead."[102]

Moreover, human law maintains its integrative place in Thomistic jurisprudence because of its relation to reality, to social and political living and governance, and to the advancement of temporal happiness. Undeniably, human or positive law can never be as comprehensive or as perfect as its relational superiors—the eternal, natural, and divine laws—and if its terminus and enforceability depend solely on its human, secular object, then such a law, if not today, will tomorrow exact an injustice. This inevitable tragedy that results when human law is the centerpiece of a legal system is easy enough to predict. Since human law is promulgated by human beings, it will always be subject to error and mistake. Nevertheless, human law is driving toward and concerned with the same goods as its counterparts. Law, as previously defined, is an exercise of reason, a rule and measure of it. Human laws directly reflect the exercise of practical reason, assessing individual facts and circumstances and then deliberating, enacting, and infusing authority by actual laws. Human laws are not, according to Thomas, the exclusive province of the positivist. Not because man is the author of the human law, but more persuasively because man, in exercising practical reason, entwines himself with the God who fashioned him.[103] It would be grotesquely inaccurate to type Thomas's human law as isolated or independent of its legal counterparts. St. Thomas, in response to whether there is such a thing as the human law, insists on its utility and unbridled necessity.[104] Human law is not only language, but the power to habituate, the strength to reign in the unreasonable and the untrue, a prescription for the virtues. Indeed, for Thomas, "it is difficult to see how man could suffice" without it.[105]

The Necessity of Human Law

One of the most striking features of Thomas's discussion of human law is its necessity, a belief that human existence would fail without legal promulgations. Human beings need commands, proscriptions, and prohibitions to carry out their individual and collective enterprise. Laws serve as a series of parameters and controls for human conduct. Although human beings are fundamentally geared to the good and by their rational nature can identify proper ends, experience delineates the value of control. Wills, passions, and appetites tug at and, at times, overwhelm rational creatures who choose conduct contrary to their nature. Indeed, St. Thomas is bold enough to assert that a morally inclined individual has little need of human law because that person already adheres to the dictates of practical reason, the mandates of the natural law, the divine law precepts, and the blueprint of the eternal law. This type of character is rare, for the theory of necessity relates to the bulk of humanity.[106] Those already disposed to virtue have less need for legal regulation, while those whose "disposition is evil are not led to virtue unless they are compelled" [sed quidam male dispositi non ducuntur ad virtutem, nisi cogantur].[107]

The necessity of human law, as St. Thomas poses, "refers to the removal of evils" from the world we inhabit.[108] Law, in the human sense, is the purifier, the fortress against the onslaught of moral barbarism. From another perspective, the necessity of human law is manifest in human activity of every sort, especially in the communal setting. Positive law involves both the "law of nations and civil law" [jus gentium et jus civile].[109]

Neither in anarchy nor in isolation does the human person carry out a social and political existence reliant upon law. Henle argues that human law is necessary not because of its own necessity, but because of the "state of fallen man."[110] The law is not inherently coercive, but is consistent with all its other purposes, "directive" of what ought to be done. To be sure, law has the power to coerce and mold, but since law is a pure exercise of reason, the human actor should be comfortable with its content. Those exercising behavior in accordance with reason are willing properly and thus not in need of coercive power of the law. In this sense, "the good are not subject to law, but only the wicked" [et ideo secundum hoc boni non sunt sub lege, sed solum mali].[111] Hence, human law is necessitous for both reasons of utility and man's current lack of perfection. It is, for lack of better description, a libation that the virtuous can avoid and the wicked must drink.

Human Law Is Derivative

Any legal professional soon discovers that most law has a precedential legacy. Cases of first instance are temporary events, since legal pronouncements eventually attract a following. When enough people praise the decision and enough support is generated amongst the legal community, a legal maxim and principle is born. To have any credibility, a law withstands the test of time and the clamor of the crowd. Good laws are not drafted in isolation, but rooted in tradition. Human law is derived from other sources, including the theological and philosophical underpinnings espoused by St. Thomas. Even speeding, jaywalking, taxes, and the like have a derivative quality, especially in the justness behind their enactment. Kings, too, derive their authority from a higher power, although history is replete with examples of those who turn the crown into an anointing, who would "usurp that right, by framing unjust laws, and by degenerating into tyrants who preyed on their subjects."[112] Human law depends upon and looks to the eternal, natural, and divine laws. Using his integrative method, Thomas finds it impossible to separate human law from the natural-law order so evident in rational creatures. At most, Aquinas places human law lower in his legal hierarchy because its enforceability depends upon human beings, while divine law "persuades men by means of rewards or punishments to be received from God. In this respect it employs higher means."[113] Since law is an exercise of human reason, and reason is the rule and measure of law, Thomas argues that human law is derived from the natural and eternal law. "Now in all human affairs a thing is said to be just from being right, according to the rule of reason. But the first rule of reason is the law of nature, as is clear from what has been stated. Consequently, every human law has just so much of the nature of law as it is derived from the law of nature."[114] Since positivism zealously excludes any rootedness beyond its promulgation, it has stripped away and gutted moral inquiry in human-law analysis. Rights are based on codifications, the mutterings of "some tiny little minority of an elite," rather than inherencies or perennial truths.[115]

The derivative relationship between the positive law and "higher" law is not one based on confrontation but one of unity and integration. Human laws that are contrary to the tenets of the natural law are, by implication, an affront to the eternal law, and not really laws in the truest sense. Radically, Thomas holds that every law is derived from the eternal law because of reason's role in the deliberation, and a law deviating from reason does not have the nature of law in any sense.[116] A human law, inconsistent with the natural, does violence to the very notion of what law is, and ergo cannot bind in conscience.[117] Neither, therefore, is it nor can it be law as popularly understood. Human laws inconsistent with the divine law receive no recognition from Thomas, since any enactment "contrary to the divine law . . . has not the nature of law."[118] Any human promulgation antagonistic to the eternal, divine, and natural laws will be an affront to any version of law and equity. Antagonistic promulgation is a radical error in jurisprudence. Thus, Thomas declares, "But in so far as it deviates from reason, it is called an unjust law, and has the nature, not of law but of violence."[119]

The "stamp of its ancestry" causes the Thomistic jurist to think teleologically, always searching for the ultimate end of man, that supernatural dimension in the human agent's existence, while simultaneously living in the trenches of legal practice and theory. From the foxholes will arise laws consistent with unity and derived from the natural and eternal law, or promulgations that trigger violence to the nature and essence of law. Laws are instituted, St. Thomas insists, for the average man with his many failings, not for the truly virtuous person.[120]

Thomas's just-law theory is a compelling and prophetic analysis of the human person's rights and obligations before the law, and further evidence of the law's derivative quality. Considered from various fronts, it is an account that deals with the justice and the equity of a law itself, the enforceability or obligatoriness of an unjust or just law, and the right to disobey its content. Thomas queries whether every law "binds" men in conscience.[121] If justly enacted, the answer is affirmative, since justice is consistent with reason and the perfect justice of God. Man is not bound to obey any unjust law, because it lacks the force and nature of a law. In both contexts, the law's legitimacy is derived from a higher order. A law is just if "ordained to the common good," the divine good, and nature itself.[122] Thomas advises direct disobedience to any law "contrary to the commandments of God," since such laws are "beyond the scope of human power."[123] For laws in contravention to these principles, the human actor is not obliged or bound; neither can the state legitimately impress such laws upon its citizenry. Scholars have debated vigorously whether St. Thomas holds to the Augustinian maxim that an unjust law is not a law at all (*lex injusta non est lex*). Thomas exhibits more caution in this language: "That which is not just seems to be no law at all" [non videtur esse lex quae justa non fuerit].[124]

At Question 96, Article 4, St. Thomas summarizes how a law can be unjust" "(1) if it is not directed to the common good; (2) if it is beyond the authority of the law-giver; and (3) if it does not impose properly proportionate burdens."[125] In any of these cases, the law loses its force as law and cannot oblige its target. Any disregard for the eternal- or natural-law principles enunciated here is surely evidence of injustice. Laws crafted in derogation to the common good, an anarchy of competing, nonaligned interests replacing a common bond with "as many rules or measures as there are things measured or ruled, . . . cease to be of use."[126]

Though derivative, human law is not a perfect undertaking. Human law, in order to be a sensible human exercise, cannot be expected to eradicate and suppress every act of vice or sin, since men are bound to err. Overzealously enforcing human laws will only produce social resistance and tumult. Thomas is completely opposed to a nation that enslaves its citizens by laws. Too much regulation and control will trigger a revolution of vice and even greater evils will appear. "Therefore it does not lay upon the magnitude of imperfect men the burdens of those who are already virtuous, viz., that they should abstain from all evil. Otherwise these imperfect ones, being unable to bear such precepts, would break out into yet greater evils."[127]

Human law images its author, the human person. Pragmatically, St. Thomas understands the limitations of human promulgations, since no human law can plausibly be expected to stamp out human error. It is not only implausible, but presumptive, since human law lacks the power to do so. Instead, Thomas suggests a recognition of limitations in the use of human law. "Human law likewise does not prohibit everything that is forbidden by the natural law."[128]

On the other hand, the objective of human law is to look to the heavens and to prod man toward a life of virtue. A Thomist discovers early on that law has a formidable relationship with virtue (see Chapter 3), and that every human law should contribute to the advancement of individual and collective virtue. Law should foster and not inhibit self-perfection.[129] Human law transforms the citizenry "who live under common legal institutions into perfect citizens."[130] The law, as an instrument of the state, wishes perfection and happiness for its community. The positive or human law cannot possibly extinguish human imperfection in every case, but it can lead men gradually to a life of virtue.[131]

SUMMARY

In Thomas's framework, law is not codification or enactment alone, but an esoteric integration of God's plan, the supreme exemplar for all being. Law encompasses man's intellectual operations and rationality; it suggests a cohesive and unified plan for social, governmental, and personal living; it lays out a schema of moral and human rights; and it insists upon an unbridled attentiveness to nature and endorses conduct consistent with our nature. More particularly, there is recognition that the law of God is neither severable nor any different from any other legal approach, for Thomas unifies and subsequently derives all from the eternal law. The Thomistic theory of natural law encourages the human player to imperfectly interact with the eternal law of God. Thomas's natural law, the blueprint implanted by God in his rational creatures, is driven by a fundamental theorem: doing good and avoiding evil. Other first principles and even secondary principles are deduced therefrom.

Fantastically, the natural-law jurisprudence of St. Thomas affords the practitioner a reliable indicator of justice. Just activities are the ambition of anything calling itself law, and just activities assume correctness, a rightness in the law's thrust. Thomas's jurisprudence posits "that there are right answers to moral questions and that lawmakers can and should be guided by such moral truths."[132] That this form of jurisprudence is allegedly out of the mainstream, supplanted by the trendy variation of positivism, makes it no less persuasive.

NOTES

1. Daniel Mark Nelson, *The Priority of Prudence: Virtue and Natural Law in Thomas Aquinas and the Implications for Modern Ethics* (University Park: Pennsylvania State University Press, 1992), 107. See also Daniel J. Sullivan, *An Introduction to Philosophy: The Perennial Principles of Classical Realist Tradition* (Rockford, Ill.: Jan Books, 1992); Bernard Beodder, *Natural Theology* (New York: Longmans-Green, 1927); Etienne Gilson, *The Christian Philosophy of St. Thomas Aquinas*, trans. L. K. Shook (New York: Random House, 1956), 266; Thomas E. Davitt, *The Nature of Law* (St. Louis: B. Herder, 1951), 39–54.

2. St. Thomas Aquinas, *Summa Contra Gentiles*, trans. Vernon J. Bourke, vol. 4 (Notre Dame: University of Notre Dame Press, 1975), bk. III, pt. II, ch. 114, 1.

3. Ibid., 115.

4. Ibid., 114.

5. St. Thomas Aquinas, "Summa Theologica," in *Basic Writings of Saint Thomas Aquinas*, ed. Anton C. Pegis, vol. 2 (New York: Random House, 1945), I–II, Q. 90, a. 1, sed contra.

6. Anton-Hermann Chroust, "The Philosophy of Law of St. Thomas Aquinas: His Fundamental Ideas and Some of His Historical Precursors," *American Journal of Jurisprudence* 19 (1975): 24.

7. Gilson, *Christian Philosophy*, 266.

8. Aristotle, "Metaphysics," in *The Basic Works of Aristotle*, ed. Richard McKeon (New York: Random House, 1941), II, 9 (200a 22); Aquinas, "Theologica," I–II, Q. 90, a. 1, c. "Quod lex quaedam regula est et mensura actuum, secundum quam inducitur aliquis ad agendum, vel ab agendo retrahitur. Dicitur enim lex a ligando, quia obligat ad agendum. Regula autem et mensura humanorum actuum est ratio, quae est principium primum actuum humanorum, ut ex praedictis patet. Rationis enim est ordinare ad finem, qui est primum principium in agendis, secundum Philosophum."

9. Walter Farrell, *The Natural Moral Law According to St. Thomas and Suarez* (Ditchling: St. Dominic's Press, 1930), 10. See also Davitt, *Nature of Law*, 39–54; Robert John Henle, "St. Thomas Aquinas and American Law," in *Thomistic Papers II*, ed. Leonard A. Kennedy and Jack C. Marler (Houston: Center for Thomistic Studies, 1986), 67.

10. Aquinas, *Summa Contra Gentiles*, vol. 3, bk. 3, pt. 1, ch. 2.

11. Aquinas, "Theologica," I–II, Q. 96, a. 2, c.

12. Ibid., I–II, Q. 96, a. 1, ad 2.

13. Ibid., I–II, Q. 96, a. 2.

14. Ibid., I–II, Q. 90, art. 2, c.

15. Jeremy Bentham, *The Principles of Morals and Legislation* (New York: Hafner, 1948).

16. Joseph V. Dolan, "Natural Law and Modern Jurisprudence," *Laval Theologique et Philosophique* 16 (1960): 40.

17. Anton-Hermann Chroust, "The Fundamental Ideas in St. Augustine's Philosophy of Law," *American Journal of Jurisprudence* 18 (1973): 67. Daniel Nelson, *Priority of Prudence*, 107, appreciates this comprehensive view of law when he states, "Law in all of its manifestations derives from God's reason."

18. Aquinas, *Gentiles*, III–II, ch. 112, 3.

19. St. Thomas Aquinas, *Treatise on Law*, ed. R. J. Henle (Notre Dame: University of Notre Dame Press, 1993), 149.

20. Aquinas, "Theologica," I–II, Q. 93, a. 3, sed contra.

21. Ibid., I–II, Q. 90, a. 1, ad 1. "Quod cum lex sit regula quaedam et mensura, dicitur dupliciter esse in aliquo: uno modo sicut in mensurante et regulante; et quia hoc est proprium rationis, ideo per hunc modum lex est in ratione sola. Alio modo sicut in regulato et mensurato; et sic lex est in omnibus quae inclinantur in aliquid ex aliqua lege; ita quod quaelibet inclinatio proveniens ex aliqua lege potest dici lex."

22. Gilson, *Christian Philosophy*, 266.

23. Chroust, "Philosophy of Aquinas," 25.

24. Aquinas, "Theologica," I–II, Q. 93, a. 1.

25. Ibid., I, Q. 45, a.3.

26. Ibid., I–II, Q. 93, a. 1, c.

27. Ibid., I–II, Q. 91, a. 1.

28. Ibid., I–II, Q. 93, a. 2, ad 1. "Quod ea quae sunt Dei, in seipsis quidem cognosci a nobis non possunt, sed tamen in effectibus suis nobis

manifestantur, secundum illud (Rom. I, 20): Invisibilia Dei, per ea quae facta sunt, intellecta conspiciuntur."

29. Ibid., I–II, Q. 93, a. 4, c.

30. Ibid., I–II, Q. 91, a. 1, c.

31. Ibid.

32. Ibid., I–II, Q. 93, a. 6, ad. 3.

33. Ibid., I–II, Q. 93, a. 6, ad. 2.

34. Ibid., I–II, Q. 93, a. 1, ad 3. "Et ideo intellectus divinus est verus secundum se; unde ratio ejus est ipsa veritas."

35. C. S. Lewis, *Studies in Words* (Cambridge: Cambridge University Press, 1961), 37.

36. Ibid., 24.

37. St. Thomas Aquinas, *On Kingship*, trans Gerald B. Phelan (Toronto: Pontifical Institute of Mediaeval Studies, 1982), ch. 2, 19.

38. Boedder, *Natural Theology*, 46.

39. Gilson, *Christian Philosophy*, 266.

40. Alasdair MacIntyre's often cited work, *Whose Justice? Which Rationality?* (Notre Dame: University of Notre Dame Press, 1988), 194, warns the critic and ally alike that the natural law is not merely a registry of pre- and proscriptions. "Obeying the precepts of the natural law is more than simply refraining from doing what those precepts prohibit and doing what they enjoin. The precepts become effectively operative only as and when we find ourselves with motivating reasons for performing actions inconsistent with those precepts; what the precepts can then provide us with is a reason which can outweigh the motivating reasons for disobeying them, that is, they point us to a more perfect good than do the latter."

41. Aquinas, "Theologica," I–II, Q. 94, a. 1.

42. Ibid., I–II, Q. 91, a. 2, c.

43. Ibid. "Inter caetera autem rationalis creatura excellentiori quodam modo divinae providentiae subjacet, inquantum et ipsa fit providentiae particeps, sibi ipsi et aliis providens. Unde et in ipsa participatur ratio aeterna, per quam habet naturalem inclinationem ad debitum actum et finem; et talis participatio legis aeternae in rationali creatura lex naturalis dicitur."

44. Ignatius T. Eschmann, *The Ethics of St. Thomas Aquinas* (Toronto: Pontifical Institute of Mediaeval Studies, 1997), 187.

45. Ibid., 166–167.

46. Aquinas, "Theologica," I–II, Q. 94, a. 6.

47. Ibid., I–II, Q. 94, a. 2, c. "Ad hoc quod veritatem cognoscat de Deo, et ad hoc quod in societate vivat: et secundum hoc ad legum naturalem pertinent ea quae ad hujusmodi inclinationem spectant, utpote quod homo ignorantiam vitet, quod alios non offendat, cum quibus debit conversari, et caetera huijusmodi qae ad hoc spectant."

48. Aquinas, *Gentiles*, III–I, ch. 4, 2.

49. Ibid., ch. 6, 5.

50. Aquinas, "Theologica," I–II, Q. 94, a. 2, ad 2.

51. See Brian Tierney, *The Idea of Natural Rights: Studies on Natural Rights, Natural Law and Church Law* (Atlanta: Scholars Press, 1998), 1150–1625.

52. Aquinas, "Theologica," I–II, Q. 94, a. 4, c. "Sic igitur patet quod quantum ad communia principia rationis sive speculativae sive practicae, est eadem veritas seu rectitudo apud omnes et aequaliter nota. Quantum vero ad proprias conclusiones rationis speculativae, est eadem veritas apud omnes, non tamen aequaliter omnibus nota: apud omnes enim verum est quod triangulus habet tres angulos aequales duobus rectis, quamvis hoc no sit omnibus notum. Sed quantum ad proprias conclusiones rationis practicae, nec est eadem veritas seu rectitudo apud omnes, nec etiam apud quos est eadem, est aequaliter nota."

53. Ibid., I–II, Q. 94, a. 4, ad 3.

54. Gratian, *The Treatise on Laws (Decretum DD. 1–20)*, trans. James Gordley (Washington, D.C.: Catholic University Press of America, 1993), I, v, prol. (I, 7); Aquinas, "Theologica," I–II, Q. 94, a. 5, sed contra. "Quod dicitur in Decretis (dist. 5, seu in Praeludio, dist. 5): naturale just ab exordio rationalis creaturae coepit, nec varitur tempore, sed immutabile permanet."

55. Aquinas, "Theologica," I–II, Q. 94, a. 2, c.

56. Gilson, *Christian Philosophy*, 266.

57. Nelson, *Priority of Prudence*, 107.

58. Even the appetitive process exhibits a certain inclination. "This certitude is based on the nature of the being. Things are constituted in a determined way, and their inclination follows and is one with their determination, so that, even without knowledge of what is and what is not appetible, a natural inclination will seek the appetible." Gustaf J. Gustafson, *The Theory of Natural Appetency in the Philosophy of St. Thomas* (Washington, D.C.: Catholic University of America Press, 1944), 71.

59. Aquinas, "Theologica," I–II, Q. 91, a. 3.

60. Ibid., I–II, Q. 94, a. 4, c.

61. Eschmann, *Ethics*, 188.

62. St. Thomas Aquinas, *Commentary on the Sentences*, 4 vols., ed. P. Mandonnet and M. F. Moos (Paris: P. Lethielleus, 1929, 1933, 1947), Suppl., Q. 65, a. 1. "Omne autem illud quod actionem inconvenientem reddit fini quem natura ex opere aliquo intendit contra legem naturae esse dicitur."

63. Aquinas, *Gentiles*, ch. 129, 4.

64. Aquinas, "Theologica," I–II, Q. 100, a. 3.

65. Ibid., I–II, Q. 94, a. 2, c. "Inest enim primo inclinatio homini ad bonum secundum naturam, in qua communicat cum omnibus substantiis, prout scilicet quaelibet substantia appetit conservationem sui esse secundum suam naturam; et secundum hanc inclinationem pertinent ad legem naturalem ea per quae vita hominis conservatur, et contrarium impeditur. Secundo inest homini inclinatio ad aliqua magis specialia secundum naturam, in qua communicat cum caeteris animalibus; et secundum hoc dicuntur ea esse de lege naturali quae natura omnia animalia docuit, ut est commixtio maris et feminae, et educatio liberorum, et similia."

66. Ralph McInerny, *Ethica Thomistica: The Moral Philosophy of Thomas Aquinas* (Washington, D.C.: Catholic University of American Press, 1982), 46, cautions interpreters not to confuse natural-law reasoning with the physical laws or imperatives: "Natural law is not simply the rational recognition of physical imperatives, nor is it a judgment of how we should

act which ignores the given teleology of the physical. Natural law relates to inclinations other than reason, which have their own ends, by prescribing how we should humanly pursue them. For Thomas, natural law is a dictate of reason, not a physical law."

67. Aquinas, "Theologica," I–II, Q. 94, a. 2, a. 4, quoted in R. A. Armstrong, *Primary and Secondary Precepts in Thomistic Natural Law Teaching* (The Hague: Martinus Nijhoff, 1966), 125.

68. Lewis, *Studies in Words*, 43.

69. Aquinas, "Theologica," I–II, Q. 100, a. 1, c.

70. Ibid., I–II, Q. 94, a. 3, ad 2. "Vel illa quae est communis homini et aliis contra naturam, sicut contra commixtionem maris et feminae, quae est naturalis omnibus animalibus, est cocubitus masculorum, quod specialiter dicitur vitium contra naturam."

71. Ibid., I–II, Q. 100, a. 11.

72. See Aquinas, *Treatise on Law*.

73. Aquinas, "Theologica," I–II, Q. 94, a. 4, c.

74. Ibid., I–II, Q. 94, a. 5.

75. Ibid., I–II, Q. 94, a. 5, c.

76. Aquinas, *Gentiles*, III–II, ch. 122, 4.

77. Ibid., III–II, ch. 122, 4.

78. Ibid., III–II ch. 124, 1.

79. Ibid., III–II, ch. 125, 7.

80. Ibid., III–II, ch. 127.

81. Ibid., III–II, ch. 127, 7.

82. Armstrong, *Primary and Secondary Precepts*, 134.

83. Aquinas, "Theologica," I–II, Q. 98, a. 1, c. "Finis autem legis divinae est perducere hominem ad finem felicitatis aeternae; qui quidem finis impeditur per quodcumque pecatum, et non solum per actus exteriores, sed etiam per interiores. Et ideo illud quod sufficit ad perfectionem legis humanae, ut scilicet peccata prohibeat, et poenam apponat, non sufficit ad perfectionem legis divinae; sed oportet quod hominem totaliter faciat ideoneum ad participationem felicitatis aeternae."

84. Jean Tonneau, "The Teaching of the Thomist Tract on Law," *The Thomist* 34 (1970): 31.

85. Noel Dermot O'Donoghue, "The Law Beyond the Law," *American Journal of Jurisprudence* 18 (1973): 158.

86. Aquinas, *Treatise on Law*, 172.

87. Aquinas, *Gentiles*, III–II, ch. 116, 3.

88. Aquinas, "Theologica," I–II, Q. 91, a. 4.

89. Ibid., I–II, Q. 91, a. 4, c.

90. Patrick M. J. Clancy, "St. Thomas on Law," in *Summa Theologica*, trans. English Dominican Friars, vol. 3 (New York: Benziger Brothers, 1947), 3275.

91. Aquinas, "Theologica," I–II, Q. 98, a. 5; Clancy, "St. Thomas on Law," 3275.

92. Aquinas, "Theologica," I–II, Q. 98, a. 5.

93. Ibid., I–II, Q. 91, a. 4, ad 1. "Quod per naturalem legem participatur lex aeterna secumdum proportionem capacitatis humanae naturae. Sed

oportet ut altiori modo dirigatur homo in ultimum finem supernaturalem. Et ideo superadditur lex divinitus data, per quam lex aeterna participatur altiori modo."

94. Ibid., I–II, Q. 91, a. 4, c.

95. Ibid. Gilson, *Christian Philosopyhy*, 333, artistically blends this divine law and human agent into a union, a unity, a bridge spanning the chasm of the temporal and the eternal, attaching him to God by means of His love.

96. Aquinas, "Theologica," I–II, Q. 100, a. 2, c; Aquinas, *Gentiles*, III–II, ch. 128, 2.

97. Aquinas, "Theologica," I–II, Q. 98, a. 2, c.

98. Ibid., I–II, Q. 100, a. 1.

99. Ibid., I–II, Q. 100, a. 8, c.

100. Ibid., I–II, Q. 99, a. 2, ad. 2.

101. Ibid., I–II, Q. 91, a. 5, ad 1. "Sicut paterfamilias in domo alia mandata proponit pueris, et alia adultis; ita etiam unus rex Deus in uno suo regno aliam legem dedit hominibus adhuc imperfectis existentibus, et aliam perfectiorem jam manuductis per priorem legem ad majorem capacitatem, divinorum."

102. Ibid., I–II, Q. 99, a. 4, ad. 1.

103. For some well-grounded discussion of positive law in Thomistic jurisprudence, see Vincent McNabb, *St. Thomas Aquinas and the Law* (London: Blackfriars, 1955); and Barry F. Smith, "Of Truth and Certainty in the Law: Reflections on the Legal Method," *American Journal of Jurisprudence* 30 (1985): 119.

104. Aquinas, "Theologica," I–II, Q. 63, a. 1; Q. 94, a.3; Q. 95, a. 1, c.

105. Ibid., I–II, Q., 95, a. 1.

106. Charles Skok, *Prudent Civil Legislation According to St. Thomas and Some Controversial American Law* (Rome: Catholic Book Agency, 1967), 119, portrays Thomas's vision as realistic rather than pessimistic: "St. Thomas often made reference to men in their present condition. Not many men are truly virtuous or highly virtuous. Laws have to be made for the general run of the people in the state in which they are found. This is not pessimism but realism."

107. Aquinas, "Theologica," I–II, Q. 95, a. 1, ad. 1.

108. Ibid., I–II, Q. 95, a. 3.

109. Ibid., I–II, Q. 95, a. 4, c.

110. Aquinas, *Treatise on Law*, 335.

111. Aquinas, "Theologica," I–II, Q. 96, a. 5, c.

112. Ibid., I–II, Q. 105, a. 1, ad 5.

113. Ibid., I–II, Q. 99, a. 6, ad. 2.

114. Ibid., I–II, Q. 91, a. 2, ad 2, c. "In rebus autem humanis dicitur esse aliquid justum ex eo quod est rectum secundum regulam rationis. Rationis autem prima regula est lex naturae, ut ex supra dictis patet. Unde omnis lex humanitus posita intantum habet de ratione legis, inquantum a lege naturae derivatur."

115. M. Gilson, *Law on the Human Level. Moral Values and Moral Life: The System of St. Thomas*, trans. L. Ward (St. Louis: B. Herder, 1931), 204.

116. Aquinas, "Theologica," I–II, Q. 93, a. 3, ad. 2.

117. Ibid., I–II, Q. 93, a 3.

118. Ibid., I–II, Q. 93, a. 3, ad 1. "Sic contrariatur legi Dei, et non habet rationem legis."

119. Ibid., I–II, Q. 93, a. 3, ad 2. "Inquantum vero a ratione recedit, sic dicitur lex iniqua, sed magis violentiae cujusdam."

120. Ibid., I–II, Q. 96, a. 2; Q. 69, a. 1; Q. 77, a. 1; Q. 78, a. 1, ad 3.

121. Ibid., I–II, Q. 96, a. 4.

122. Ibid., I–II, Q. 96, a. 4, c.

123. Ibid., I–II, Q. 96, a. 4, ad. 2.

124. Ibid., I–II, Q. 95, a. 2; Q 96, a. 4

125. Ibid., I–II, Q. 96, a. 4, c. "Dicuntur autem leges justae, et ex fine, quando scilicet ordinantur ad bonum commune; et ex auctore, quando scilicet lex lata non excedit potestatem ferentis; et ex forma, quando scilicet secundum aequalitatem proportionis imponuntur subditis onera in ordine ad bonum commune." See Damich, "Essence of Law," 92.

126. Aquinas, "Theologica," I–II, Q. 96, a. 2, ad 2.

127. Ibid., I–II, Q. 96, a. 2, ad 2. "Et ideo non statim multitudini imperfectorum imponit ea quae sunt jam virtuosorum, ut scilicet ab omnibus malis abstineant; alioquin imperfecti hujusmodi praecepta ferre non valentes in deteriora mala prorumperent."

128. Ibid., I–II, Q. 96, a. 2, ad 3. "Unde etiam lex humana non omnia potest prohibere quae prohibet lex naturae."

129. Raymond Dennehy, "The Ontological Basis of Human Rights," *The Thomist* 42 (1978): 455–457, addresses the law's ultimate aim: "For, as a rational being, man attains his self-perfection by transcending the limitations of his finite, temporal self. Through the immanence of knowing, he achieves ever higher levels of reality as he identifies himself ontologically with Being and its facets. Truth, Goodness, Beauty, and ultimately with the fullness of Being, God; and all the while he retains his own unique selfhood."

130. Hemrich A. Rommen, *The Natural Law*, trans. Thomas R. Hanley (St. Louis: B. Herder, 1948), 54–55.

131. Aquinas, "Theologica," I–II, Q. 96, a. 2.

132. Henry Mather, "Natural Law and Right Answers," *American Journal of Jurisprudence* 38 (1993): 334. See also Skok, *Prudent Civil Legislation*, 22.

CHAPTER 3

St. Thomas on Virtue and Law

Being a virtuous person is synonymous with the moral practice of law. Virtue is about proper ends and dispositions. Virtuous conduct is consistent with the rule and measure of reason. Whether the virtue's end tends toward intellectual or applied activity, each virtue habituates and disposes the human actor to those goods which preserve personal and spiritual integrity. Wisdom and understanding, for example, are perfections of the speculative intellect, while justice, temperance, fortitude, and prudence represent the capacity to act on reason's commands. A just lawyer or judge selects courses of conduct that restore the equilibrium between individuals and governing bodies. The prudential judge chooses habitually correct resolutions to specific dilemmas. Virtue is the mean, the power to choose and do righteously.

Virtuous activity is that conduct consistent with the proper ends of the human person. A virtuous life and its corresponding activity correspond to happiness in the human species, both from a natural and a supernatural perspective. For Aristotle, virtue was seen as the means to pure happiness in the earthly domain. A virtuous disposition makes the human player happy and contented. So compelling is the virtuous life, according to Aristotle, that the subject not only performs good activity, but enjoys it. Virtuous conduct becomes so pleasing that vice is pleasingly shunned. Character arises "out of like activity."[1]

St. Thomas agrees with the Aristotelean perspective, but goes further. Virtuous conduct, to be sure, is geared to the human person's proper ends, but these ends extend to a higher, supernatural order. Human happiness can only culminate in the truest, most complete end of man—God. Virtue is a reflection of not only the human player's essential perfections in the material world, but that of God's supreme perfection. Thus, St. Thomas dictates, happiness is only achievable, in its purest sense, in the supernatural order. Law facilitates both individuals and communities toward these perfections.

THE RELATIONSHIP OF VIRTUE AND LAW

The relationship between any notion of virtue and legal jurisprudence prompts a host of initial reactions, some confused, some happily concurrent. How virtue, that disposition to do what is right, to be righteous in deed and orientation, intersects with law is one of St. Thomas's finest and most remarkable insights. At its heart, St. Thomas's theory of virtue accepts and presumes that man, as a creature, is inherently ordered to the good, this condition being indelibly imprinted on man by the God who creates him. This orientation, this tendency, this inherency is the essential component of the being in question, in tune with its fundamental nature, moving toward the proper ends and objects of its very existence. God's "architectonic plan" is part of God's reason, from the origin of the universe to the fluidity of the present.[2]

As both Plato and Aristotle deduced, certain attributes constitute excellence in the fullness of any being.[3] What, for example, makes the excellent musician or craftsman? How can art and artistry achieve their highest perfection? How does a gardener cultivate crops most productively? All things and all beings are seeking and desiring to fulfill and achieve the fullest extent possible of their perfection. Rational creatures naturally desire knowledge, hoping to learn and find out about their basic ends, and "nothing can completely satisfy man's desire which does not comprehend universal goodness."[4] This purpose or end is not what is contrary or antagonistic to man, but complimentary to his or her fruition, "leading man to virtue, by habituating him to good works."[5] So the task of the Thomistic legal thinker is to identify and dwell upon those ends, those objects pertinent to man's very existence, and to utilize that portion of man's being that gives the human species its unique identity. Within this framework, man is determined and defined by his or her intellect, soul, and rationality. Reason defines and distinguishes the human actor from other species. Intentionality exclusively resides in the human person, and this component of being deciphers proper ends. Thus, St. Thomas holds, first and foremost, that virtue is a direct relative to the activities of reason: "The good of each thing is its end: and therefore, as truth is the end of the intellect, so to know truth is the good act of the intellect. Whence the habit which perfects the intellect in regard to the knowledge of truth, whether speculative or practical, is a virtue."[6]

Virtue, for St. Thomas, represents a proper and comparative ordering of reason, a disciplined disposition to do what is good for the human person, a power and a strength to achieve the suitable ends of the created being. In his analysis of love and friendship, St. Thomas puts virtue on a pedestal when compared to other earthly goods: "Virtue is much more honorable than money, whence those who feign virtue are more malicious than those who counterfeit money."[7] Gilson succinctly analyzes this aspect of St. Thomas:

Each thing's good is what is suited to it in view of its form. Each thing's evil is whatever contradicts this form and tends, consequently, to destroy its order. Since man's form is his rational soul itself, every act conforming to reason must be called good, and every act contrary to it called evil. If we consider each individual act which conforms to reason, we shall find that it does so insofar as it is ordered to an end and to a series of means which the reason, after some investigation, declares good. So, the many particular good acts which man does are an ensemble of acts ordered to their end and justifiable by reason.[8]

Virtue is a power that stimulates the human agent to perfect. Since the "good for anything whatever consists in the fact that its action is in agreement with its form," virtue is the means by which reason will act in accordance with the essence of the being and avoid those things "repugnant to the nature of reason."[9]

That reason is the conduit for virtuous activity is consistent with Thomas's overall philosophy. Reason, if correctly applied, only deliberates and guides activities compatible with preservation. Virtue is critical to the unfolding of human capacity, and influences contrary to it must be cast off. Even longtime friendship "should be dissolved toward those who do not remain in virtue."[10] Since the rule of reason is the measure of human activity, "the virtuous habit, for St. Thomas, is its agreement with reason. Man is marked by rationality as his specific difference: to become a morally perfected human being is to develop all four moral powers in accord with right reason."[11]

No thinker, except Aristotle, has so aggressively and decisively advanced this theory of virtue relating to reason as has St. Thomas. In the soul of man we find either virtue or vice. In reason, if acting in accordance with our form, we find an inclination, a disposition to do good, to achieve proper ends. Virtue is the "perfection of a power" to perfect oneself according to our nature.[12] Virtue's prime act is what is true "in making man's deed good."[13]

Remembering that law, according to Thomistic jurisprudence, is nothing more than reason's rule and measure of human activity, it makes perfect sense to integrate the doctrine of virtues. Man's very essence is in the form of a rational soul, and as a result there is in "every man a natural inclination to act according to reason; and this is to act according to virtue."[14]

VIRTUE, LAW, AND THE ENDS OF THE HUMAN PERSON

Now that the relationship between virtue and law has been established, what ends should the law promote and foster? Law is in the business, states St. Thomas, of promoting the virtuous life of individual and community. Addressing whether human laws pertain to virtues, St. Thomas instructs lawmakers to never lose sight of the law's virtuous purposes, since "all the objects of the virtues can be referred either to the private good of an individual, or to the common good of the multitude."[15] Therefore, the law is an instrument, a tool of moral perfection. Law facilitates individual and communal perfection, it assists the human agent in being virtuous, and it aids human beings in the contemplation of proper objects and ends. In these ways, law is far more influential than its mere promulgation. Because the positivist looks no further than the enactment of law, questions of ends seem irrelevant to law. Thomistic jurisprudence has loftier aims and ends in mind for its law. The law's effects are thoroughly consistent with the effects of the virtuous disposition. Law directs men to their true goal; it fashions good men. That which is lawful gently coerces the citizen by permission, common prohibition, and penalty toward the virtuous life. Unlawfulness achieves the opposite result.

But what ends are the virtues compatible with? What ends should the lawmaker seek? How does one know what ends promote virtue? As noted, the proper ends of a creature are its own good. Virtue is the perfection and achievement of what constitutes the good in human activity, whether in the social, political, or spiritual sphere. Virtue is the result of a correct intellectual activity, the employment of reason's function consistent with the ends of man. Virtue is an ordered, habituated disposition of the human soul to the goods it needs to sustain itself. Jean Porter claims that the *Summa Theologica's* massive content encapsulates a "general theory of goodness."[16] Every creature, including man, has certain goods and corresponding ends to its formal existence.[17] Thomas's treatise, *On Kingship*, corroborates how a theory of goods, of happiness, weaves its way back into a theory of virtue: "This is also clearly shown by reason. It is implanted in the minds of all who have the use of reason that the reward of virtue is happiness. The virtue of anything whatsoever is explained to be that which makes its possessor good and renders his deed good."[18]

The end of human life is "happiness or beatitude," in both an earthly and eternal sense.[19] Laws should promote virtuous conduct, thereby generating the good conducive to the creature's enhancement. Thomas, like Aristotle and Plato, weighed the quality of goodness with the goods bestowed on human life. The goods range from the ephemeral to the divine.

From another perspective, Thomas's thought is often described as being as psychological as it is philosophical. Human development, fullness of operations, and realization of potentiality envision the unfolding of the human person toward the most attainable perfection. Virtue empowers man to seek and reach the requisite ends for human happiness. It is the power of the soul that reaches for the perfection of human operation and beyond. Each operation is generated and proceeds from the power of the soul. Because virtue disposes the human player to perfection, the end being the best, Thomas concludes that the "power of the soul is the subject of virtue" [potentia animae sicut in subjecto].[20]

The Thomistic human being is neither predestined nor predetermined, nor locked into a series of modes or operations that are inherently static, but free to roam in a unified, modifiable, and intellectually "dynamic, potential whole."[21] Man has the capacity to progress and achieve, scaling moral encounters with confidence. Thomas says, "Whence, since virtue is the proper perfection of man, and a virtuous man is perfect in the human species, it is fitting that the virtuous man should be taken as the measure for the whole human genus."[22]

Aside from these personal effects, virtue also tends to enhance or secure the common good of the community. In Chapter 6 the collective good and its centrality in Thomas's legal thought is analyzed. That "law is ordained to the common good" further represents Thomas's penchant for stability, advancement, and permanency, since a culture, just as the individual, seeks not its ruination but its fixation and its flowering.[23] Enacting laws that expressly disregard the common good is a sure prescription for cultural collapse, since individualism offers an unpredictable and unstable legal landscape. St. Thomas declares that the common good is the end of law, the reason for its existence. Not the particular, unique, individualized good, but the good that promotes and protects the common welfare of a society is the good Thomas speaks of. The common good sought is one that catapults a culture toward the goods and ends appropriate to man, that affords a stable communal atmosphere, and that preserves the moral, cultural, and intellectual values of the nation.

Goods can also be identified according to inclinations in the species. Of course, Thomas's entire natural-law theory presupposes a series of goods that man, by nature, clings to and desires. The fundamental maxim "do good and avoid evil" comprises the natural law. Some of these inclinations are *per se nota*, others derivative, but in any event, these principles, whether first or secondary, are evidence of proper goods and ends for man. Some are naturally known goods, a product of both inherent attributes and common experience, inherent representations of human nature. Automatically, these inclinations are discoverable.[24] Thomas instructs that the good is easily discerned, even in particularized situations and moral dilemmas, and virtue habituates us toward those goods, just as vice makes us blind to what is true and good. Common precepts are known to all, and these "cannot in any way be blotted out from men's hearts" [nullo modo potest a cordibus hominum deleri].[25] The secondary precepts, the more contingent and particularized determinations, "can be blotted out from the human heart, either by evil persuasions, just as in speculative matters errors occur in respect of necessary conclusions; or by vicious customs and corrupt habits, as among some men, theft, and even unnatural vices."[26]

Because the natural law is man's participation in the eternal law of God, the penultimate good of man is God Himself. The purest of virtues and the perfection of law culminates in the divine essence of God. Virtue leads the human player to participate in the truth. Virtue is the instrument that aids man in the pursuit of God. Man is perpetually wanting the divine presence, if exercising the law inherent in reason and being attentive to the messages of the natural law. Virtue assists the moral agent, molds and frames the paths of activity, and finally makes the journey to this ultimate and final good effortless. Human beings inherently know this, for every other good lacks the permanency and substantive depth to perpetually refresh us.

Only in this final state with God will real happiness be achieved. Only here will the complete fullness of good be met. Only here will man reach the plateau of perfection. Only in pure, unreserved, unrestrained, wholly unified virtue will God reside. St. Thomas identifies the perfection of virtues with God Himself:

Consequently the exemplar of human virtue must needs pre-exist in God, just as in Him pre-exist the exemplars of all things. Accordingly, virtue may be considered as existing originally in God, and thus we speak of *exemplar* virtues, so that in God the divine mind itself may be called prudence; while temperance is the turning of God's gaze on Himself, even as in us temperance is that which conforms concupiscence to reason.[27]

The topic of virtue is treated with regularity in the works of St. Thomas, and his coverage impressively includes not only a definitive review of the virtues but also a cogent look at the nature of habituation, the processes of corruption, the increase or addition in virtues, the interconnectedness and equality of the virtues, and, finally, the various categories of virtue. Whether the theological virtues of faith, hope, and charity; the intellectual virtues of the speculative and practical order; or the moral virtues of temperance, justice, fortitude, and prudence, whose subject matter is application, Thomas masters the topic. Thomas particularly focuses on the cardinal or "hinge" virtues of temperance, fortitude, justice, and prudence, because of their centrality in moral decision making.

When carrying out either practical or theoretical legal exercises, virtuous tendencies or traits are, by most accounts, beneficial. Who would disavow the lawyer who is just and equitable? What judge would be condemned because of a tendency to judge wisely and prudentially? Who would be adverse to the intellectually prepared judge, whose reasoning exudes wisdom, common sense, and an understanding of individual and collective ramifications? Here again, St. Thomas cannot divide the character of the professional from the activities of the profession. This integrative view of man—virtue and performance—causes the judge or the advocate to think from a multiplicity of vantage points, including the traditional ones of precedent and legal language, common and case law. Virtue mandates a legal practice in conjunction with the goods spoken of, with perennial and universal truths. Therefore, any discussion of St. Thomas's jurisprudence must take account of the virtues. A lawmaker lacking prudence knows neither how to legislate wisely nor what the subject matter of his or her laws should be. This is also true for the lawmaker lacking the moral courage and fortitude to legislate morally or the judge who caves into fads or political pressure. In St. Thomas's world, the lawmaker's laws are in part or whole the lawmaker's being. In sum, virtue is the assurance that law, in either a practical or a theoretical sense, will be just and good.

Virtue, Habituation, and Law

One of the most compelling observations generated by St. Thomas was that virtue is a form of habituation. While there is slight support for the idea that certain habits may be infused by divine grace, or knowledge of the natural law's first principles could be called, as Thomas relays, "a natural habit," Thomas is resolute in describing habits as "formative."[28] By formative one means that the activity creates the habit. In turn, habits fall into two categories: virtue and vice. Virtue leads to the good and vices the opposite. Thomas terms a habit as a "certain disposition in relation to nature or to operation," and this disposition is "caused by acts."[29] The acts causing the habit are never singular, but multiple, says St. Thomas:

> For everything that is passive and moved by another is disposed by the action of the agent; and therefore if the acts be multiplied, a certain quality is formed in the power which is passive and moved, which quality is called a habit; just as the habits of the moral virtues are caused in the appetitive powers, according as they are moved by the reason, and as the habits of science are caused in the intellect, according as it is moved by first propositions.[30]

Of course, the repetition of acts can cause either virtue or vice, excess or defect, more or less of a disposition. Habits can be altered, changed, increased or decreased, corrupted or purified. Even sin causes man to lose "a habit of virtue."[31]

The view that a human agent is separable from personal activity is at odds with Thomas's opinion of habit. In legal circles, it is crucial to be judged by one habituated to virtue. Legal science is a moral science that requires not simply legal acumen, but also a virtuous disposition.[32] A lawmaker on the take, a district attorney subject to extortion and bribes, or a lawyer prone to falsehoods will be occupationally influenced by these negative, vicelike habituations.

Virtue, Law, and the Intellect

St. Thomas categorizes the subjects of virtues by their agency. In general, almost everything in a rational being can be habituated. Some argue that physical training, or lack thereof, is directly relational to virtue. What is surely true in Thomas's eyes is that virtue is primarily an orderly disposition consistent with rationality. Virtue "disposes to that which is best," and the "soul is the subject of virtue."[33] The intellect is also subject to the power of virtue, both practically and speculatively. At Question 56, Article 3, we see the confirmation: "Hence the subject of a habit which is called a virtue in a relative sense can be the intellect, and not only the practical intellect, but also the speculative, without any reference to the will."[34]

From this point, St. Thomas categorizes the content of the speculative intellect's virtues; namely wisdom, science, and understanding.[35] It would be absurd to argue that a *habitus* does not pertain to those engaging in intellectual pursuits. Thomas says that perfection of knowledge is perfection of truth. To truly know and understand any principle in law, the speculative intellect is habituated by the virtue of "understanding" [intellectus].[36] As understanding presumes knowledge of a principle, it is appropriately labeled "the habit of principles" [habitus principiorum].[37]

Prudence, the subject matter of Chapter 5, receives considerable attention from Thomas's cutting intellect. While prudence is construed as both an intellectual and a moral virtue, it is clear that the virtue of choosing means, tackling problems, and identifying a course of conduct is more applicative than consultative and deliberative. Despite these subtleties, prudence is a virtuous habituation as well, and for Thomas the virtue "most necessary for human life."[38] Prudence is about means, courses of conduct, and the manner of doing, not the end sought. Prudence is "rectitude of choice" based upon experience, effects, impacts, and individual and communal ramifications.

Virtue, Law, and Moral Activity

Thomas fundamentally divides virtue into two kinds: the intellectual and the moral.[39] In the former case, the habituation is primarily speculative; in the latter case, the virtue has application to a particular determination. Another contrast between the two would be the intellectual virtue's locus primarily in reason or intellect, while the moral virtue resides more within the appetitive realm, rather than in pure speculation and contemplation. Moral virtues, tied to appetites, "move all the powers to their acts" [movere omnes potentias ad agendum].[40] As a consequence, the moral virtues are more disposed to matters of passion than thought, though, as St. Thomas cautions, the passions are also intricately tied to reason by their moderation. "Conformity to reason" signifies the virtuous act.[41] Passions, however, are not synonymous with virtues, but, more descriptively, nothing more than "movements of the sensitive appetite."[42] Virtue does not extinguish the passions but moderates them.[43] As many appetites as there are, there will be a correlative number of moral virtues to temper them. Quoting Aristotle, Thomas lists the moral virtues "according to their diverse matter, passion, or objects."[44] The list includes "ten moral virtues about the passions, viz., fortitude, temperance, liberality, magnificence, magnanimity, love of honor, gentleness, friendship, truthfulness and wittiness. All of them are distinguished according to their diverse matter, passions or objects; so that if we add justice, which is about operations, there will be eleven in all."[45]

Special attention is then given to the four cardinal or moral virtues: justice, prudence, temperance, and fortitude. "Cardinal" is used interchangeably with the term "principal." These terms indicate the importance of the four moral virtues in the life of man and the society inhabited. Prudence, since it is about choosing means to appropriate ends, is labeled by Thomas the "principal of all the virtues."[46] Despite this preference, St. Thomas describes these four moral virtues as the building blocks of a nation and the standards by which an individual and community thrive. St. Thomas touts their importance above all others:

First, according to their common formal principles. In this way, they are called principal, being general, as it were, in comparison with all the virtues; so that, for instance, any virtue that causes good in reason's act of consideration may be called prudence; every virtue that causes good of rectitude and the due in operations, be called justice; every virtue that curbs and represses the passions, be called temperance; and every virtue that strengthens the soul against any passions whatever, be called fortitude. Many, both holy doctors, as also philosophers, speak about these virtues in this sense.[47]

These virtues are principal because of their subject matter and their indispensability. Question 61, Article 3, relays the pinnacle roles these cardinal virtues carry out in a lawful society. Prudence commands, justice distributes and differentiates, temperance "suppresses desires for the pleasures of touch" [quae reprimit concupiscentias delectationum tactus], and fortitude "strengthens against dangers of death" [quae firmat contra pericula mortis].[48] Later, Thomas typifies their significance by function: assuring political and legal stability, perfecting the citizenry for temporal affairs, and reconciling one's soul to the perfect God. These four virtues Thomas calls perfect, the virtues "of a now cleansed soul" [virtutes jam purgati animi].[49] These perfect virtues reign higher than other virtues because of their proximity to and identicality with God. "Thus, prudence now sees nought else but the things of God; temperance knows no earthly desires; fortitude has no knowledge of passion; and justice, by imitating the divine mind, is united thereto by an everlasting covenant. Such are the virtues attributed to the blessed, or in this life, to some who are at the summit of perfection."[50] Justice and prudence, covered extensively in Chapters 4 and 5, represent giving what and when is due and choosing proper means to ends.

Virtue, Law, and the Mean

It would be derelict not to feature some analysis of the mean in moral and virtuous inquiry. As his beloved Aristotle, Thomas wholeheartedly finds solace in the theory of the mean, that judgment of human activity that resists radicalness and extremes of every sort. Virtue, for Aquinas, is not simply an ordered disposition in a personal or analytical sense, but a slide rule by which conducts can and are measured. By mean, we do not imply compromise or accommodation, since many conducts in the criminal or moral sphere will always be opposed to the rule of reason (e.g., murder, pedophilia, etc.). Depending upon circumstances, one evaluates moral conduct using a moral norm. By way of illustration, the sorrowful man is just as out of kilter as the gregarious, continually laughing man. The mean is between, Thomas comments:

In actions and passions, the mean and the extremes depend on various circumstances. Hence nothing hinders something from being extreme in a particular virtue according to one circumstance, while the same thing is a mean according to other circumstances, through its conformity with reason. This is the case with magnanimity and magnificence. For if we look at the absolute quantity of the respective objects of these virtues, we shall call it an extreme and a maximum; but if we consider the quantity in relation to other circumstances, then it has the character of a mean, since these virtues tend to this maximum in accordance with the rule of reason, *i.e., where* it is right, *when* it is right, and for an *end* that is right.[51]

It is more appropriately termed the "mean of reason," not a mathematical, computational, or political mean. This is true for intellectual virtues, prudential judgments, and theological insights as well. Every virtue is good only if it "consists in a mean, according to which it is conformed to a rule or measure which it is possible to overstep or to fail to reach, as was stated above. Now intellectual virtue, like moral virtue, is directed to the good."[52] Each virtue focuses on the just mean of human activity. To be in conformity with right reason the just mean is

removed from excess and defect in each given case. Sometimes it happens that the mean fixed by reason is the mean of the thing itself, as in the case of justice which regulates operations relating to external acts, and must assign to each his due, neither more nor less. Sometimes, on the contrary, it happens that the mean fixed by reason is not the mean of the thing itself, but one that is a mean in relation to us.[53]

VIRTUE AND LEGAL PRACTICE

In conclusion, St. Thomas's esoteric treatment of virtue edifies and elucidates his complex psychology. The human person is not a drifter, a persona without cause or purpose, an ignorant and empty player bereft of moral dimension. Thomas would disagree with those who allege a person is ill-equipped to live life according to the nature imparted to him or her or the basic inclinations that show just the periphery of virtuous possibilities. To be sure, virtue is formative and habitual. Virtue and its corresponding activity make it possible for the justice professional to succeed and to actualize the potency to happiness that resides in virtue.

We are confronted with a contemporary legal system, and even more markedly, a bureaucracy of legal education that doesn't even pay lip service to the virtuous aspect of human activity. By contrast, those who quietly, almost timidly decry this horrid state of moral training are relegated to the status of an elitist or moral tyrant judgmentally imposing values. As Aristotle and Thomas agree, the lawyer and judge who lack theological faith and an unequivocal belief in a deity will still benefit from the virtuous disposition.[54] Happiness comes even to the nonbeliever since virtuous conduct is in accord with reason, comportable with nature, and consistent with advancing the ends appropriate to the human species. Lawyers and judges clinging to virtue are guaranteed a life of professional fulfillment.

Virtue and the practice of law are indispensably joined. A reasoned person has mastered appetites and passions, acts in accord with nature, understands and comprehends ends and purposes, chooses suitable means, and can identify legal decision making from both the individual and collective perspectives. Virtue is the assurance that the law is right. For lawyer, judge, and humanity, law assists, facilitates, and enables in the most complete sense of what happiness means. The legal professional using virtue as guide will assuredly advocate and decide correctly, but will also be happy and contented in his or her work. Virtue maximizes happiness and allows the justice professional not only to be proficient and competent in function, but also at peace internally and externally.

NOTES

1. Aristotle, "Nicomachean Ethics," in *The Basic Works of Aristotle*, ed. Richard McKeon (New York: Random House, 1941), bk. II, 952–953.

2. See Vernon J. Bourke, "Right Reason in Contemporary Ethics," *The Thomist* 38 (1974): 113. See also Brian T. Mullady, "The Meaning of the Term 'Moral' in St. Thomas Aquinas," in *Studi Thomistica*, vol. 27 (Vatican City: Libreria Editric Vaticana, 1986), 90; Robert J. Kreyche, "Virtue and Law in Aquinas: Some Modern Implications," *Southwestern Journal of Philosophy* 5 (1974): 130.

3. Plato, *The Laws of Plato*, ed. Thomas L. Pangle (New York: Basic Books, 1980), b X 886a. Aristotle, *Nicomachean Ethics*, trans. Martin Ostwald (New York: Bobbs-Merrill, 1962), X, 9, 1180a.

4. Numerous thinkers express this relationship between God and creation with an enviable clarity. See Kevin Staley, "Happiness: The Natural End of Man?" *The Thomist* 53 (1989): 221.

5. St. Thomas Aquinas, "Summa Theologica," in *Basic Writings of St. Thomas Aquinas*, ed. Anton C. Pegis, vol. 2 (New York: Random House, 1945), I–II, Q. 100, a. 9, sed contra.

6. Ibid., I–II, Q. 56, a. 4, ad 3. "Quod bonum uniuscujusque est finis ejus. Et ideo cum verum sit finis intellectus, cognoscere verum est bonus actus intellectus; unde habitus perficiens intellectum ad verum cognoscendum vel in speculativis, vel in practicis, dicitur virtus."

7. St. Thomas Aquinas, *On Aristotle's Love and Friendship*, trans. Pierre Conway (Providence: Providence College Press, 1951), IX, ch. 3.

8. Etienne Gilson, *The Christian Philosophy of St. Thomas Aquinas*, trans. L. K. Shook (New York: Random House, 1956), 260.

9. Bourke, "Right Reason," 108.

10. Aquinas, *Love and Friendship*, IX, ch. 3.

11. Bourke, "Right Reason," 107.

12. Aquinas, "Theologica," I–II, Q. 56, a. 1.

13. St. Thomas Aquinas, *Summa Theologica*, trans. English Dominican Friars, vol. 2 (New York: Benziger, 1947), II–II, Q. 109, a. 2, c.

14. Aquinas, "Theologica," I–II, Q. 94, a. 3, c.

15. Ibid., I–II, Q. 96, a. 3, c. "Omni autem objecta virtutum referri possunt vel ad bonum privatum alicujus personae, vel ad bonum commune multitudinis."

16. Jean Porter, *The Recovery of Virtue* (Louisville, Ky.: Westminster/John Knox Press, 1990), 35.

17. Porter's view is keenly stated in ibid., 62:

The ordering of the universe, for Aquinas, includes not only what we might call a macro-ordering of all creatures into an array of species. It also includes the fundamental ordering of all creatures toward the attainment of their own proper good and the exercise of their own proper causality. . . . Even though we recognize that our own existence, as individuals or as a species, is not the greatest created good, nonetheless, it is only right—that is, in accordance with the ordering of ourselves and all other things by God—for us to be concerned first of all with our own well-being, rather than with the good of the universe as a whole.

18. St. Thomas Aquinas, *On Kingship*, trans. Gerald B. Phelan (Toronto: Pontifical Institute of Mediaeval Studies, 1982), bk. I, ch. 8, 63.

19. Aquinas, "Theologica," I–II, Q. 90, a. 2, c.

20. Ibid., I–II, Q. 56, a. 1, c.

21. Rose E. Brennan, *The Intellectual Virtues According to the Philosophy of St. Thomas* (Washington, D.C.: Catholic University of America Press, 1941), vii.

22. Aquinas, *Love and Friendship*, IX, ch. 4.

23. Aquinas, "Theologica," I–II, Q. 90, a. 2, c.

24. The level of this type of understanding is the subject of constant scholarly review. See Walter Farrell, *The Natural Moral Law According to St. Thomas and Suarez* (Ditchling: St. Dominic's Press, 1930). See also Kreyche, "Virtue and Law"; Porter, *Recovery*; Alasdair McInerny, *After Virtue*, 2d ed. (Notre Dame: University of Notre Dame Press, 1984).

25. Aquinas, "Theologica," I–II, Q. 94, a. 6, c.

26. Ibid. "Potest lex naturalis deleri de cordibus hominum, vel propter malas persuasiones (eo modo quo etiam in speculativis errores contingunt circa conclusiones necessarias), vel etiam propter pravas consuetudines et habitus corruptos, sicut apud quosdam non reputabantur latrocinia peccata, vel etiam vitia contra naturam."

27. Ibid., I–II, Q. 61, a. 5, c. "Vel prout est exemplariter in Deo; et sic dicuntur virtutes exemplares; ita scilicet quod ipsa divina mens in Deo dicatur prudentia; temperantia vero conversio divinae intentionis ad seipsum, sicut in nobis temperantia dicitur per hoc quod concupiscibilis conformatur rationi."

28. Ibid., I–II, Q. 51, a. 4, a. 1.

29. Ibid., I–II, Q. 50, a. 2; Q. 51, a. 2.

30. Ibid., I–II, Q. 51, a. 2. c. "Nam omne quod patitur et movetur ab alio, disponitur per actum agentis. Unde ex multiplicatis actibus generatur quaedam qualitas in potentia passiva et mota, quae nominatur habitus; sicut habitus virtutum moralium causantur in appetitivis potentiis, secundum quod moventur a ratione; et habitus scientiarum causantur in intellectu, secundum quod movetur a primis propositionibus."

31. Ibid., I–II, Q. 53, a. 1.

32. Naus treats this interplay in John E. Naus, *The Nature of the Practical Intellect According to Saint Thomas Aquinas*, in *Analecta Gregoriana*, vol. 108 (Rome: Libreria Editrice Dell' Universita Gregoriana, 1959), 49.

33. Aquinas, "Theologica," I–II, Q. 56, a. 2.

34. Ibid., I–II, Q. 56, a.3, c. "Subjectum igitur habitus, qui secundum quid dicitur virtus, potest esse intellectus non solum practicus, sed etiam intellectus speculativus absque omni ordine ad voluntatem."

35. Ibid., I–II, Q. 57, a. 2.

36. Ibid., I–II, Q. 57, a. 2, c.

37. Ibid., I–II, Q. 57, a. 5.

38. Ibid., I–II, Q. 58, a. 2.

39. Ibid., I–II, Q. 58, a. 1, c.

40. Ibid., I–II, Q. 58, a. 1, c.

41. Ibid., I–II, Q. 58, a. 3.

42. Ibid., I–II, Q. 59, a. 1.

43. Ibid., I–II, Q. 59, a. 2.

44. Ibid., I–II, Q. 60, a. 5.

45. Ibid., I–II, Q. 60, a. 5, c. "Decem virtutes morales circa passiones, scilicet fortitudo, temperantia, liberalitas, magnificentia, magnanimitas, philotimia, mansuetudo, amicitia, veritas, et eutrapelia, et distinguuntur secundum diversas materias, vel secundum diversas passiones, vel secundum diversa objecta. Si igitur addatur justitia, quae est circa operationes, erunt omnes undecim."

46. Ibid., I–II, Q. 61, a. 3.

47. Ibid., I–II, Q. 61, a. 3, c. "Uno modo secundum communes rationes formales; et secundum hoc dicuntur principales, quasi generales ad omnes virtutes; ut puta quod omnis virtus quae facit bonum in consideratione rationis, dicatur prudentia; et quod omnis virtus quae facit bonum debiti

et recti in operationibus, dicatur justitia; et omnis virtus quae cohibet passiones et reprimit, dicatur temperantia; et omnis virtus quae facit firmitatem animi contra quascumque passiones, dicatur fortitudo. Et sic multi loquuntur de istis virtutibus tam sacri doctores quam etiam philosophi."

48. Ibid.

49. Ibid., I–II, Q. 61, a. 5, c.

50. Ibid. "Ita scilicet quod prudentia sola divina intueatur; temperantia terrenas cupiditates nesciat; fortitude passions ignoret; justitia cum Davina menthe perpetuo foedere societur, eam scilicet imitando; quas quidem virtutes dicimus esse beatorum vel aliquorum in hac via perfectissimorum."

51. Ibid., I–II, Q. 64, a. 1, ad 2. "Quod medium et extrema considerantur in actionibus et passionibus secundum diversas circumstantias. Unde nihil prohibet in aliqua virtute esse extremum secundum unam circumstantiam, quod tamen est medium secundum alias circumstantias per conformitatem ad rationem; et sic est in magnificentia et magnanimus. Nam si consideretur quantitas absoluta ejus in quod tendit magnificus et magnaimus, dicetur extremum et maximum; sed si consideretur hoc ipsum per comparationem ad alias circumstantias, sic habet rationem medii, quia in hoc maximum tendunt hujusmodi virtutes secundum regulam rationis, id est, ubi oportet, et quando oportet, et propter quod oportet."

52. Ibid., I–II, Q. 64, a. 3, c. "Quod bonum aliqujus rei consistit in medio secundum quod conformatur regulae vel mensurae, quam contingit transcendere, et ab ea deficere."

53. Gilson, *Christian Philosophy*, 264.

54. Aristotle, "Nicomachean Ethics," bks. I, V, VI, X.

CHAPTER 4

Law and Justice

In designing a jurisprudence of right, a distinction between just and unjust activities needs to be made. Commencing with the perfect justice, God the Creator, St. Thomas lays out a definitional and essential blueprint for the notion of justice. First, justice is a rational exercise, while its counterpart, injustice, is contrary to reason. Second, justice is a virtuous disposition, an habituation, in which the human actor gives both citizen and community what is due. Third, justice is generally a measure of the mean in human conduct, that balance of behavior and result that keeps interrelationships and political and communal entities in balance. Finally, St. Thomas categorizes justice by its forms: *distributive* and *commutative*. He then declares that when applied to communal contexts, justice evolves to a special category: legal justice. Without justice, neither lawyers nor judges perform their occupational roles lawfully.

THE INTERPLAY BETWEEN JUSTICE AND LAW

The purpose and goal for any justice system, whether criminal or civil, is justice itself. The label "criminal justice" implies a systematic attempt to dispense consequence by reward or punishment, to assure order and tranquility in the culture, and to employ a machinery (e.g., courts, prisons, police and other justice entities) that functionally do justice for both individuals and society. Justice is the cornerstone of a just person and a just society. Thomas proclaims that the "order of justice arises by relation to the first cause, who is the rule of all justice."[1]

Indeed, any Thomistic insight on justice immediately appreciates the interrelationship between a state and an individual that is just or unjust. Thomas firmly believes that the lifeblood of a person and a people depend on justice for "it is of the essence of a nation that the mutual relations of the citizens be ordered by just laws."[2] No place is this position more apparent than in Thomas's suggestion that unjust laws, the promulgations crafted contrary to reason, the natural law, and the divine and eternal laws, are really illusory enactments.[3] Unjust laws lack an obligatory force and should be disregarded, attacked as injurious to the common and individual good, and, in a way, disobeyed.[4] In contrast to the legal positivist, whose legal earth germinates exclusively in the words of the law and whose legitimacy depends upon the power of the entity or individual promulgating it, St. Thomas views justice as the handmaiden of law. Legitimacy, enforceability, and obligatoriness do not arise because a law is a law. The content and end of law are justice and justice alone. Murder is not wrong because the legislator legislates or sexual assault is not grotesque because a special interest group for victims zeroes in on the injustice. Such criminal acts "violate the natural order and, consequently, outrage[s] reason. For such actions use a being who is an end in himself as a mere means to an end, as a mere object of scientific or social purpose."[5]

As in all other aspects of Thomas's work, justice is an eclectic concept, inexorably finding its meaning in teleology from God to man, from perfection to imperfection, from the ultimate, purest goods to temporal ones.[6] God, the eternal lawmaker, consists of pure and perfect justice. Just laws are consistent with the divine exemplar and unjust laws are an affront to this perfection. Just laws oblige in conscience depending on the eternal law and the eternal lawmaker. Hence, the justice of any law is derived from its relationship to its end, the common good, the legitimacy of the lawmaker, its form and sensibility, and its proportionality and equity.[7] Derivatively, the lawfulness and justness of human activity descend from God's justice. From another point of view, justice is virtuous habituation for individual and communal living. Consistent with Thomas's virtue theory, justice is an ordered disposition of the soul, a habituation consistent with the rule and measure of reason, and a rectification of the will to render to each person what is due.[8] Justice is mandatory for the human species because of the will's capacity to stray, whether by avarice, sexual lust, greed or envy, inordinate desire, or anger. Willing more than one is due inevitably produces an injustice.[9]

Justice is one of Thomas's four cardinal virtues, the hinge activities of human existence. It is the virtue of interrelationship and social interaction, but its essence, "dealing with others," is virtuous because of its attentiveness to the rule of reason.[10] Thomas describes this moral virtue with clarity:

A human virtue is one *which renders a human act and man himself good* and this can be applied to justice. For a man's act is made good through attaining the rule of reason, which is the rule whereby human acts are regulated. Hence, since justice regulates human operations, it is evident that it renders man's operations good, and, as Tully declares (*De Officiis* i. 7), good men are so called chiefly from their justice, wherefore, as he says again (*ibid.*) *the luster of virtue appears above all in justice.*[11]

What is so consistently evident in Thomas's treatment of justice is its relational quality. Justice cannot exist in the human sphere without others, and is about "external actions and things," about operations not passions, and, unlike charity, which supremely envelops all the virtues, it is especially concerned with relational interaction.[12] Justice is about external operations and activities, whether person or government entity. Giving each his or her due "according to equality of proportion" is the proper act of justice.[13] Justice is, as MacIntyre interprets Thomas, relational and communal: "To every human being every other human being thus owes, and of all the virtues *iustitia* is the one peculiarly concerned with relations to others. In so characterizing it Aquinas unified within a single complex account the definitions of justice provided by Aristotle, Cicero, and Augustine."[14]

In sum, it is impossible to segregate individual activity from that of the collective where justice is concerned. Realizing this, the contemporary judge, jurist, and advocate are incapable of articulating any idea of justice without weighing the impact on the culture at large. Individual rights are not based upon a just theory if robbed of their teleological qualitites. In every context, justice is primarily concerned with doing the right. Right is the object of justice itself.[15] Justice is the same as its very object, the right, and in this way it towers over all other virtues, being its "own special proper object over and above the other virtues" [Et propter hoc specialiter justitiae prae aliis virtutibus].[16]

JUSTICE AS THE MEAN

Continuing the Aristotelian conception of virtue, Thomas sees justice, as well as other virtues, in measurable terms, particularly the mean—that balance of intellect, appetites and passions, reason and will—that behavioral modicum representing the human agent doing what is in accord with nature and reason.[17] The mean, in most cases, is neither mathematical nor political. Justice "is a mean between having too much and too little."[18] Compromise is not the mean as if the moral agent could choose conduct if only in reasonable amounts. Nor is the mean an avoidance of extremes (e.g., the drunkard versus the prohibitionist, the chaste versus the promiscuous). Thomistic psychology is more multidimensional. The mean is only discoverable when evaluated in light of human reason and rationality. Thomas states,

Moral virtue derives its goodness from the rule of reason, while its matter consists in passions or operations. If, therefore, we compare moral virtue to reason, then if we look at that which it has of reason, it holds the position of one extreme, viz., conformity; while excess and defect take the position of the other extreme, viz., deformity. But if we consider moral virtue in respect of its matter, then it has the nature of a mean, in so far as it makes the passion conform to the rule of reason.[19]

Both excess and defect of reason disregard the mean. Every virtue, whether temperance, prudence, fortitude, or the like, directs itself toward a specific object, and to be properly called a virtue the measure of its quality as virtue is its "conformity to reason."[20] Gilson illustrates the mean of any intellectual virtue as truth, since it "is the just mean, determined by the thing itself. And it is this very truth which confers moral excellence upon a virtue."[21] The mean consists not of political accommodation, but of a balance, an accord with natural traits, attributes, and dispositions.

Justice, just as its virtuous counterparts, searches for the mean. Its object may differ, driven more by external, relational, and operational issues when compared to the internal habituation regarding lust, anger, or other passions. Thomas precisely distinguishes the mean of justice from the other moral virtues, whose chief concern is the irascible and concupiscible. Passions are about internal operations, while justice concerns itself with the external relations common to humanity. The mean of temperance or fortitude, by way of comparison, differs from justice, since its measure is internally computed "by comparison with the virtuous man himself" [comparationem ad ipsum hominem].[22] On the other hand, justice's mean is calculated using the external dynamic, consisting "in a certain proportion of equality between the external thing and the external person."[23]

Justice's elemental concern with equality, proportionality, and equity leads Thomas to conclude that justice's mean is more or less "arithmetical" when compared to the means of other virtues.[24] Justice is about commerce, crime and punishment, political authority and citizenry, property and ownership, and distribution of money and usury. "Justice, then, is a virtue whereby men fulfill their judicial obligations."[25] Its operative quality imputes a relational, interpersonal rationality, Thomas claims: "The reason for this is that justice is about operations, which deal with external things, wherein the right has to be established absolutely and in itself, as was stated above. Hence the mean of reason in justice is the same as the real mean, in so far, namely, as justice gives to each one his due, neither more nor less."[26] To sustain and preserve a friendship, that emotional bond between persons, requires a "proportionate return" of thoughts, emotions, and interpersonal acts.[27] In other words, the mean of justice cannot be determined without reference to others.

Justice is conformity, balance, and equilibrium, in stark contrast to "injustice, deformity, discordance and inequality."[28] The external qualitites of justice for every larceny entail the capture of another's property. In other moral virtues, this relational quality is absent, and for this reason the legal and justice system appreciates the virtue of justice over its counterparts.[29]

Thomas's articulation of what constitutes justice's mean is foundationally tied to reason itself:

Law is reason ordaining what must be done to bring about justice, i.e., the just, or, the right. It tells us how equality, that is to say, a proper commensuration, ought to be achieved, what the *debitum* is, and how it should be rendered. Our enduring desire to render what is due another is the virtue of justice; the enactment of rules whereby the *debitum* will be recognized and rendered is part of the virtue of prudence—its legislative aspect.[30]

Within every aspect of virtue analysis, Thomas enumerates reason as the rule and measure of existence. So the mean of justice is "also the rational mean."[31] Wanting too much, craving, envying, and avariciously desiring what others have are antagonistic to justice.

To further explain justice, Thomas expends energy cataloguing the nature of injustice. Injustice is contrary and confrontational to the rational mean: It is disproportionate and defamatory, zealously desiring, or inordinately possessing. Thomas calls injustice a "special" form of vice because it negatively influences both the individual actor and society.[32] Individual acts of injustice taint the sanctity of the multitude, are repugnant to the common good, and such "contempt of the common good may lead to all kinds of sins."[33] Wisely, Thomas suggests that individual injustices negatively affect an entire community. Thomas is so convinced of injustice's severity and opposition to his rational mean that he terms any act of injustice a mortal sin.[34] Injustice is classified as not only an irrational act, but one that can only be involuntarily accepted, since the human agent never yearns for injustice, and "no man suffers an injustice except against his will."[35] It is therefore inconsistent with our nature to desire injustice, nor to willingly heap it upon our being. For St. Thomas, even choosing to do an unjust thing is more difficult than doing justice: "It is not easy for any man to do an unjust thing from choice, as though it were pleasing for its own sake and not for the sake of something else."[36]

THE FORMS OF JUSTICE

Legal practitioners, both novice and experienced, soon learn that justice can be differentiated according to purpose or goal. While justice is to give each person his or her due, justice is "suitably assigned," depending upon circumstances.[37] Thomas, as Aristotle, divides justice into two basic species, (1) commutative and (2) distributive, and when either of these are applied to a communal setting, he further differentiates legal justice. Thomas defines commutative justice in a relational sense, between two individuals or between individuals and particular groups. Contractual law is an illustration of this type of justice. So, too, is the law of real estate or other legal activity dependent upon monetary or performance equality. Commutative justice exists when both parties engage wilfully in their dealings, neither at an advantage nor disadvantage, but reciprocally. In his *Commentary on Aristotle's Ethics*, Thomas relates how parties are voluntarily involved "in selling and buying, . . . in barter, . . . in bail, . . . in a loan, . . . in a deposit, . . . in rent."[38] Voluntary transactions are just, while involuntary ones "like theft, by which one takes a thing belonging to another who is unwilling; adultery, by which a man secretly approaches the wife of another for sexual intercourse; poisoning, by which a person poisons another with intent either to kill or injure in some way" are unjust.[39] Thomas terms this type of justice as *equalizing*: "Hence it is necessary to equalize thing with thing, so that the one person should pay back to the other just so much as he has become richer out of that which belonged to the other. The result of this will be equality according to the arithmetical mean which is gauged according to equal excess in quantity."[40] Commutative justice is therefore about "mutual dealings."

In the second designation, distributive, Thomas reviews the relation between individual action and that of the state, the community, and the societal whole. Distributive justice perceives individual identities not in a contractual, egalitarian sense, but more as citizens in the collective, who may or may not have more or less than others, whose status may be higher or lower, and whose power, governance, or legal authority may differ. Instead of an arithmetical mean, Thomas says that this type of justice is "geometrical": "Hence in distributive justice the mean is observed, not according to equality between thing and thing, but according to proportion between things and persons: in such a way that even as one person surpasses another, so that which is given to one person surpasses that which is allotted to another."[41]

Legal justice relates to its paramount interest in the common good, and thus it is considered by some a distinct or special form of justice. Legal justice is more perfect, more relational, and more developed because of its interactive and applied quality. Thomas is insightful enough to craft a narrower definition for legal justice, since "legal justice alone seems to be the good of another (that is, relates to our neighbor) inasmuch as it aims to perform actions useful to another, viz., to the community or the ruler of the community."[42] Certainly, justice in a general sense is concerned with what is due and owed others, a penchant for reciprocity and equality. When Thomas defines legal justice, its bent is primarily upon collective impacts and communal goods. Here, any system of law asserting a just operation will have to achieve the virtue of legal justice and direct "man in his relations with individuals as such but with others in general—others as parts of a community."[43]

Commutative Justice

The chief concern of commutative justice is reciprocity, the equality between people and circumstance. Concerned more with strict equality than its distributive counterpart, this form of justice "governs man's civil intercourse and thus by far the greater part of his social life."[44] Commutative justice, with its emphasis on equality, encompasses the equilibrium, the reaction to action, and the price for the product. Punishment for criminal conduct is a prime illustration, since the judicial imposition of sentence attempts to restore balance. Judges try "to equalize this by subtracting from the gain and allotting compensation for the loss."[45] Retaliation, restitution, and imprisonment similarly embrace the notion of commutation. Murder, as an example, cannot go unanswered or left unjudged, for to avoid judgment is a certain injustice. Commutative justice deals with an arithmetical exchange, mean, or rule (e.g., this amount of money for a car or a house, this wage for this work, or this sum for that result). The commercial exchange, the act of buying and selling, represents the commutative equilibrium. Cheating, deceit, and fraud in negotiations and dealings, on the other hand, are affronts to justice. Contract law does not escape Thomas's attention and represents a perfect illustration of the equality of thing and thing. It is unjust and fraudulent to sell an item for more than its inherent worth; buying and selling imply an equality of product and price.[46]

Thomas's consumerist suggestions predate our present notion of unconscionability, and his legal foresight does not end here. St. Thomas expects the seller of any good or service to voluntarily disclose the existence of defects, latent or otherwise.[47] Without this affirmative disclosure, the equilibrium and the reciprocity of justice are in abeyance. A buyer should not suffer a loss from this injustice, whether a "man sells a lame for a fleet horse, a tottering house for a safe one, rotten or poisonous food for wholesome."[48] In demanding each man "to tell everyone the truth about matters pertaining to virtue," Thomas appreciates the destruction of justice caused by falsehood.[49]

Doing good and avoiding evil, the primordial quality of natural-law reasoning, perfectly typifies this commutative idea. If one does the good, both individual and community flourish. The opposite conclusion is easy enough to deduce. Those bypassing the first principle of the natural law and its secondary precepts inevitably engage in injustice. Commutative justice, embracing all the tenets of natural-law theory, attempts to reestablish the equilibrium lost when a victim suffers at the hands of a fraud artist, rapist, or other malefactor, or when cheating or other harm occurs. Commutative justice, as Aristotle defines it, hopes for equal footing in the social complex, a restoration of the balance lost in the moral imperfection, the personal injury, the criminal harm, or other negative result. When discussing the theory of restitution, Thomas insists on its importance for justice's sake, since it "re-establishes equality" and proportionality.[50] Only when restitution, or other proportionate resolution is insisted upon will a "just thing" be discovered.[51] Restitution is mandatory when one individual causes loss to another, and without its recognition a permanent imbalance remains uncured:

Restitution re-establishes the equality of commutative justice, which equality consists in the equalizing of thing to thing, as stated above. Now this equalizing of things is impossible, unless he that has less than his due receive what is lacking to him: and for this to be done, restitution must be made to the person from whom a thing has been taken.[52]

If restitution can only be accomplished by restoration of stolen or damaged property, that practice is just as obligatory.[53]

The commutative quality of Thomistic justice is also evident in the advocacy of the death penalty. Of primary concern to Thomas are the needs and wants of those other than the executed. By slaying the wicked, we enhance the safety of the virtuous.[54] It may even be praiseworthy and good to inflict execution to assure communal tranquility.[55] Retaliation, the vengeful fomenting of the harmed and injured party, is at times properly within the province of commutative justice. To retaliate is to parlay passion for passion. But Thomas warns that passion for passion is not the same equation as act for act. Equality of an act heavily depends upon a theory of proportionality. One cannot retaliate with the death penalty for a theft of food, or, as Thomas remarks, one's stolen chattel repossessed under a theory of retaliation.[56] Thomas insists that the retaliator, in order to be just, equalize both passions and corresponding acts of retaliation. Passions of the inordinate variety are beyond the horizon envisioned in commutative justice. Passion need "be equal to the action" [sit aequalis actioni].[57] Proportionality assures justice; disproportionality fosters injustice.

Thomas's inquiry into vengeance continues this logical line of reasoning. Obviously, vengeance for ulterior or hateful motives nurtures not justice, but hatred in the avenger.[58] Vengeance is compatible with justice if directed toward some good, or for the reformation of the sinner, "for instance that the sinner may amend, or at least that he may be restrained and others be not disturbed, that justice may be upheld, and God honored."[59] But vengeance has no place for those acting in ignorance or by accident, mistake, or other involuntary means. Early on Thomas evaluates intentionality as the criteria for exerting commutative justice and tolerates it only when the party whose aim it focuses upon acts with pure, unaffected will. That party "suffers something that is contrary to his will" [aliquid contra suam voluntatem patitur]; namely vengeance, because reciprocity, sees vengeance as the agency necessary for equilibrium.[60] Those sinning by will may be punished by those willing vengefully.

Commutative justice fosters individual tranquility and peace and is an indispensable condition of social existence. Complementing commutation, that relation of the individual to the state, distributive justice is allocative and proportionally determinative.

Distributive Justice

Distribution of goods, services, material possessions, or political positions will be neither uniform nor identical, but proportionate to what each is due. Distributive justice resists any redistribution of goods, services, and authority, but is at ease with a diversity of stations in life. There is nothing unjust about differences, Thomas says, because "in distributive justice a person receives all the more of the common goods, according as he holds a more prominent position in the community."[61] Differences do not imply a disproportionate sharing of resources. In fact, Thomas insists on basic distributions for each citizen.[62] Unreasonable and disproportionate "burdens in taxation or military, partiality and favoritism in public appointments, in the award of honors or of grants of public funds, are incompatible with distributive justice."[63] For example, "payment for laborious work" is expected, while the involuntary forfeiture or taking of property is condemned.[64] Distributive justice obliges the state to socially contract with its citizenry. If this is not done, and the individual citizen is left in a state of material and personal neglect, theft is excused. Thomas views human necessaries as subject to communal ownership. If the need is urgent enough, criminal culpability is not present. It is even "lawful" to take either "openly or secretly" [sive manifeste, sive occulte] to satisfy these fundamental human needs.[65]

"Distributive Justice orders the relationship between individuals or groups of individuals and the whole community or the state. It has to do with the distribution of goods, benefits, burdens, etc. to the citizens of the state. This type of Justice regulates the sharing in the Common Good."[66] Doubtless, Thomas presumes fundamental governmental protections for its citizenry, some coherent and equitable distribution of what is materially available to the individual rank and file. A state that neglects its individual citizens' primordial needs is not a just state. Jean Porter intelligently summarizes Thomas's account of distributive justice: "Distributive justice, on the other hand, preserves the proper proportion between what an individual deserves from the community, and what he receives from it."[67]

Legal Justice

As mentioned, most commentators ascribe two basic forms of justice in Thomistic thought: the distributive and the commutative. Further down the continuum, Thomas's presentation in the *Summa Theologica* mentions legal justice in a separate sequence of arguments. Legal justice is directly addressed at Question 58, Articles 5, 6, and 7. The sum and substance of the articles are that as justice pertains to every type of virtuous disposition, legal justice is primarily a relational virtue whereby "man is in harmony with the law which directs the acts of all the virtues to the common good."[68] Legal justice addresses general relationships and "does indeed direct man sufficiently in his relations towards others."[69] Legal justice encompasses the virtuous, whose central object is the common good. Thus, legal justice is measuring what is due the whole as it recommends individual justice. Legal justice "tends to the common good."[70]

Legal justice is the virtuous disposition of a ruler, a king, or one entrusted with the body politic, because that leader's promulgations affect the whole rather than its individual parts. Justice—the interior, virtuous, individual disposition—gives each its due and becomes collectivized in the politician or ruler. Those empowered with governance can never be just if they cave in to the constituents' demands or vote everyone's conscience but their own, for in each of these cases they lose sight of the whole. Legal justice is undoubtedly a disposition desirable not only in those that govern and legislate, but those who judge. When the advocates and parties stand before the tribunal, they are asking for individual justice in their respective cases. Not to be forgotten is the connectedness that the individual dispensation of justice will have on the entire community. It will be an injustice to have a sitting judge who looks no further than the parties pleading. That judge will be deficient in the virtue of legal justice, just as the "ruler who contributes towards the destruction of the common good by enacting no just laws, and that subject who disobeys all the precepts of just law, have no virtue in them but are sunk in illegal injustice to the extent that it is the whole of vice."[71] The just judge operates from a justice underpinning that is both individual and communitarian.

Commutative and distributive justice are certainly in the forefront of legal reasoning. Weigh the collective impact of such justice and a legally just judge exists. Judges who are personally virtuous may lack a communal perspective and thus be poor jurists. Thomas gets to the heart of the matter declaring that many "can practice virtue in things pertaining to themselves but not in the things pertaining to others."[72] What Thomas hopes for is a judge or lawyer blessed by both aspects of the virtue of justice. He wants a "law-abiding just man [who] is most virtuous" and a professional who appreciates that "legal justice is the most perfect of virtues."[73]

Thomas's emphasis and distinction may be more educational than substantive. His coverage is a perpetual reminder that individual justice is bound up in the sea of individuals who constitute the community.

JUSTICE: THE CORNERSTONE OF THE LEGAL SYSTEM

Justice is a key component in any legal system imagined by St. Thomas, because justice is primarily about operations, the external mechanics between individuals, groups, and the state. "Justice alone, of all the virtues, implies the notion of duty."[74] When just, the actor is habituated to the proper object or end of justice: the good. Lawyers and judges, to perform lawfully, need to exhibit the virtuous dispositions and inclinations germane to justice: giving individual and nation their due, establishing and reestablishing balance and level relations, and resolving legal problems in light of perennial truths and communal goods.

Virtue, too, as an orderly disposition, is compatible with Thomas's theorem on reason being the rule and measure of man's existence. But justice is also about choices, consent to certain means, applications, or uses. This being so, justice is a rectification of the will to give another what is his or her due. Justice manifests itself in the "virtuous person being well disposed to another."[75] It is a perfection of human interaction and interrelationships; it is a confirmation that man "owes certain duties to God and to his neighbor."[76] By implication, the virtuous person has good relations with family and the community.

Justice is both commutative and distributive, individual and communal. In either category, justice seeks equilibrium, a balance and proportional distribution between individual actors and communities, whether by commerce, punishment, or the distribution of material. Only rational and free willing creatures are capable of being habituated toward justice. To be just requires not only the will to be so, and the corresponding inclination, but the actual carrying out of the just activity.[77]

From both the commutative and distributive viewpoints, justice encapsulates a restoration of order, balance, adjustment, and modification of interrelationships, both in an individual and communal sense. Social beings require these two species of justice. Person-to-person dealings are an impossibility without some idea of equilibrium. Without justice, the individual and the community suffer from a paralyzing indecision.

Legal justice is the art of assuring just results for the entire culture. Legal professionals have special obligations to foresee and foretell the impacts of their advocacy and decision making. For some legal professionals, justice is solely about outcomes, litigious tactics, or victories in advocacy. This is not the justice of which Thomas speaks. A legal system that allows criminals to victimize and then allows perpetrators to walk free lacks justice. Thieves who neither restore nor remit restitution live in a similar world of imbalance. Phony and exaggerated injury claims that result in damage awards represent injustice. Legal-aid lawyers insisting on a redistribution of wealth because capitalism is allegedly unjust fail to understand Thomistic justice. Thomas looks to judges to "lead the way to what is just."[78]

Justice is what is due, not what is demanded. Justice is what is proportionate to effort, sacrifice, and varying degrees of status, whether by education, inheritance, conquest, or plain luck. Justice is what is deserved, earned, and calculated in life's columns of debits and credits. What is acutely intuitive in Thomas's perspective on justice is how the human person's very essence, being imbued with the fundamental precepts of the natural law, already has the capacity to do justice. For reason conveys justice, just as the other virtues, and "whatever kind of justice Aquinas analyzes it will have to be some sort of personal quality, in God, in angels, or in humans."[79]

NOTES

1. St. Thomas Aquinas, *Summa Theologica*, trans. English Dominican Friars, vol. 1 (New York: Benziger, 1947), Question and objection I, Q. 105, a. 6, ad 2. "Ad secundum dicendum, quod contraria etsi dissentiant quantum ad fines proximos, conveniunt tamen quantum ad finem ultimum, prout concluduntur sub uno ordine universi."

2. Ibid., I, Q. 105, a. 2. c.

3. Ibid., I–II, Q. 96, a. 2.

4. St. Thomas Aquinas, "Summa Theologica," in *Basic Writings of St. Thomas Aquinas*, ed. Anton C. Pegis, vol. 2 (New York: Random House, 1945), I–II.

5. Raymond Dennehy, "The Ontological Basis of Human Rights," *The Thomist* 42 (1978): 450.

6. Alasdair MacIntyre, *Whose Justice? Which Rationality?* (Notre Dame: University of Notre Dame Press, 1988), 198, ably points out how justice is encased in the divine exemplar:

In its primary application "Justice" is one of the names applied to God. . . . It is not of course that it is by reference to this divine exemplar that *we* acquire the concept of justice; Aquinas' theory of concept-acquisition was Aristotlean, not Platonist, in its starting point, although it moved beyond Aristotle. But that there is such a timeless standard of justice is a claim ultimately grounded on a theological understanding of the ordering of things.

7. James F. Ross, "Justice Is Reasonableness: Aquinas on Human Law and Morality," *The Thomist* 58 (1974): 100.

8. Aquinas, *Theologica*, vol. 1, I–II, Q, 57–58.

9. Paul J. Weithman, "St. Thomas on the Motives of Unjust Acts," *Proceedings of the Catholic Philosophical Association* (1990): 218.

10. Aquinas, *Theologica*, vol. 2, II–II, Q. 58, a. 2.

11. Ibid., II–II, Q. 58, a.3, c. "Quod virtus humana est quae bonum reddit actum humanum, et ipsum hominem bonum facit; quod quidem convenit justitiae. Actus enim hominis bonus redditur ex hoc quod attingit regulam rationis, secundum quam humani actus rectificantur. Unde cum justitis

operationes humanas rectificet, manifestum est quod opus hominus bonum reddit; et ut Tullius dicit (De offic. Lib. I, in tit. De justitia, circa princ.), ex justitia praecipue viri boni nominantur; unde, sicut ibidem dicit, in ea virtutis splendor est maximus."

12. Ibid., II–II, Q. 58, a. 8, 9.

13. Ibid., II–II, Q. 58, a. 11, c. "Secundum proportionis aequalitatem."

14. MacIntyre, *Whose Justice?* 199.

15. Aquinas, *Theologica*, vol. 2, II–II, Q. 57, a. 1.

16. Ibid., II–II, Q. 57, a. 1, c.

17. St. Thomas Aquinas, *Commentary on the Nicomachean Ethics*, trans. C. I. Litzinger (Chicago: Henry Regnery, 1964); Aristotle, *Nicomachean Ethics*, trans. Martin Ostwald (New York: Bobbs-Merrill, 1962).

18. Aquinas, *Commentary*, V. L.X:C 998.

19. St. Thomas Aquinas, *Basic Writings of St. Thomas Aquinas*, vol. 2, ed. Anton C. Pegis (New York: Random House, 1944), I–II, Q. 64, a. 1, ad 1. "Ad primum ergo dicendum, quod virtus moralis bonitatem habet ex regula rationis; pro materia autem habet passiones vel operationes. Si ergo comparetur virtus moralis ad rationem, sic secundum id quod rationis est, habet rationem extremi unius, quod est conformitas; excessus vero et defectus habet rationem alterius extremi, quod est deformitas. Si vero consideretur virtus moralis secundum suam materiam, sic habet rationem medii, inquantum passionem reducit ad regulam rationis."

20. Aquinas, "Theologica," I–II, Q. 64, a. 1.

21. Etienne Gilson, *The Christian Philosophy of St. Thomas Aquinas*, trans. L. K. Shook (New York: Random House, 1956), 264.

22. Aquinas, *Theologica*, vol. 2, II–II, Q. 58, a. 10, c.

23. Ibid. "Et ideo medium justitiae consistit in quadam proportionis aequalitate rei exterioris ad personam exteriorem."

24. Ibid., II–II, Q. 58, a. 8.

25. J. Messner, *Social Ethics: Natural Law in the Modern World*, trans. J. J. Doherty (St. Louis: B. Herder, 1952), 213.

26. Aquinas, *Theologica*, vol. 2, II–II, Q. 64, a. 2, c. "Cujus ratio est, quia justitia est circa operationes quae consistunt in rebus exterioribus, in quibus rectum institui debet simpliciter et secundum se, ut supra dictum est."

27. St. Thomas Aquinas, *On Aristotle's Love and Friendship*, trans. Pierre Conway (Providence: Providence College Press, 1951), bk. IX, ch. 2.

28. Aquinas, "Theologica," I–II, Q. 64, a. 1.

29. Aquinas, *Theologica*, vol. 2, II–II, Q. 58, a. 9, ad. 2.

30. E. T. Gelinas, "Right and Law in Thomas Aquinas," in *Myth and Philosophy*, ed. George F. McLean, vol. 45 (Washington, D.C.: American Catholic Philosophical Association, 1971), 132.

31. Aquinas, *Theologica*, vol. 2, II–II, Q. 58, a. 9.

32. Ibid., II–II, Q. 59, a. 1.

33. Ibid.

34. Ibid., II–II, Q. 59, a. 4.

35. Ibid., II–II, Q. 59, a. 3.

36. Ibid., II–II, Q. 59, a. 2, ad 2. "Quod non est facile cuiquam facere injustum ex electione, quasi aliquid per se placens, et non propter aluid."

37. Ibid., II–II, Q. 60, a. 6.

38. Aquinas, *Commentary*, V. L.II:C 929.

39. Ibid., V. L.II:C 930.

40. Aquinas, *Theologica*, vol. 2, II–II, Q. 61, a. 2, c. "Et ideo oportet adaequare rem rei, ut quanto iste plus habet quam suum sit, de eo quod est alterius, tantumdem restituat ei cujus est. Et sic fit aequalitas secundum arithmeticam medietatem, quae attenditur secundum parem quantitatis excessum."

41. Ibid. "Et ideo in justitia distributiva non accipitur medium secundum aequalitatem rei ad rem, sed secundum proportionem rerum ad personas, ut scilicet sicut una persona excedit aliam, ita etiam res quae datur uni personae, excedat rem quae datur alii."

42. Aquinas, *Commentary*, V. L.II:C 909.

43. Jeremiah Newman, *Foundations of Justice* (Cork: Cork University Press, 1954), 3.

44. Messner, *Social Ethics*, 219.

45. Aquinas, *Commentary*, V. L.II:C 952.

46. Aquinas, *Theologica*, vol. 2, II–II, Q. 77, a. 1, c. "Et ideo carius vendere vel vilius emere rem quam valeat, est secundum se injustum et illicitum."

47. Ibid., II–II, Q. 77, a. 3.

48. Ibid., II–II, Q. 77, a. 3, c.

49. Ibid., II–II, Q. 77, a. 3.

50. Ibid., II–II, Q. 62, a. 4.

51. Aquinas, *Commentary*, 406.

52. Aquinas, *Theologica*, vol. 2, II–II, Q. 62, a. 5, c. "Restitutionem fit reductio ad aequalitatem commutativa justitiae, quae consistit in rerum adaequatione, sicut dictum est. Hujusmodi autem rerum adaequatio fieri non posset, nisi ei qui minus habet quam quod sum est, suppleretur quod deest. Et ad hanc suppletionem faciendam necesse est ut ei fiat restitutio a quo acceptum est."

53. Ibid., II–II, Q. 62, a. 6.

54. Ibid., II–II, Q. 64, a. 2, ad 1.

55. Ibid., II–II, Q. 64, a. 2.

56. Ibid., II–II, Q. 61, a. 4.

57. Ibid., II–II, Q. 61, a. 4, c.

58. Ibid., II–II, Q. 108, a. 1.

59. Ibid., II–II, Q. 108, a. 1, c. "Puta ad emendationem peccantis, vel saltem ad cohibitionem ejus et quietem aliorum, et ad justitiae conservationem, et Dei honorem."

60. Ibid., II–II, Q. 108, a. 4, c.

61. Ibid., II–II, Q. 61, a. 2, c. "Et ideo in distributiva justitia tanto plus alicui de bonis communibus datur, quanto illa persona majorem habet principalitatem in communitate."

62. Ibid., II–II, Q. 66, a. 7.

63. Messner, *Social Ethics*, 218.

64. Aquinas, *Theologica*, vol. 2, II–II, Q. 61, a. 3.

65. Ibid., II–II, Q. 66, a. 7, c. See also ibid., Q. 66, a. 7, sed contra. "In cases of need all things are common property, so that there would seem to be no sin in taking another's property, for need has made it common" [Sed contra est quod in necessitate sunt omnia communia; et ita non videtur esse peccatum, si aliquis rem alterius accipiat propter necessitatem sibi factam communem].

66. St. Thomas Aquinas, *Treatise on Law*, ed. R. J. Henle (Notre Dame: University of Notre Dame Press, 1993), 72.

67. See Jean Porter, *The Recovery of Virtue* (Louisville, Ky.: Westminster/John Knox Press, 1990), 153.

68. Aquinas, *Theologica*, vol. 2, II–II, Q. 58 a. 5, c.

69. Ibid., II–II, Q. 58, a. 7, ad. 1

70. Aquinas, *Commentary*, V. L.II:C 911. Jeremiah Newman, *Foundations*, 6, wisely interprets the slant in Thomas's legal thinking:

Hence there is an essential connection between legal justice and law, which connection must be stressed. The citizen has a double vocation, one which is proper to him as a man and one which he, as citizen, has in common with all other citizens. His private vocation, whatever it be, as long as it is within the law and consequently good, is not only a private affair; it is also a work of social importance. As long as it is in harmony with the law it is for the common good and is a work of the virtue of legal justice. Thus the private.individual's part in the procuration of the common good consists in the fulfilment of his legal obligations.

71. Newman, *Foundations*, 11.

72. Aquinas, *Commentary*, V. L.II:C 908.

73. Ibid., V. L.II:C 910.

74. Aquinas, *Theologica*, vol. 2, II–II, Q. 99, a. 5, ad 1.

75. Ibid., II–II, Q. 58, a. 12.

76. Ibid., II–II, Q. 100, a. 5, ad 1.

77. R. J. Araujo, "Thomas Aquinas: Prudence, Justice, and the Law," *Loyola Law Review* 40 (1995): 909, dwells upon man's social nature to typify justice as functionally mandatory for personhood. See also Vernon J. Bourke, "Justice as Equitable Reciprocity: Aquinas Updated," *American Journal of Jurisprudence* 27 (1982): 19.

78. Aquinas, *Commentary*, V. L.II:C 955.

79. Bourke, "Justice," 19.

CHAPTER 5

Law and Prudence

Knowing what to do, identifying proper ends, legal or otherwise, is fundamentally a speculative exercise. The prime aims of prudence are to know how to achieve the ends identified and the suitable means to success. Judges and lawyers earnestly need the practical wisdom that accompanies the virtue of prudence. Prudence is an habituation that forges in the legal professional the best strategic and tactical plan. Without prudence the judge conceives and conceptualizes law, but is decisionally frozen regarding the means to implement decision making. Prudence disposes the judge to correct decision making about the law and particular circumstances. Prudence calculates and evaluates courses of conduct. Prudence affords the judge the power and the disposition to judge sensibly, to counsel and command, and to choose properly. Lawyers lacking prudence will fall short in other virtuous dispositions, for the neglect of prudence invariably leads to inactivity in all other facets of the virtuous life. A lawyer lacking prudence will surely be impoverished in truth, courage, and justice. Prudence, St. Thomas holds, is preeminent amongst the virtues.

THE RELEVANCY OF PRUDENCE

Already covered in the assessment of virtue and law is how virtue, in contrast to vice, orders the soul, inclines toward the good, and directs its possessor to proper objects and ends. Just as the ultimate end of the human species is the perfect goodness that is God, the common good of any society simultaneously corresponds to that perfection, and the law's general care is the human, common, and final goods of man and society, virtue is a disposition to similar ends. Virtue is a perfection of a power, a natural inclination, or a desire residing in the human species. Virtue is an interior, internal disposition by which the human agent acts correctly. Virtues are to some extent innate, and some even divinely infused, but for the most part they are acquired. Habituation garners virtue or vice, and each virtue is distinguished by its respective objects.

As discussed earlier, virtues, whether theological, intellectual, or moral in scope, dispose the human being toward the proper ends. For example, justice trains and inclines the agent toward giving others their due as to goods and services, punishments, and the like; temperance regulates sensual appetites; and fortitude is the mean between recklessness and cowardice. By examining St. Thomas's text, the essence of virtue can be summed up as a *perfection*:

As we have said above, virtue implies a perfection of power, and therefore the virtue of a thing is fixed by the peak of its power. Now the peak of any power must needs be good, for all evil implies defect. Hence Dionysius says that every evil is a weakness. And for this reason the virtue of a thing must be regarded in reference to good. Therefore human virtue, which is an operative habit, is a good habit, productive of good works.[1]

Virtue is "formally, or absolutely, good when it confers not only facility for well-doing, but the right use of such facility."[2]

Virtue is relevant within the legal province, especially as to practice and decision making. A judge must do the right thing when sentencing or deliberating a decision or appeal, just as a lawyer advancing or advocating a claim. Who could dispute that the virtuous man or woman will make the better lawyer or judge? Ethics, in the truest sense of the word, connotes a fondness for virtue and a disdain for vice. The lawmaker and the legal advocate should possess moral virtue to effect proper and appropriate ends for person and civilization: to be temperate, to be just and equitable, and to be strong and courageous, as examples.

That same judicial professional cannot function in a completely legal or moral sense if bankrupt of virtue. A virtuous disposition is crucial in judicial decision making. Without it, the lawyer or lawmaker decides or advocates without a meaningful or proper end. Instead of reason moving the professional, the vagaries of will and appetite control. That is why the human person can intellectualize the proper and correct end, but still neglect the choices promoting the same. One's appetites and passions subsume or overwhelm the actor to choose actions contrary to the good, and in turn prudential "judgement is corrupted."[3] One may know that fornication is wrong, and "in the abstract" be capable of issuing intelligent judgments about its suitability. Yet despite this realization, passions will dominate the intellectual truth of the matter. Fear, trepidation, or other anxiety may cause right reasoning to be replaced with inadequate reaction.[4]

But being just, temperate, or courageous are only partial pieces in the human edifice, and St. Thomas is salient enough to suggest a fourth category of moral virtue; namely, prudence. The just man or temperate woman may lack the sense of what to do or in exactly what way to do it. "Prudence is the quality of an integrated personality."[5] Prudence is the perfection of the practical intellect, of practical reason, and of choice. Prudence is a cardinal virtue upon which other virtues must depend. The attainment of prudence means the moral agent is habituated toward proper choice and is adept at selecting the right means to a good end. At its heart, prudence is the practical reason's perfection. Temperance, fortitude, and justice are not visible in the person; the regulation of our sensual appetites and the distinguishing of courageous acts is not possible without prudence.[6]

From a legal perspective, prudence is a virtue of integral importance. Since decision making is the fruit of prudence whether the decision is an appellate decision or the moral quandary of abortion, the jurist's decision may manifest prudential or imprudential qualities. Prudence implies a sort of wisdom, a reflection of practical intelligence that is consistent with the goods so often evaluated in this work. The prudent person successfully deliberates desires with actions, passions with obligations, and imperatives with relative circumstances. For St. Thomas, prudence dictates not only knowledge of the moral law, but also application of moral decision making in specific circumstances. Prudence "respects the right order of means to ends."[7] Prudence requires not only moral correctness, but that the means be suited (morally so) to those same ends.

Legal professionals, whether judges or lawyers, do more than play the parts of their respective roles, for it is incumbent upon them to do justice. Prudence assures the "justness" of legal action. R. J. Henle poignantly integrates prudence into the life of a judge:

Prudence is *the* virtue of the good judge. The judge has to apply the law and judicial doctrine—including "Natural Justice" to individual cases. Reasoning, factual investigation, etc. must precede the judicial prudential judgment, but, in the last analysis, the judge must judge. There are no rules for rule application, otherwise there would be an infinite regress of rules.

The ancient tradition said that judges should be "Justice Personified." We may add that the judge should be "Prudence Personified."[8]

THE ESSENCE OF PRUDENCE

Prudence is labeled a cardinal virtue because, according to St. Thomas, "Prudence is absolutely the principal of all the virtues."[9] Prudence's centrality to reason, its perfecting role in how the human agent chooses courses of activity and selects the means toward proper ends, is what gives rise to its preeminent position among the virtues. Only in prudence does reason achieve its most superlative capacity, since the prudent man possesses "a certain rectitude of discernment in actions or matter whatever."[10]

Plainly, all the moral virtues promote the proper ordering of the soul, moderating and equalizing passions and operations. However, in one sense, prudence, even though compatible with the other moral virtues, is partially distinct. It is the province of prudence alone to discern, to discover, and to weigh and calculate courses of conduct, and in this way it is a distinct enterprise compared to the other virtues. Intricate as the argument may be, St. Thomas subtly points out the distinction:

It is only in the point of having discernment, which we ascribed to prudence, that there seems to be a distinction from the other three, inasmuch as discernment belongs essentially to reason; whereas the other three imply a certain share of reason by way of a kind of application to passions or operations. According to this explanation, then, prudence would be distinct from the other three virtues, but these would not be distinct from one another; for it is evident that one and the same virtue is both habit, and virtue, and moral virtue.[11]

In another sense, prudence exhibits some of the qualities that typify intellectual virtues, especially since portions of its content are judgment, counsel, and command. These parts of prudence portray the stages of prudential insight. The prudent person weighs and evaluates alternative courses of conduct and simultaneously considers the means for accomplishing a moral end. Once this inquiry is done, what is to be done is formulated by actual judgment. At the end of the process, the will commands what is to be omitted or performed. As such, prudence appears to be a virtue with both intellectual and moral qualities.[12] Gilson appears hesitant to narrowly define this central virtue:

Moral virtue cannot do without intellectual virtue. Moral virtue must determine a good act. Now an act supposes election; and, as we have seen in our analysis of the structure of the human act, election supposes the deliberation and judgment of reason. So intellectual virtues, which are not directly related to the action can, indeed, dispense with moral virtues. But prudence cannot do so. It must terminate in precise acts. The intellectual virtue of prudence does not merely determine what should be done in general.[13]

Others engage in compromise, readily admitting, as St. Thomas urges, that prudence is a moral virtue, but then making claims like, "Prudence has more to do with our cognitive power than with our appetitive power. Therefore prudence does not belong to the active life. . . . Prudence falls half way between the moral virtues and the intellectual virtues."[14]

Not surprising, prudence is often compared to art, since the former is about doing and selecting proper conduct, while the latter concerns making or producing things in the right way. Upon closer inspection, art is an activity about what is to be created, while prudence is the way to fashion the means to the end result. While art is about things to be crafted, prudence deals with the way to share it. St. Thomas distinguishes the art of prudence from art itself:

Consequently, it is requisite for prudence, which is right reason about things to be done, that man be well disposed with regard to ends; and this depends on the rectitude of his appetite. Therefore, for prudence there is need of moral virtue, which rectifies the appetite. On the other hand, the good of things made by art is not the good of man's appetite, but the good of the artificial things themselves, and hence art does not presuppose rectitude of the appetite. The consequence is that more praise is given to a craftsman who is at fault willingly, than to one who is unwillingly; whereas it is more contrary to prudence to sin willingly than unwillingly, since rectitude of the will is essential to prudence, but not to art. Accordingly, it is evident that prudence is a virtue distinct from art.[15]

Prudence is more comprehensive in its applicability because human activity is boundless. Prudence is labeled the centerpiece of human activity because it stands watch over all moral activity.

The preeminence of prudence within the virtuous domain is evident throughout St. Thomas's works. Lacking the power, the capacity, or the inclination to act, to choose, or to differentiate good and bad results is disastrous for the moral agent. Thus, prudence is the virtue "most necessary for human life" [maxime necessaria ad vitam humanam].[16] The moral being must not only choose correctly but do so from rational choice, "not merely from impulse or passion" [non solum ex impetu aut passione].[17] A shortage of prudence is a guarantee for at least a vapid moral existence, for "prudence is necessary to man that he may lead a good life, and not merely that he may become a good man."[18] Argued from another vantage point, prudence is a compass, a map for the virtuous good life. Prudence is picking and selecting avenues of action that are in accord with reason, consistent with our nature, and compatible with divine providence. In Book 1 of St. Thomas's *On Kingship*, man is characterized as having "the light of reason placed [by nature] to guide him in his acts towards his end."[19] Comparing the life of reason to the navigation route of a ship, St. Thomas speaks of the moral life with poetic simplicity:

A ship, for example, which moves in different directions according to the impulse of the changing winds, would never reach its destination were it not brought to port by the skill of the pilot. Now, man has an end to which his whole life and all his actions are ordered; for man is an intelligent agent, and it is clearly the part of an intelligent agent to act in view of an end. Men also adopt different methods in proceeding towards their proposed end, as the diversity of men's pursuits and actions clearly indicates. Consequently man needs some directive principle to guide him towards his end.[20]

Further on, the work suggests nature, the natural law as a participant in the eternal law, as that guide. But man can intellectualize this without much effort. The first principles of the natural law, those things naturally knowable to each member of the human community, are discoverable with minimal reflection. Further down the self-evident continuum are the secondary precepts of the natural law, whose content emerges in moral decision making and inquiry into our inherent being. While the clarity of these principles will differ from person to person, knowledge of its content is imputable to those who reflect. In a range of moral choices, means, and ends, man can know and simultaneously follow or disregard these instructions.

Considered in a narrower vein, our legal system is confronted daily with judges, lawmakers, and advocates who have knowledge of these self-evident propositions yet feel duty bound to purge any moral qualities in their roles. Judges frozen by occupational fear and moral trepidation often issue incomplete, incoherent rulings. Other rulings lack insight, common sense, and any measure of legal logic. Or the decision announced may be delivered for all the wrong motives. In each of these cases, the human player, still in possession of reason, is prudentially inadequate. To be effective, legal action, whether by judge or lawmaker, must address issues squarely, resolve factual dilemmas, and mete out justice. The average citizen knows when his or her legal system is imprudent; for example, absurd U.S. Supreme Court decisions, IRS audits of twelve-year-olds, tax assessments of home-run balls, sexual-harassment petitions lodged against six-year-olds, and the passage of petty and demoralizing ordinances. Where is the prudential wisdom in such cases? Prudence is knowing what works and what doesn't in the larger society.

Prudence is cogently described as a perfection of the practical intellect and practical reason. The speculative intellect is the theoretical knowledge base that prudence will try to make reasoned application, but by no means is speculation exclusively the province of prudence. Prudence is better suited to application than contemplation, since its framework resides in deliberation and choice. Pure thinking without corresponding activity is not prudential.[21] Nor is it right to claim that any resulting activity coming from and arising from speculation will be prudent. At its core, prudence is a virtue of actions, choices, and means to ends. Prudence is knowledge put to use. Prudent activities are those consistent with our final end, our proper goods.

Another quality of prudence, as every other virtue, is its capacity to be increased or diminished, made stronger or weaker, or lost altogether. Prudence's power, its habituation, "is abolished when right appetite ceases."[22] In a series of cognitive steps and stages, St. Thomas relates how the practical intellect psychologically operates. At the first stage, the individual engages in counsel, *eubulia*, an ordering of particular facts or circumstances to particular choices. In legal circles, concepts like precedent, *stare decisis*, jurisdiction, relevancy, and materiality represent this weighing, evaluating, and fitting facts and law into a particular scheme. St. Thomas characterizes this activity as within the speculative intellect, since no action or means has arisen. Hence, counsel is "a kind of inquiry."[23]

In the next phase of cognition, the individual makes a judgment, *synesis*, about what is to be done. Even though still speculative in nature, it is easy to see why judgment comes closer to giving the virtue of prudence reality. St. Thomas clearly sets out this second phase: "Judgment about what is to be done is directed to something further; for it may happen in some matter of action that a man's judgment is sound, while his execution is wrong. The whole process does not attain its perfection until reason commands with rightness on what ought to be done."[24]

Once at the final phase of the suggested continuum, command, the actor is applying choices and means, the primary quality of prudence itself. At this juncture, prudence emerges or is indiscernible, since the commanded act triggers reality from previous counsel and judgment: "But the third is proper to the practical intellect in so far as the practical intellect is ordained to operation, for reason does not have to command in things that man cannot do. Now it is evident that in things done by man the chief act is that of command, to which all the rest are subordinate."[25]

Thus, the central and essential act of prudence is *praeceptum*. The virtue of prudence is therefore not evident in a man of inactivity or reticence, but drawn from the direction of human movement. Prudence is not comfortable with languid inactivity, but expects, demands, and commands. The strength of command doesn't emerge instantaneously, but is, as Gilson remarks, "a life's work."[26] Prudence is not solely experiences of the war-storied litigator or judge, but an esoteric habituation. In Gilson's inimitable style, prudence is labeled a life-long ambition:

In sum, in deciding every particular case he must know how to begin, in order to arrive at its ends. What he has to acquire in order to become prudent is the ability to discern the particular act that must be done if the desired result in a given case is to be obtained. This is truly an art. How am I to deal with such and such a man in particular circumstances without humiliating or injuring him? This is the kind of problem which the virtue of prudence places before the understanding.[27]

In fact, choosing proper means to ends should become effortless and habitually natural to the evaluator. When capable and at ease in choice, Thomas states the moral agent is endowed with the virtue of *synderesis*. St. Thomas defines *synderesis* as consisting "primarily in the habitual knowledge of the general self-evident principles of the practical order."[28] The practical intellect prudentially chooses, without much deliberation and counsel, and quickly targets courses of conduct that are consistent with virtue. Since there is in man a natural tendency or inclination toward the proper ends of human action, the human being already knows ends are the suitable objects. Developing a natural recognition or a more automatic understanding of them is the disposition of choice. All rational creatures are imbued with *synderesis*. Following the tenets of the natural law is never burdensome, but joyous. Avoiding excessive sensuality and dysfunctional appetites brings glee to the man or woman habitually disposed to *synderesis*. Bad things are to be shunned, and the good which maintains life, which "ensure[s] the continuation of their species by reproducing and caring properly for the young, seeking truth and shunning ignorance, maintaining society, and cultivating virtue," is habitually desired.[29]

THE PRUDENT JUDGE AND LAWYER

Thomistic prudence is a mandatory attribute for any professional in the justice system. Judges and lawyers must be virtuous, since a virtuous life stands for those goods inexorably bound up in the human person's makeup. How could a judge who scoffed at equity and equality before law, who rested easily in capriciousness and arbitrariness, who was timid, politically motivated, a slave to drink, lust, sloth, and other intemperate behaviors, dispense justice? What of lawyers, policemen, or correctional officials laboring under the same deficits? Will they deliver justice? Prudence implies, or better yet, mandates, a virtuous habituation. All virtue, including prudence, orders the soul correctly, inclines to goods and means consistent with nature, and ultimately leads the human agent to the final destiny of God. The prudent justice professional is virtuous, morally upright, and driven by good rather than evil. The prudent justice professional knows how to analyze and apply facts and circumstance, and can deliberate with rational consistency, doing all in accordance with right reason and the inherent nature of man. The prudent lawyer and judge acknowledge truth and truth alone as the measure of legal decision making, and promote "the true good, in all our actions and life."[30] The prudent justice employee does not react with isolated introspection, but is attentive to consequence, "using powers of circumspection, of weighing the individual circumstances of a situation, of exercising caution lest good intentions ultimately do more harm than good. Reasoning, foresight, circumspection, precaution are all essential elements of prudence, and there is no real prudence without them."[31] Gilson holds that "prudence seems principally to depend upon that freedom of mind by which a man judges accurately the particular data of a practical problem, appreciates the moral quality of acts, and assesses their significance. Whatever disturbs this balance of judgment diminishes prudence."[32] Prudence brings to "perfection that part of the intellect which calculates or deliberates about contingent things."[33] A judge blessed with deliberative powers but crippled by inactivity and nonapplication is not prudent. Thomism would declare inactivity as inconsistent with the practical intellect, for man does not deliberate without means, purposes, or ends. Practical reason determines what one should or could do. Prudence is the impetus for making it happen.

Judges, as functionaries, depend upon disputes and dilemmas as well as the existence of contrary positions. In this divide, Thomas asserts, judges are reconcilers of doubts, because the primary reason "judges are appointed among men is that they may decide doubtful points in matters of justice."[34] Prudence aids the judge in the reconciliation of disputes. The practice of law depends just as heavily upon the fruits of prudence. At a minimum, the lawyer who fails to weigh and assess facts—for example, seeing wrong when the harm is excusable, advocating a legal cause of action when the legal argument is unmeritorious—is devoid of prudential wisdom. Prudence is equally applicable to the end sought by the advocate, whether it is just or unjust. Prudence's demands are geared only to virtuous application. Lawyers whose cases and tactics foster distrust and chaos in the courtroom and justice system are not prudential. Advocating cases without regard for their long-term cultural and moral impact and in contravention to natural-law principles—for example, pro-abortion, pro-same sex marriage, pro-euthanasia—is antagonistic to prudence. Prudence cannot accept the occupational excuses so prevalent today: "I'm doing my job; Everyone needs a lawyer; I can't separate myself from the case I represent." Prudence mandates correct moral application consistent with our operations. Making a living and collecting a fee is not a manifestation of prudence. Instead, the prudent lawyer chooses not only his or her strategy, tactic, and plan of representation wisely, but his or her life.

St. Thomas holds resolutely to a unified view of the human agent, dependent upon reason, infused with certain innate characteristics, and endowed with free will and natural-law imprints, but in need of prudential development. Prudence is not inbred but learned, solidified by experience and application.[35]

Those who exhibit prudence touch not only the individual case or circumstance before it, but are attentive to the needs of the whole community, that "common good of the multitude" [bonum commune multitudinis] that rests atop any "private good of the individual" [bonum privatum unius hominis].[36] Prudence, as enunciated by St. Thomas, can influence kings, governments, domestic economies, political systems, rulers, and subjects. Every person, says St. Thomas, "for as much as he is rational, has a share in ruling according to the judgment of reason, he is proportionately competent to have prudence."[37]

In addition to these basic ideas, St. Thomas further treats prudence according to its military and regnative functions. What is so compelling about arguments posed by St. Thomas is the eclectic role prudence plays in the life of any viable society or subsystem within it. Clearly, any justice system must manifest prudential judgment. Prudence towers over the civilization, or at least hopefully so. Expressed from another perspective, St. Thomas proclaims, "Hence prudence in its special and most perfect sense, belongs to a king who is charged with the government of a city or kingdom: for which reason a species of prudence is reckoned to be regnative."[38]

Prudence and justice are the most pertinent virtues for king or ruler because each exhibits relational and collective qualities and each points to communal concerns. The king, by edict and rule, touches the whole of the realm, and justice, if delivered, proportionately is dispensed to all in the kingdom.[39] Prudence is a great unifier by directing all the actions of the individual toward the true human and communal good. While this observation is right enough, prudence does even more: It assures tranquility, temporal happiness, and individual and social growth, and guarantees that the individual will achieve the grand purpose of human existence.

NOTES

1. Thomas Aquinas, "Summa Theologica," in *Basic Writings of St. Thomas Aquinas*, ed. Anton C. Pegis, vol. 2 (New York: Random House, 1945), I–II, Q. 55, a. 3, c. "Sicut supra dictum est, virtus importat perfectionem potentiae. Unde virtus cujuslibet rei determinatur ad ultimum in quod res potest, ut dicitur. Ultimum autem in quod unaquaeque potentia potest, oportet quod sit bonum; nam omne malum defectum quemdam importat; unde Dionysius dicit quod omne malum est infirmum. Et propter hoc oportet quod virtus cujuslibet rei dicatur in ordine ad bonum. Unde virtus humana, quae est habitus operativus, est bonus habitus, et boni operativus." Henle interprets Thomas accurately in St. Thomas Aquinas, *Treatise on Law*, ed. R. J. Henle (Notre Dame: University of Notre Dame Press, 1993), 67. See also Rose E. Brennan, *The Intellectual Virtues According to the Philosophy of St. Thomas* (Washington, D.C.: Catholic University of America Press, 1941), 1.

2. Brennan, *Intellectual Virtues*, 9.

3. John E. Naus, "The Nature of the Practical Intellect According to Saint Thomas Aquinas," in *Analecta Gregoriana*, vol. 108 (Rome: Libreria Editrice Dell' Universita Gregoriana, 1959), 62.

4. A solid examination of the phenomena is provided in Daniel Westberg, *Right Practical Reason: Aristotle, Action and Prudence in Aquinas* (Oxford: Clarendon Press, 1994), 221.

5. Ignatius T. Eschmann, *The Ethics of St. Thomas Aquinas* (Toronto: Pontifical Institute of Mediaeval Studies, 1997), 179.

6. Aquinas, *Treatise on Law*, 73–74.

7. Robert J. Kreyche, "Virtue and Law in Aquinas: Some Modern Implications," *Southwestern Journal of Philosophy* 5 (1974): 127.

8. Aquinas, *Treatise on Law*, 75.

9. Aquinas, "Theologica," I–II, Q. 61, a. 3.

10. Ibid., I–II, Q. 61, a. 4.

11. Ibid., I–II, Q. 61, a. 4, c. "Solum autem hoc quod est discretionem habere, quod attribuebatur prudentiae, videtur distingui ab alii tribus, inquantum hoc est ipsius rationis per essentiam, alia vero tria important quamdam participationem rationis per modum applicationis cujusdam ad passiones vel operationes. Sic igitur secumdum praedicta, prudentia quidem esset virtus distincta ab aliis tribus; sed aliae tres non essent virtutes distinctae ab invicem. Manifestum est enim quod una et eadem virtus et est habitus, et est virtus, et est moralis."

12. Ignatius Eschmann's remarkable work, *The Ethics of Saint Thomas Aquinas*, indicates the twofold aspects of prudence, both intellectual and moral.

To be prudent is to be human, to be moral; the moral human being is the prudent person. Let the disillusioned lover of Nirvana be the moral ideal of Buddha, and the stoically unperturbed bearer of misfortune that of Epictetus, the successful tradesman that of Jeremy Bentham, the believer in unlimited progress that of John Dewey, the television announcer selling every soap that of Bertrand Russell; Saint Thomas's ideal is the prudent human being. Such as conceived by Thomas Aquinas, prudence is connected on the one hand with the virtues residing in the will and on the other hand with certain dispositions residing in the intellect or reason. Prudence will not work unless it functions within this context. (pp. 178–179)

13. Etienne Gilson, *The Christian Philosophy of St. Thomas Aquinas*, trans. L. K. Shook (New York: Random House, 1956), 261.

14. St. Thomas Aquinas, *An Apology for the Religious Orders*, ed. John Procter (St. Louis: B. Herder, 1902), Q. 181, a. 2.

15. Aquinas, "Theologica," I–II, Q. 57, a. 4, c. "Et ideo ad prudentiam, quae est recta ratio agibilium, requiritur quod homo sit bene dispositus circa fines; quod quidem est per appetitum rectum. Et ideo ad prudentiam requiritur moralis virtus, per quam fit appetitus rectus. Bonum autem artificialium non est bonum appetitus humani, sed bonum ipsorum operum artificialium; et ideo ars non praesupponit appetitum rectum. Et inde est quod magis laudatur artifex qui volens peccat, quam qui peccat nolens; magis autem contra prudentiam est quod aliquis peccat volens quam nolens, quia rectitudo voluntatis est de ratione prudentiae, non autem de ratione artis. Sic igitur patet quod prudentia est virtus distincta ab arte."

16. Ibid., I–II, Q. 57, a. 5, c.

17. Ibid.

18. Ibid., I–II, Q. 57, a. 5, ad 1.

19. St. Thomas Aquinas, *On Kingship*, trans. Gerald B. Phelan (Toronto: Pontifical Institute of Mediaeval Studies, 1982), bk. I, ch. 1, 3.

20. Ibid.

21. See Eugene F. Miller, "Prudence and the Rule of Law," *American Journal of Jurisprudence* 24 (1979): 195; R. J. Araujo, "Thomas Aquinas: Prudence, Justice and the Law," *Loyola Law Review* 40 (1995): 907.

22. Naus, "Nature of the Practical Intellect," 141.

23. Aquinas, "Theologica," I–II, Q. 57, a. 6, c.

24. Ibid., I–II, Q. 57, a. 6, ad 2. "Judicium in agendis ad aliquid ulterius ordinatur; contingit enim aliquem bene judicare de aliquo agendo, et tamen non recte exequi; sed ultimum complementum est, quando ratio jam bene praecepit de agendis."

25. Ibid., I–II, Q. 57, a. 6, c. "Sed tertius actus est proprie practici intellectus, inquantum est operativus: non enim ratio habet praecipere ea quae per hominem fieri non possunt. Manifestum est autem quod in his quae per hominem fiunt, principalis actus est praecipere, ad quem alii ordinatur."

26. Gilson, *Christian Philosophy*, 287.

27. Ibid.

28. Aquinas, "Theologica," I, Q. 79, a. 12, c.

29. Miller, "Prudence," 199.

30. Eschmann, *Ethics*, 200.

31. Gilson, *Christian Philosophy*, 288.

32. Ibid.

33. Miller, "Prudence," 193.

34. Aquinas, "Theologica," I–II, Q. 105, a. 2, ad. 7. "Judices ad hoc inter homines constituuntur ut determinent quod ambiguum inter homines circa justitiam esse potest."

35. St. Thomas Aquinas, *Summa Theologica*, trans. English Dominican Friars, vol. 2 (New York: Benziger, 1947), bk. II, pt. II, Q. 47.

36. Ibid., II–II, Q. 47, a. 10, c.

37. Ibid., II–II, Q. 47, a. 12, c. "Sed quia quilibet homo, inquantum est rationalis, participat aliquid de regimine secundum arbitrium rationis, intantum convenit ei prudentiam habere."

38. Ibid., II–II, Q. 50, a. 1, c. "Et ideo regi, ad quem pertinet regere civitatem vel regnum, prudentia competit secundum specialem et perfectissimam sui rationem; et propter hoc regnativa ponitur species prudentiae."

39. Ibid., II–II, Q. 50, a. 1, ad 1.

CHAPTER 6

Law and the Common Good

That law as an activity directed to the common good is a central feature in Thomistic jurisprudence. By common good Thomas takes in the entire social and political system, and insists that lawmaker, judge, and lawyer think how their activities will effect not simply the individual plaintiff and defendant, but the multitude. The good of the person is synonymous with the good of the state. The common good represents the proper ends for both individual and collective. The common good includes, but is not limited to, objects and ends conducive to the happy life, paths to perfection ultimately residing in God, and virtuous dispositions and habits in conformity with right reason. For legal practitioners any inquiry into the common good will be at odds with our current penchant for resolution of individualized case and circumstance. Since the common good includes the divine exemplar, these practitioners will have little choice but to view the perfection of the whole rather than the isolation of the singular.

COMMUNAL GOODS, LAW, AND THOMISTIC JURISPRUDENCE

Any cursory understanding of Thomistic jurisprudence will quickly glean its collective rather than singular tendencies. Law, in both the abstract and practical senses, is not rooted in individualistic need, nor the whimsy of relative circumstance. In a much grander way, law pertains to the whole, the totality, the fullness of community and communal life. Law is ordained always to the common good and its prime purpose is to direct man and society to their final end.[1] For St. Thomas, any law, lawgiver, judge, or jurist must gauge decision making not by the sounding board of individual needs, but by its effects on the multitude, on the social and communal order. As St. Thomas relates,

Now the intention of every lawgiver is directed first and chiefly to the common good; secondly, to the order of justice and virtue, whereby the common good is preserved and attained. If, therefore, there be any precepts which contain the very preservation of the common good, or the very order of justice and virtue, such precepts contain the intention of the lawgiver, and therefore are indispensable.[2]

In the framework of a commonwealth, St. Thomas presents a panorama of law that unites the individual citizen to the collective whole, as if parts to a composite, rather than isolated actors drifting through time. "The common good of a human society is similarly at the service of the person. The 'good' is a communion of life between all the members of society."[3] Just as law is the rule and measure of individual human activity, that exercise of reason so often described by St. Thomas, the community is nothing more than a mass or multitude of individuals simultaneously exercising reason. A legal system at odds with communal goods, emphasizing private goods and gains at the expense of the social order, will be an unjust enterprise. Thomas's *On Kingship* recites this idea: "Moreover, a government becomes unjust by the fact that the ruler, paying no heed to the common good, seeks his own private good. Wherefore the further he departs from the common good the more unjust will his government be."[4]

Put another way, the particular action, whether legal ruling or tactic in advocacy, cannot be sequestered from its impact on the whole, the general, and the legal system. For lawyer and judge engaged in immoral and unethical legal practices ruin more than the individual client or cause. Each professional corruption negatively impacts the larger system. Legal systems rot one player at a time. Justice professionals often conveniently dismiss the impact of their individual corruption, and Thomas discerns its corrosive, communal effects. Each individual action travels to a common, communal end: "Actions are indeed concerned with particular matters, but those particular matters are referable to the common good, not as to a common genus or species, but as to a common final cause, according as the common good is said to be the common end."[5]

Dwelling firmly in the community is a major concern for St. Thomas, whose citizen respects not only legal, political, and spiritual authors, but "behave[s] well towards those who are his fellows and partners in the community."[6] A law that fails to advance the common good lacks the true attributes of a law. Neither virtue nor law exists in the tyrant's domain, whose chief aim is not commonality, but private elevation and gain. Kings or other leaders rule the collective body, not the individual personality. Laws direct fundamental energies to identical interests, since "the making of a law belongs either to the whole people or to a public personage who has care of the whole people; for in all other matters the directing of anything to the end concerns him to whom the end belongs."[7]

St. Thomas characterizes precepts or rules devoted exclusively to individual demands as being "devoid of the nature of law."[8] Individuals and states, therefore, relate interdependently. On the one hand, a community would be absolutely bankrupt of laws if there were no individuals, while on the other hand, a horde of isolated individuals, with little or no interaction, could neither invent or institute anything remotely resembling law. A communal society "will be the more perfect the more it is sufficient unto itself to procure the necessities of life."[9] Individuals showing scant concern for the whole community are incapable of being good, and in many cases corrupted states or nations generate weak citizens. Both whole and parts share a unity of purpose and end, for "the common good of the state cannot flourish, unless the citizens be virtuous, at least those whose business it is to govern."[10] In essence, the common good depends upon substantially more than individual development alone, for "common good is that state of society through which the attainment of the existential ends of its members is made possible."[11]

In this collective framework of the common good, the community, and the commonwealth, law functions as far more than command or prohibition, but as a mechanism to advance the communal welfare, for "the good of the multitude is greater and more divine than the good of one man."[12] St. Thomas confidently proclaims that laws failing to enhance the common welfare are "without binding power."[13] He radically urges disobedience when a legal case arises "wherein the observance of that law would be injurious to the general welfare."[14] Human beings form into groups, not by optional selection, but naturally, "for the purpose of *living well* together, a thing which the individual man living alone could not attain, and *good life* is virtuous life."[15] The human agent is neither isolated nor communized in Thomistic thinking, but integrated as part of the whole. Individual goods inexorably rely on common goods and common goods cannot be deduced or fathomed without assessment of individual goods. St. Thomas's elaborate review of the virtue justice, or any virtue for that matter, recognizes this fact of interdependency. The "good of a part can be directed to the good of the whole" [quodlibet bonum partis est ordinabile in bonum totius], and the chief end is the individual and collective whole, "so that all acts of virtue can pertain to justice, in so far as it directs man to the common good."[16] So much of contemporary jurisprudence is ardently dedicated to the division and dissection of individual and community. The language of personal preferences, rights, privacies, and regulatory protections replaces the collective imagination. The long-term implication of supplanting the common good with individual demands is a recipe for cultural demise and disorder.[17] At the heart of St. Thomas's view is the recognition that individual goods elevated in derogation of the common welfare is a prescription for cultural and legal anarchy.

THE COMPOSITION OF THE COMMON GOOD

Doing good and avoiding evil, the structural basis of the natural law, provides a partial backdrop in the search for exactly what the common good is. More accurately, St. Thomas tells both legislator and lawyer that goods, common or otherwise, are understood by both ends and respective objects. Goods vary according to their nature, purpose, or end. By nature, the human species is constructed with good and purposes. The major premise of natural-law reasoning is the centerpiece of both individual and common goods. Each agent is ordered to its proper end and purpose. The eternal plan of creation imprints these fundamental ends into our operations. Being social, being communal, and acting toward the common end represent what is natural in our very essence.[18] Creation participates and shares in this order, this universe of objects and ends. Beings seek their perfection, their ultimate good, and rational beings yearn for happiness and beatitude. Rulers, governments, kings, and queens carry out their governance not independent of their subjects, but always mindful of them. Both king and lawmaker, says St. Thomas, are insurers of the good life, their concern being threefold: "First of all, to establish a virtuous life in the multitude subject to him; second, to preserve it once established; and third, having preserved it, to promote its greater perfection."[19]

Thus, the common good can properly be equated with human happiness. Common good is a society, a civil community seeking perfection, an "organic society" achieving its ultimate end of stability and providing happiness for its individual members.[20] The civil community is the vehicle for human agents to live collectively, to be social animals. Operating within this civil community is a legal system that must also achieve the ends and purposes for its institution, and since it is the adjudicatory arm of the community, must just as readily and attentively advance the common good. The common good consists not only of a practical, functional ends—the operational and efficiently just society—but is geared to a more comprehensive, universal scheme. In other words, how a community, culture, or society promotes the common good is not merely a temporal question, but one inherently woven into creation itself:

Now the first principle in practical matters, which are the object of the practical reason, is the last end: and the last end of human life is happiness or beatitude, as we have stated above. Consequently, law must needs concern itself mainly with the order that is in beatitude. Moreover, since every part is ordained to the whole as the imperfect to the perfect, and since one man is a part of the perfect community, law must needs concern itself properly with the order directed to universal happiness.[21]

In this sense, Thomas's common good is teleological as opposed to utilitarian, divine in addition to human, and ultimately geared to the perfect beatitude that is God.

God, the Human Person, and the Common Good

Nothing could be more adverse to the spirit of Thomism than the assertion that the collective state reigns supreme in any determination of the common good. Plainly, St. Thomas has already signaled his preference for legal decision making in a collective versus an individual sense, but this preference should not be construed as a forum for dictatorships. Temporal kings and kingdoms are of the earth—their time and authority are at best ephemeral. It is dangerous to give more credit to secular governors than they are due. Heinrich Rommen, a philosopher whose depth and breadth emerged from his experiences with Hitler's Third Reich, issues a warning worth remembering:

A science of pure law is consequently unsatisfying. For law is at bottom founded on the essentially teleological character of social being, and in practice its concrete contents are always social life which requires the form of law. But this is not to assert that sociologism is alone warranted in law. For the sociological school of law is indeed able to explain the origin and effect of positive legal norms from the actual sociological facts, but it cannot explain law itself. The two schools of thought constitute a positivist's cleavage of the natural-law doctrine. Natural law, of course, implies an ultimate unity of essential being and oughtness.[22]

St. Thomas's conception of the common good is divinely hierarchical in design, cascading from God to His creation. The divine "God is the universal common good and humans are directed toward him as to their end and ultimate fulfillment."[23] Goods are not merely temporal pleasantries, but spiritual and universal realizations. Self-fulfillment in the social reality, the communal context, that "union with others," extends into eternity.[24] Every creature, being the product of God, is good. God is the perfect good toward whom all creatures strive. In this way, God is the ultimate end, the primordial and preeminent good. Rational creatures, of course, can achieve or participate more in this end than the nonrational. God, by and through His law, is the exemplar for all human activity. Hence, the common good is first and foremost God Himself, for He is the primary and complete end every creature longs for.[25]

The human person naturally strives for the perfection of being. God is that ultimate end in the path to perfection, for the imperfect hope for the perfect, the less beautiful for the more attractive, the lower for the higher. Any concept of the common good in legal decision making is unattainable without consideration of this hierarchical order. Stated another way, what is the common good without God? It is folly to assert any definition of the common good while neglecting God—the exemplar for creation, the perfection and ultimate end of life, and the seat and fullness of what can be or is the common good. Only in God will man identify the purest and unequivocal common good, for God is the common good. Every law, as discussed previously, emanates and is derived from the eternal law, the divine exemplar. God, St. Thomas holds, can "command the whole of nature" [Deus dicitur praecipere toti naturae].[26] Each action and every movement in nature is the result of God's "imprints on the whole of nature" [Deus imprimit toti naturae].[27] In sum, the common good is that which advances human perfection and happiness and the subjective enjoyment of God Himself.

Human Law, Virtue, and Common Good

St. Thomas's lucid expositions on virtue in human activity inevitably find their way into his legal analysis, for virtue resides in and inclines to the good. Any being pursuing its good, its end, must develop suitable habits. The habits can either be virtues or vices, the former developing propensities or inclinations to do what is right, just, or lawful, the latter the opposite. Reason alone is insufficient to achieve goodness. Reason coupled with a virtuous disposition forges the good agent. Gilson writes,

Thus, it is as completely impossible to reduce one of these two orders to the other as it is to isolate them. Moral virtue cannot do without intellectual virtue. Moral virtue must determine a good act. Now an act supposes election; and, as we have seen in our analysis of the structure of the human act, election supposes the deliberation and judgment of reason. So intellectual virtues, which are not directly related to the action can, indeed, dispense with moral virtues. But prudence cannot do so. It must terminate in precise acts. The intellectual virtue of prudence does not merely determine what should be done in general.[28]

Virtuous acts are in conformity with right reason. Law is a rule and measure in conformity with reason, *recta ratio*, and virtue is the disposition to do good. And the common good is what perfects the creature, directing it to its proper end. When discussing habits generally, St. Thomas generously accepts the idea that habituation in human activity, whether for good or bad, produces a pattern, an inclination, not inherently impressed but driven to the level of a propensity. Since every virtue is a habit, a multiplicity of acts generates a particular human trait ("De generatione habituum ex actibus in generali"). Virtue makes the man good. Virtue is a perfecting act, a strength, a power toward the being's proper and ultimate end. Since God is perfect goodness, only virtuous acts will be compatible with the divine plan. The truly virtuous person is happy in being virtuous, since when the virtuous act, they do so consistently and rationally. Appetites are controlled in due course, will is comfortable with reason's dictates, and the human actor takes pleasure in the virtuous disposition. Man, in pining for the ultimate end, yearns for perfection, for God. The only proper way to yearn is to be virtuous, choosing good ends over bad. Here, the concept of the common good is directly relational, for as noted already, the common good is also a perfection of the individual social and civil order. Even though a temporal and imperfect existence, human activity and human government can only achieve goodness if virtuously done. The virtuous life provides the best chance for happiness in earthly governance.[29] Absent a virtuous order and lacking truth in the community guarantees the demise of social and political order. Indeed, St. Thomas observes that human relationships and communal interrelations would be impossible without some semblance of virtuous disposition.[30]

Human law plays a crucial role in the advancement of both the virtuous life and the common good. St. Thomas is realistic enough to see the necessity of human laws in the curbing of vice and the advancement of virtue. Human laws "are most necessary for mankind."[31] Whether by coercion, fear, or punishment, human laws are habituations in both a good and a bad sense. Judges and legislators whose opinions and statutes promote immorality habituate toward vice. Lawmakers who legislate responsibility, accountability, and moral parameters are more likely habituate virtue. St. Thomas realizes that man has a fundamental aptitude for virtue, but must be constantly corralled in, controlled, restricted, and cajoled by human laws.[32] He states,

And as to those young people who are inclined to acts of virtue by their good natural disposition, or by custom, or rather by the gift of God, paternal training suffices, which is by admonitions. But since some are found to be dissolute and prone to vice, and not easily amenable to words, it was necessary for such to be restrained from evil by force and fear, in order that, at least, they might desist from evil-doing, and leave others in peace, and that they themselves, by being habituated in this way, might be brought to do willingly what hitherto they did from fear, and thus become virtuous. Now this kind of training, which compels through fear of punishment, is the discipline of laws. Therefore, in order that man might have peace and virtue, it was necessary for laws to be framed.[33]

The law's discipline is formative for both person and state. Human laws perform an integral function in shaping a nation of virtuous citizens. St. Thomas could not be clearer about the interplay between human law, virtue, and the common good when responding to the query:

Whether human law prescribes the acts of all the virtues?
There is no virtue whose act is not ordainable to the common good.[34]

St. Thomas consistently cautions his readers to avoid making any effort to stamp out all vice through legal means, but to concentrate instead on those activities that provide security and tranquility to the society.[35] He says to give little credence to either the radical or the extremist or those whose views of morality are impossibly unenforceable, but pay heed to policies supportive of the common good. Human laws, being consistent with virtue, and thereby being compatible with the common good, should not oppress the citizen but foster an environment and a culture conducive to betterment. Be wary of those who see human law as the remedy for all human error, Thomas suggests. Vice cannot be stamped out or eradicated in full. Attempting to purge the community of any form of vice is both unrealistic and likely to nurture a tyrant. St. Thomas continues his practical insights:

Now human law is framed for the multitude of human beings, the majority of whom are not perfect in virtue. Therefore human laws do not forbid all vices, from which the virtuous abstain, but only the more grievous vices, from which it is possible for the majority to abstain; and chiefly those that are injurious to others, without the prohibition of which human society could not be maintained. Thus human law prohibits murder, theft and the like.[36]

In the Thomistic framework, human law is heavily dependent and unavoidably intersects with virtue. Law must promote the good. It must foster and nurture the virtuous. It must never become so oppressive that it bludgeons virtue into the subject. "The purpose of human law is to lead men to virtue not suddenly, but gradually" [Lex humana intendit homines inducere ad virtutem, non subito, sed gradatim].[37]

This purpose is so unreserved that St. Thomas advocates civil disobedience to those laws that are inconsistent with this schema. Recognizing that laws are either just or unjust in design, St. Thomas disavows the binding effect of the unjust law. More to the point, Thomas mentions laws contrary to the common good as acts of "*violence rather than laws*," and states such laws "do not bind *in conscience*."[38] St. Thomas goes even further in tolerating the nonobservance of laws enacted that are contrary to the common good. He remarks, "Laws may be unjust through being opposed to the divine good. Such are the laws of tyrants inducing to idolatry, or to anything else contrary to the divine law. Laws of this kind must in no way be observed, because as is stated in *Acts* v. 29, *we ought to obey God rather than men*."[39]

THE COMMON GOOD IN JUDICIAL PROCESS

The judge, jurist, and lawyer engaging in legal practice should not lose sight of a common good that is attentive to the ultimate end of the human person—God. Beginning here, St. Thomas avoids the pitfalls of history, refusing to promote a developmental psychology for individuals alone, and just as fervently rejecting the totality of state. It is an old and repeated temptation, the idea that perfect communities produce perfect people, that governments and dictatorships with promises of utopia are the common good. This is an absurd rendition of the common good.

For the positivists, the law can never achieve the comprehensive conception of St. Thomas. The law is what it is *because* it is. For St. Thomas, it will only be law if consistent with the hierarchy of goods, the universal, eternal, and perennial truths of God, the plan of perfection, the purity of virtue, the achievement of the beatific vision. For the lawyer or judge engaged in the trench warfare of legal practice, it is easy to forget the collective impact. As the judge prepares to render a decision, his or her reasoning is too often myopically attentive to the case before the bench. Judicial rulings leap quickly into the world at large. When abortion is legalized for the individual Roe, it is not long before the Roes multiply, and even shorter still before a negative culture of death becomes an easier pill to swallow. Euthanasia evolves into a mainstream practice, so too partial-birth abortion practice, suicide, and other activities historically shown to undermine the collective enterprise.

Lawyers, when advocating individual falsehoods before the tribunal, can be as effective in subverting the common good. Hiding behind a theory of "zealous" representation will not support or justify the lawyer who withholds evidence, proffers untrue claims and defenses, or lies to opposing counsel and the tribunal itself. These untruths ripple far beyond the individual adjudication. In time, immoral legal tactics serve as mortar in the construction of an immoral legal system. Sure to follow will be the corruption of the community where these advocates reside.

Ultimately, the Thomistic grounding for the common good remains the province of the divine. Judicial conduct and legal advocacy inattentive to the divine dimension are at odds with Thomistic philosophy. Without God, without universal goodness, perfection, and truth, how can the legal system justify the permanency of its judgment?[40]

NOTES

1. George Quentin Friel, *Punishment in the Philosophy of Saint Thomas Aquinas and among Some Primitive Peoples* (Washington, D.C.: Catholic University of America Press, 1939), 118.

2. Thomas Aquinas, "Summa Theologica," *Basic Writings of Saint Thomas Aquinas*, ed. Anton C. Pegis, vol. 2 (New York: Random House, 1945), I–II, Q. 100, a. 8, c. "Intentio autem legislatoris cujuslibet ordinatur primo quidem et principaliter ad bonum commune; secundo autem ad ordinem justitiae et virtutis, secundum quem bonum commune conservatur, et ad ipsum pervenitur. Si qua ergo praecepta dentur quae contineant ipsam conservationem boni communis, vel ipsum ordinem justitiae et virtutis, hujusmodi praecepta continent intentionem legislatoris; et ideo indispensabilia sunt."

3. Cornelius F. Murphy, "Distributive Justice, Modern Significance," *American Journal of Jurisprudence* 17 (1972): 157.

4. St. Thomas Aquinas, *On Kingship*, trans. Gerald B. Phelan (Toronto: Pontifical Institute of Mediaeval Studies, 1982), bk. I, ch. III, 24. J. Messner *Social Ethics: Natural Law in the Modern World*, trans. J. J. Doherty (St. Louis: B. Herder, 1952), 130, describes the common good as "intrinsically a dynamic process . . . neither at any moment finished and completed nor ever ceasing to assimilate fresh driving forces from the perpetual development of the human mind, human interests and technical means."

5. Aquinas, "Theologica," I–II, Q. 90, a 2, ad. 2. "Operationes quidem sunt in particularibus; sed illa particularia referri possunt ad bonum commune, non quidem communitate generis vel speciei, sed communitate causae finalis, secundum quod bonum commune dicitur finis communis."

6. Ibid., I–II, Q. 100, a. 5, c.

7. Ibid., I–II, Q. 90, a. 3, c. "Et ideo condere legem vel pertinet ad totam multitudinem, vel pertinet ad personam publicam, quae totius multitudinis curam habet; quia et in omnibus aliis ordinare in finem est ejus, cujus est proprius ille finis."

8. Ibid., I–II, Q. 90, a. 2.

9. Aquinas, *Kingship*, I, ch. I, 14.

10. Aquinas, "Theologica," I–II, Q. 92, A. 1, ad 3. "Unde impossibile est quod bonum commune civitatis bene se habeat, nisi cives sint virtuosi, ad minus illi quibus convenit principari."

11. Messner, *Social Ethics*, 137.

12. Aquinas, *Kingship*, I, ch. IV, 70.

13. Aquinas, "Theologica," I–II, Q. 96, a. 6.

14. Ibid.

15. Aquinas, *Kingship*, II, ch. III (I, 14), 106.

16. St. Thomas Aquinas, *Summa Theologica*, trans. English Dominican Friars, vol. 2 (New York: Benziger, 1947), bk. II, pt. II, Q. 58, a. 5, c. "Et secundum hoc actus omnium virtutum possunt ad justitiam pertinere, secundum quod ordinat hominem ad bonum commune."

17. James V. Schall, "The Natural Law Bibliography," *American Journal of Jurisprudence* 40 (1995): 168, warns the legal thinker that the substitution of a communal jurisprudence with an individual one has adverse consequences: "There should be no doubt, then, that natural law and civilization are intimately related. To the degree that they are not, right order of soul as well as of the city collapse. When the collapse does occur, we can only begin to think about the disorder and wonder how it occurred."

18. Martin P. Golding, "Aquinas and Some Contemporary Natural Law Theories," *Proceedings of the American Catholic Philosophical Association* 48 (1974): 242. See also Frank Yartz, "Virtue as an *Ordo* in Aquinas," *Modern Schoolman* 47 (1970): 311; Jean Porter, *The Recovery of Virtue* (Louisville, Ky.: Westminster/John Knox Press, 1990), 177.

19. Aquinas, *Kingship*, II, ch. IV (I,15), 117.

20. Messner, *Social Ethics*, 141.

21. Aquinas, "Theologica," I–II, Q. 90, a 2, c. "Primum autem principium in operativis, quorum est ratio practica, est finis ultimus. Est autem ultimus finis humanae vitae felicitas vel beatitudo, ut supra habitum est. Unde oportet quod lex maxime respiciat ordinem qui est in beatitudine. Rursus cum omnis pars ordinetur ad totum, sicut imperfectum ad perfectum (unus autem homo est pars communitatis perfectae), necesse est quod lex proprie respiciat ordinem ad felicitatem communem."

22. Heinrich A. Rommen, *The Natural Law*, trans. T. Hanley (St. Louis: B. Herder, 1948), 244.

23. Michael Sherwin, "St. Thomas and the Common Good. The Theological Perspective: An Invitation to Dialogue," *Angelicum* 70 (1993): 308.

24. Messner, *Social Ethics*, 143.

25. Charles De Koninck, "In Defense of Saint Thomas," *Laval Theologique et Philosophique* 2 (1945): 42; Messner, *Social Ethics*, 143.

26. Aquinas, "Theologica," I–II, Q. 93, a. 5, c.

27. Ibid.

28. Etienne Gilson, *The Christian Philosophy of St. Thomas Aquinas*, trans. L. K. Shook (New York: Random House, 1956), 261.

29. Ralph McInerny, *Ethica Thomistica: The Moral Philosophy of Thomas Aquinas* (Washington, D.C.: Catholic University of American Press, 1982), 1–2.

30. Aquinas, "Theologica," I–II, Q. 96, a. 3, ad. 3.

31. Ibid., I–II, Q. 95, a. 1.

32. Ibid.

33. Ibid., I–II, Q. 95, a. 1, c. "Et quidem quantum ad illos juvenes qui sunt proni ad actus virtutum ex bona dispositione naturae, vel consuetudine, vel magis ex divino munere, sufficit disciplina paterna, quae est per monitiones. Sed quia inveniuntur quidam protervi, et ad vitia proni, qui verbis de facili moveri non possunt; necessarium fuit quod per vim vel metum cohiberentur a malo, ut saltem sic malefacere desistentes, et aliis quietam vitam redderent, et ipsi tandem per hujusmodi assuetudinem ad hoc perducerentur quod voluntarie facerent quae prius metu implebant, et sic fierent virtousi. Hujusmodi autem disciplina cogens metu poenae est disciplina legum. Unde necessarium fuit ad pacem hominum et virtutem, quod leges ponerentur."

34. Ibid., I–II, Q. 96, a. 3, ad 3.

35. Ibid., I–II, Q. 96, a. 2.

36. Ibid., I–II, Q. 96, a. 2, c. "Et ideo lege humana non prohibentur omnia vitia, a quibus virtuosi abstinent, sed solum graviora, a quibus possibile est majorem partem multitudinis abstinere, et praecipue quae sunt in nocumentum aliorum, sine quorum prohibitione societas humana conservari non posset; sicut prohibentur lege humana homicidia, furta, et hujusmodi."

37. Ibid., I–II, Q. 96, a. 2, ad 2.

38. Ibid., I–II, Q. 96, a. 4.

39. Ibid., I–II, Q. 96, a. 4, c. "Leges possunt esse injustae per contrarietatem ad bonum divinum, sicut leges tyrannorum inducentes ad idololatriam, vel ad quodcumque aliud quod sit contra legem divinam; et tales leges nullo modo licet observare, quia, sicut dicitur (Act. IV), obedire oportet Deo magis quam hominibus."

40. See Kevin M. Staley, "Happiness: The Natural End of Man?" *The Thomist* 53 (1989): 221.

CHAPTER 7

Law, Justice, and Judgment

Thomistic jurisprudence is integrative, for it perceives lawyer and judge not as mere functionaries with roles and tasks to carry out, but as human persons endowed and constructed with essential components. Judgment emerges from reason's dictate and the will's freedom. Judgment occurs in unity with human personhood, not apart from it. When judges and lawyers deliberate and issue judgments, they internally process information, causes and effects, and other data. Judgments never arise in a vacuum, but are the stunning by-products of reason and the rational capabilities of the human agent. To judge effectively, the legal professional must adequately deliberate, counsel, and weigh options and, after sufficient time, choose courses of action. To be right, judgment needs to be in accord with our basic rationality. Here, St. Thomas lifts up reason to a superior position to will, for judgment knows its irrefutable dictate, though the will can choose contrarily. Hence, to find a just judgment, the legal decision maker will act in accordance with reason. Judging requires the assertion of the right.

JUDGMENT AND REASON

Judgment is only possible in rational, intellectual creatures, since it is the rational being that has ends and objects. These objects, these ends, from the finite to the infinite, so frequently referenced in St. Thomas's work, serve as the intellectual backdrop to human judgment. In the *Summa Contra Gentiles*, Thomas types each and every human activity "for the sake of some perfection."[1] The human agent intends to bring about perfection, but this is utterly unlikely if the skill at making sound judgments is absent. Judgment calls upon the human player to deliberate and decide, to counsel and select, to choose and discard any series of options. Judgment, in order to be correct, needs to conform to right reason and to its necessary, self-evident principles as its starting point.

Since reason is the distinguishing force and characteristic in human operations, judgment cannot occur without intellectual reflection. Reason and reason alone comprises the intellectual ordering of man, making judgmental activities about the proper objects and ends of human existence a reality. By contrast, will is the decision making relative to choice, to means, and not the known ends of judgments. More precisely, will chooses amongst alternatives posed and shaped by reason. The intellect has no choice, in Thomas's panoramic picture of man, about ends. Will or choice can disregard what reason knows is true. Gilson elaborates on the close yet strikingly different functions of intellect and will in the human agent:

They act here upon each other, but under different relations. Let us consider their objects. That of the intellect is universal being and truth. But universal being and truth constitute the first formal principle that it is possible to assign. And the formal principle of an act is also that which puts it in a determinate species. For example, the action of warming is only such by reason of its formal principle, heat. Now that intellect moves the will by presenting its object to it. This object is universal being and truth.[2]

The will, as common sense dictates, clearly influences reason, and not surprising, reason effects will. This blended relationship delivers similar but not identical definitions. The intellect (reason) knows what is good and the will (free choice) can accept or alter the plan. Man is not a creature of necessity, but of free choice and free willing, as Thomas poignantly describes: "For man can will and not will, act and not act; and again, he can will this or that, and do this or that. The reason for this is to be found in the very power of the reason. For the will can tend to whatever the reason can apprehend as good."[3]

Yet man in the willing mode is not in a superior position to the thinking being. Reason "orders the operations of the will."[4] Reason, intellect, "presents the will with a good as a plan for acting," and the human will may accept or reject any specific good presented.[5] After presentation of proper ends and goods, the will does will or does not will, but assuredly the will commands the sensory appetites and passions in the rational creature. Will comes after judgment. Judgment, therefore, is not an act of will, but one of reason. Reason, by its normative operation, identifies and focuses upon the requisite goods for human fulfillment.

In the practice of law, judgment, the centerpiece of judge and lawyer, requires a virtuous disposition, especially prudence. Law is a dispassionate exercise, more accurately and appropriately an application of prudential judgment. Being capable of discovering proper ends and goods is dependent upon virtue, that ordered disposition of the soul. Justice, by way of example, is the most relevant virtue to judgment itself. A judgment can be just or unjust. Assuming this interplay, it is safe to say that Thomas's view of judgment is compatible with his general philosophical underpinnings. Judgment is primarily teleological in design and intellectual in scope, rather than a by-product of utilitarian or positive inclinations. Judgment, as a human activity, leans toward the ends consistent with men. Judgment cannot separate itself from that which is part of our very essence, our inclinations and habituations, our tendencies and imperatives. Ends cannot be hacked away from the form of the human actor.

JUDGMENT AND DELIBERATION

Any further look into the Thomistic theory of judgment will expose his usual psychological, intellectual, and spiritual depth. Judgment is never robotic. Judgment is never exercised in a vacuum or in isolation from a being's condition. As we pass from the universal truth of our nature, impressed and imprinted upon our very essence, to the particular determinations of a civil society and the "various states and conditions in which men live," judgments will vary.[6] Gilson poses the descent into the particular with his usual clarity: "Now, when we pass from the universal to the particular, we leave behind the immovable and certain to enter the realm of the variable and uncertain. Hence the knowledge of what ought to be done is inevitably filled with uncertainty. Reason does not risk making a judgment in doubtful matters without preliminary deliberation."[7]

Here, Thomas calls upon those entrusted with the activities of judgment, whether they are judges or legal fact finders, to evaluate in deliberation, to counsel, and to mentally examine the circumstances before judging. Inquiry, reflection, and internal questioning are critical steps that precede judgment in particular determinations. St. Thomas relays, "Now in things doubtful and uncertain, the reason does not pronounce judgment without previous inquiry. Therefore the reason must of necessity institute an inquiry before deciding on what is to be chosen; and this inquiry is called counsel."[8] Reason pursues the inquiry because inquiry or deliberation is an intellectual undertaking rather than an exercise or application of choice. Deliberation, Thomas declares, can and should result in a chosen activity, a selected means to the ends, but said deliberation may or may not evolve into human activity. Indeed, St. Thomas signals that deliberation and counsel imply a resolution by their very nature, but implication is no guarantee. Mindless, purposeless inquiry is contrary to the ends of judgment, since judgment is about resolution, which leads to what must be done.[9]

Even so, this propensity toward resolution does not force deliberation into the realm of application. Judges who merely deliberate and avoid decisions lack the true meaning of judgment. Lawyers unable to implement a course of trial conduct or litigation, frozen in motion as to legal argument, are locked into deliberation. Competent lawyers or judges deliberate with purpose, since judgment, according to St. Thomas, inevitably leads to "things we do."[10] Hence, proper judicial function expects decision making; judgment precedes the legislative enactment of the lawmaker. Case defense or prosecution by the professional advocate commences with judgment itself.

Laws, if properly reflected upon, formulated, and enacted, are the product of deliberation, St. Thomas claims, "Although that which is laid down by the law is not due to the action of him who seeks counsel, nevertheless it directs him in his action; for the mandate of the law is one reason for doing something."[11] In this sense, deliberation and counsel can and should "conclude with a judgment of the practical reason" that manifests itself in singular or multiple choices of conduct.[12] Deliberation poses the alternatives; it is the will that chooses and consents.[13] When desire exerts its compulsion, reason and therefore judgment itself are now partially or wholly directed by the will. Judgment's function terminates and is replaced by consent, free choice (*electio*), actual application (*usus*), and inevitable enjoyment (*fruito*).[14] Only after deliberation can the moral agent intend or will anything. St. Thomas points out that the will needs instruction to effect choice: "The will does not ordain, but tends to something according to the order of reason. Consequently, this term *intention* indicates an act of the will, presupposing the act by which the reason orders something to the end."[15]

It is only by weighing the alternative avenues of resolution, of assessing and evaluating circumstances, that the decision maker can judge correctly. Implementing any strategy and adopting singular or multiple courses of conduct presupposes some level of deliberation. In this way, the will awaits the cognitive analysis before implementing a sensible directive.[16] For these and other reasons, deliberative counsel assumes a major role in any theory of Thomistic judgment. Aside from the self-evident, *per se nota*, indemonstrable principles of the natural law, the human species deliberates about most things. Action without thought is charitably blind, as Thomas asserts: "Choice presupposes counsel because of its judgment or decision. Consequently, when the judgment or decision is evident without inquiry, there is no need for the inquiry of counsel."[17] That "choice presupposes counsel" indicates St. Thomas's preference for prudential reasoning.

From this vantage point, the free, unfettered, and unshackled human person—who can do or not do, will nor not will, think or not think, or pose resolutions or reject them—again appears. Tantamount to St. Thomas is the freedom not only to judge, but to will contrarily in conformity with what judgment instructs. Reason, judgment, and deliberation portray a thriving and vibrant intellectual being whose power is further liberated by consent, choice, application, and delight. On both sides of thought and desire, human beings display freedom in its fullest sense. Opposed to predestination and predetermination, St. Thomas recoils at the thought of man's will or reason being controlled or dominated, compelled or coerced, or knowingly or unknowingly moved by some external force. Thomas's person is the free being, acting not in necessity, but from judgment and free will. Judgment is neither command nor dictate, but a decision on how things are or must be. Law and its corresponding judgments live in the land of the intellect, not the land of desire. When intellect and will work harmoniously, legal judgment will be rational and reasonable.[18] Relaying the example of Socrates, St. Thomas says to sit or not sit, to do or not do, is the essence of human judgment: "Thus, that Socrates is sitting is not necessary; but that he is sitting, as long as he continues to sit, is necessary; and this can be known with certainty."[19]

JUDGMENT AND JUSTICE

St. Thomas's treatment of judgment inexorably weaves its way into the virtue of justice. As witnessed in Chapter 4, justice, as both a universal good and a measure of virtuous conduct, is an integral component of Thomistic legal reasoning. Giving someone his or her due is the benchmark for all interpersonal acts, whether legal or otherwise. Only God is capable of dispensing the perfection of justice and rational creatures hope for partial participation in this splendid perfection.

Justice pertains to the right, the equitable, the equilibrious, and the balanced. Justice is the regulatory mechanism, the standard, and the parameter for human interaction, and it is in a superior position to its virtuous counterparts. Quoting Aristotle, Thomas regards justice as *"more glorious than either the evening or the morning star."*[20]

Justice, being designated cardinal, is relevant in individual, social, political, and civic activity. It is applicable to business and commerce, crimes and punishment, restitution and compensation, and other interrelationships. Judgment cannot avoid the essence and nature of justice in any sense, for the law "exists for those between whom justice exists—it follows that it is for those between whom there is unjust action and for those between whom there is just action."[21] In fact, judgment implies the right, and demands, as enunciated already, right reason, a virtuous disposition. Thomas's jurisprudence is quite capable of disavowing a law not attentive to the order of reason. He argues flawlessly: "Again, men receive from divine providence a natural capacity for rational judgment, as a principle for their proper operations. Now, natural principles are ordered to natural results. So, there are certain operations that are naturally suitable for man, and they are right in themselves, not merely because they are prescribed by law."[22]

Judgment, in another sense, is the fruition of justice or injustice, depending upon how it is arrived at. Derived from the very act of judging, the very notion of a judge's occupational role, Thomas states judgment promotes the right (*jus dicens*) and imputes or infers a form of right reasoning.[23] "The other is the disposition of the one who judges, on which depends his aptness for judging aright. In this way, in matters of justice, judgment proceeds from justice, even as in matters of fortitude, it proceeds from fortitude. Accordingly judgment is an act of justice in so far as justice inclines one to judge aright, and of prudence in so far as prudence pronounces judgment."[24]

On a more functional level, Thomas finds judgment not only an act of righteousness, but a mandatory trait for anyone filling the role of a justice professional (e.g., judge, lawyer, or law enforcement officer). Judgment is appropriate for order and maintenance of civilization, but is recognizable only when just. Judgments contrary to justice are "perverted or unjust" or are promulgated or delivered by those lacking the proper authority.[25] Labeling the latter category "judgment by usurpation," St. Thomas disregards and disavows the judgments of those not entrusted with the power to make judicial determinations.[26] There is little doubt of St. Thomas's respect for formal authority and his disdain for those who imitate it without privilege or right. Public authority and qualification assure better legal decision making, because just as it would be unjust to enforce a law not yet enacted, it would be equally unjust to compel "another to submit to a judgment that is pronounced by other than the public authority."[27]

Nor will Thomas give credence to any judgment made in haste or founded upon mere suspicion.[28] As to the question of suspicion, Thomas demands a level of evidentiary scrutiny that casts a sure footing for the case at hand: "Some kind of certainty is found in human acts, not indeed the certainty of a demonstration, but such as is befitting the matter in point, for instance when a thing is proved by suitable witnesses."[29] Stingily granting credibility to doubt, judges and lawyers are bound to "proceed according to law, testimony, and witnesses."[30] Judgments, to be just, should rest upon solid facts, not assumptions or presumptions riddled with inconsistencies and doubts. Again, Aquinas offers an evidentiary insight that insists on legal rigor and grants the general benefit of the doubt to those accused of wrongdoing. Human beings should be judged as presumptively good "unless there is evident proof of the contrary" [nisi manifesta ratio in contrarium appareat].[31] Judges are obligated to skeptically weigh doubtful evidence and to insist upon a reliable evidentiary record. It is better to presume credibility, even to the dishonest and disingenuous, unless the record indicates otherwise. Interpret "doubtful matter[s] for the best" [meliorem partem interpretatur].[32]

In addition to these general characteristics of judgment, St. Thomas lays out his propensity for strict constructionism at Question 60, Article 5 of the *Summa Theologica*. In answering whether judgments should be made according to written law, Thomas displays little hesitancy in overturning a judicial decision inattentive to the law's actual wording. This stance, which at first appears inflexible, images Thomas's general position on the validity or invalidity of human or positive laws. Assuming that a law is only a law, just as it is only just if consistent with the hierarchical schema of the eternal–natural–divine–human, Thomas is predictably consistent. Unjust, immoral, or unnatural promulgations oblige no one, whether written or not. Thomas knows full well that human laws cannot abrogate divinely, eternally, and naturally infused rights. Unjust laws are incapable of diminishing the essential power of a true right and are incapable of annulling its force.[33]

Otherwise, St. Thomas painstakingly sets out the rationale for why written laws are the anchors for legal decisions and, if enacted properly, bind not only a judge but all men: "Now laws are written for the purpose of manifesting both these rights, but in different ways. For the written law does indeed contain natural right, but it does not establish it, for the latter derives its force, not from the law but from nature: whereas the written law both contains positive right, and establishes it by giving it force of authority."[34] Cases where the law's content and subsequent enforcement will cause injustice do not escape Thomas's eye. When legal remedies are inadequate, when an injury or unconscionable unfairness result from a correct interpretation of an existing law, St. Thomas advances a doctrine of legal "equity." Even when the law is "just" but its enforcement causes extreme and disproportionate results, it should "fail" in some cases.[35] St. Thomas holds, "Wherefore in such cases judgment should be delivered, not according to the letter of the law, but according to equity which the lawgiver has in view."[36] Judgment, therefore, is simultaneously an act of rationality and the virtuous disposition.

JUDGMENT AND LAW

Jurisprudence, from both a practical and a theoretical perspective, must inevitably be in the business of judgment. Judgment is resolution. Judgment is decision making. Judgment is a finding, a determination, a mediation of some issue. Law, for all intents and purposes, would be an impossible exercise if judgment did not occur. Judgment, as held by St. Thomas, is part and parcel of man's every internal operation, a product of rational inquiry and an intellectual decision concerning courses of conduct in the human sphere. Judgment is essentially "an act of reason, because it belongs to the reason to pronounce or define."[37]

Judgment for St. Thomas is both necessary and essential to any idea of the just person or society. In a modern world where "being judgmental" is scandalous at best and tyrannical at worst, when courts and the justice system itself are critiqued for issuing judgments of any form, it seems almost arcane to claim the indispensability of judgment. Although Thomas portrays judgment as a sort of functional necessity, an attribute of an ordered culture, he more compellingly argues that judgment is the culmination, the fruition of justice itself. Consciously or not, the human actor lives in a world of judgment. By nature, judgment is the undeniable by-product of reason discovering ends, deliberating and counseling internally over their content, and then willing the means, by consent, election, and application. Judgment implies activity, for it would be folly to live in the transfixed, intellectually trapped world of pure deliberation. Resting judgments exclusively on a positivist's foundation, looking solely to judicial officers and courts "for pronouncements about the state of the law," represents a partial and parochial understanding of Thomistic judgment.[38]

Judgment is inexorably an internal operation of the human species, intricately wed to reason and rationality. The judgment of law is not right because of its promulgation or deliberative bill making, but because it is consistent and compatible with the ends reason identifies. So much of current legal practice is glowingly short on this type of rational scrutiny. Reason is the vehicle, the barometer for how judgments are to be made. To be a true judgment, the outcome can only be just. A judge or other legal player must be just, possess lawful authority, operate on facts and dependable information, be attentive to the written law, and exhibit justice in operations. Not a bad recipe for those entrusted and empowered with the task of legal judgment.

NOTES

1. St. Thomas Aquinas, *Summa Contra Gentiles*, trans. Vernon J. Bourke, vol. 4 (Notre Dame: University of Notre Dame Press, 1975), III, I, ch. 3, 5.

2. Etienne Gilson, *The Christian Philosophy of St. Thomas Aquinas*, trans. L. K. Shook (New York: Random House, 1956), 252.

3. St. Thomas Aquinas, "Summa Theologica," in *Basic Writings of Saint Thomas Aquinas*, ed. Anton C. Pegis, vol. 2 (New York: Random House, 1945), bk. I, pt. II, Q. 13, a. 6, c. "Potest enim homo velle et non velle, agere et non agere; potest etiam velle hoc aut illud; cujus ratio ex ipsa virtute rationis accipitur. Quidquid enim ratio potest apprehendere ut bonum, in hoc voluntas tendere potest."

4. Frank Yartz, "Order and Right Reason in Aquinas' Ethics," *Mediaeval Studies* 37 (1975): 416. See Joseph V. Dolan, "Natural Law and Modern Jurisprudence," *Laval Theologique et Philosophique* 16 (1960): 37; John Finnis, "Object and Intention in Moral Judgments According to Aquinas," *The Thomist* 55 (1991): 5.

5. Yartz, "Order and Right Reason," 416.

6. John E. Naus, "The Nature of the Practical Intellect According to Saint Thomas Aquinas," in *Analecta Gregoriana*, vol. 108 (Rome: Libreria Editrice Dell' Universita Gregoriana, 1959), 54–55.

7. Gilson, *Christian Philosophy*, 253.

8. Aquinas, "Theologica," I–II, Q. 14, a. 1, c. "In rebus autem dubiis et incertis ratio non profert judicium absque inquisitione praecedente: et ideo necessaria est inquisitio rationis ante judicium de eligendis. Et haec inquisitio consilium vocatur."

9. Ibid., I–II, Q. 14, a. 5, c.

10. Ibid., I–II, Q. 14, a. 3.

11. Ibid., I–II, Q. 14, a. 3, ad 2. "Id quod est lege positum, quamvis non sit ex operatione quaerentis consilium, tamen est directivum ejus ad operandum; quia ista est una ratio aliquid operandi scilicet mandatum legis."

12. Gilson, *Christian Philosophy*, 254.

13. Aquinas, "Theologica," I–II, Q. 15, a. 1.

14. Ibid.; Q. 13, a. 6; Q. 16, a. 2; Q. 15, a. 3.

15. Ibid., I–II, Q. 12, a. 1, ad 3. "Voluntas quidem non ordinat, sed tamen in aliquid tendit secundum ordinem rationis. Unde hoc nomen intentio nominat actum voluntatis, praesupposita ordinatione rationis ordinantis aliquid in finem."

16. Ibid., I–II, Q. 12, a. 4; Q. 15, a. 3. See Finnis, "Object and Intention," 8–9.

17. Aquinas, "Theologica," I–II, Q. 14, a. 4, ad 1. "Electio praesupponit consilium ratione judicii, vel sententiae. Unde quando judicium vel sententia manifesta est absque inquisitione, non requiritur consilii inquisitio."

18. The interactivity of reason, will, and legal thought is convincingly portrayed in Daniel Westberg, "Reason, Will and Legalism," *New Blackfriars* 68 (1987): 434.

19. Aquinas, "Theologica," I–II, Q. 14, a. 6, ad 3. "Socratem enim sedere non est necessarium: sed eum sedere, dum sedet, est necessarium; et hoc per certitudinem accipi potest."

20. St. Thomas Aquinas, *Summa Theologica*, trans. English Dominican Friars, vol. 2 (New York: Benziger, 1947), bk. II, pt. II, Q. 58, a. 12, c. "Et neque est Hesperus, neque Lucifer ita mirabilis."

21. St. Thomas Aquinas, *Commentary on the Nicomachean Ethics*, trans. C. I. Litzinger (Chicago: Henry Regnery, 1964), V. L.XI:C 1008.

22. Aquinas, *Summa Contra Gentiles*, III–II, ch. 129, 3.

23. Aquinas, *Theologica*, vol. 2, II–II, Q. 60, a. 1.

24. Ibid., II–II, Q. 60, a. 1, ad 1. "Aliud autem est dispositio judicantus, ex qua habet idoneitatem ad recte judicandum; et sic in his quae pertinent ad justitiam, judicum procedi ex justitia; sicut et in his quae ad fortitudinem pertinent, ex fortitudine. Sic ergo judicium est quidem actus justitiae sicut inclinantis ad recte judicandum; prudentiae autem sicut judicium proferentis."

25. Ibid., II–II, Q. 60, a. 1.

26. Ibid.

27. Ibid., II–II, Q. 60, a. 6, c. "Si aliquis compellat aliquem ferre judicium quod publica auctoritate non fertur."

28. Ibid., II–II, Q. 60, a. 3.

29. Ibid., II–II, Q. 60, a. 3, ad 1. "In humanis actibus invenitur aliqua certitudo, non quidem sicut in demonstrativis, sed secundum quod convenit tali materiae, puta cum aliquid per idoneos testes probatur."

30. George Quentin Friel, *Punishment in the Philosophy of Saint Thomas Aquinas and among Some Primitive Peoples* (Washington, D.C.: Catholic University of America Press, 1939), 128.

31. Aquinas, *Theologica*, vol. 2, II–II, Q. 60, a. 4, ad 2.

32. Ibid., II–II, Q. 60, a. 4, ad 1.

33. Ibid., II–II, Q. 60, a. 5, ad 1. "Lex scripta sicut non dat robur juri naturali, ita nec potest ejus robur minuere vel auferre, quia nec voluntas hominis potest immature naturam."

34. Ibid., II–II, Q. 60, a. 5, c. "Leges autem scribuntur ad utriusque juris declarationem, aliter tamen et aliter; nam legis scriptura jus quidem

naturale continet, sed non instituit: non enim habet robur ex lege, sed ex natura; jus autem positivum scripturam legis et continet et instituit, dans ei auctoritatis robur."

35. Ibid., II–II, Q. 60, a. 5.

36. Ibid., II–II, Q. 60, a.5, ad 2. "Et ideo in talibus non est secundum litteram legis judicandum, sed recurrendum ad aequitatem, quam intendit legislator."

37. Ibid., II–II, Q. 60, a. 1, ad 1.

38. Barry F. Smith, "Of Truth and Certainty in the Law: Reflections on the Legal Method," *American Journal of Jurisprudence* 30 (1985): 101.

CHAPTER 8

Law, Justice, Judges, and Judicial Process

St. Thomas's holistic picture of the human player makes it impossible for him to separate judicial function from personhood. The just man or woman will be the just judge. The virtuous disposition lends itself to a determination of what is due or not due. Other features of the judgeship do not escape Thomas's cutting mind. To judge one must be in public officialdom and not occupy any ecclesiastical position and title. To judge laws correctly, St. Thomas favors the school of textualism known as "strict constructionism." To judge soundly, St. Thomas exhorts judicial officers to weigh and assess the credibility of witnesses and evidence, to afford a series of procedural and judicial rights, to rely on proper documentation, and to permit legitimate defenses. An elaborate procedural code is made available to defense and prosecution so that the truth may be tested in the legal arena. Most critically, St. Thomas permits judges to disregard, and even disavow, the "unjust" law that is contrary to his jurisprudence of the *telos*.

THE JUDGE IN THOMISTIC JURISPRUDENCE

Any key role or position in the justice system envisioned by St. Thomas can only carry out its task and function when in accord with Thomas's overall philosophy. Judges are not only expected to pay more than glancing attention to the ideals of Thomistic jurisprudence, but to live and abide by its content. Judges short on justice and other virtues, or devoid of any teleological conception of law, will perform the most basic of judicial functions poorly, whether judgment, sentencing, evidentiary analysis, or testimonial evaluation. Judges, as ordinary men and women, are not another category of human species, but endowed like any other rational being. Thomas calls judging a "craft," indistinguishable from human identity.[1] The judicial capacity to deliver any version of justice is tied to our operative powers, Thomas comments: "Just as there pre-exists in the mind of the craftsman an expression of the things to be made externally by his craft, which expression is called the rule of his craft, so too there pre-exists in the mind an expression of the particular just work which the reason determines, and which is a kind of rule of prudence."[2]

Being a judge is not only a job or occupational description, but a vocation, arising in and from the human person who happens to engage in the particular role. The Thomistic impression of vocation and profession inevitably winds its way back to human capacity. Each person, including any judge, employs reason, that rule and measure, and the internal law of human existence. Each person is imprinted with the natural law, its self-evident and indemonstrable precepts naturally known by man, and can easily discern the secondary principles with minor reflection.[3] The natural law itself is man's participation in the eternal law of God and woven into the fiber of the human person.[4] Thomas resists the divisibility of person and craft and instead unifies them. Law is more than a craft, more than a series of competencies and behavioral obligations. It is a reflection of our unceasing and unquenchable thirst for what is true and good and for justice itself.

At the forefront, judges serve as gatekeepers to the judicial process and as arbiters of disputes and disputants. Judges must be persons of virtue and integrity. St. Thomas disqualifies those unfit in soul or spiritual health from the judicial role, or those "who stand guilty of grievous sins should not judge those who are guilty of the same or lesser sins."[5]

A judge deficient in moral or intellectual virtue is incapable of judging correctly. A judge failing to exercise right reason will predictably issue improper and incoherent rulings. An unjust judge not only lacks justice but all the other virtues necessary for the good life and acts not in accordance with the prescription for the moral life but contrary to its ends.[6] Thomas's judge labors not solely in a functional sense but in a holistic way, blending competency of task with competency of soul. A judge's "task is justice."[7] The perfectly good person is the perfectly good judge "subject to the overruling of providence as is all creation."[8] The Thomistic judge implores for more than respect or a jurisprudence exclusively dependent on "social practice and usages."[9] The validity or regularity of judicial decision making is not rooted in the chimerical theme of respect, that chameleon of amorality, but upon a natural moral law that generates and announces some fundamental precepts for human living. Judges judge correctly when being attentive to reason and the divine imprint, as Thomas outlines in the *Summa Contra Gentiles*: "Moreover, it is the function of every lawmaker to determine by law the things without which observation of the law is impossible. Now, since law is proposed to reason, man would not follow the law unless all the other things which belong to man were subject to reason. So, it is the function of divine law to command the submission to reason of all the other factors proper to man."[10]

The true judge does all in accord with reason, while the malicious and errant judge subverts human nature and disregards reason's instructions and the indelibly imprinted inclinations in our being. Gilson contrasts the just versus the unjust judge:

The judge who in justice condemns on mere suspicion commits the most serious of sins against justice, since instead of judging according to rights, he is violating them. His act is a direct offense against the very virtue it is his duty to exercise. Where there is no certitude, the benefit of the doubt should be given to the accused. The judge's duty, to be sure, is to chastise the guilty, and all of us must condemn the wicked in our inner forum. But it is better to err many times by acquitting the guilty than even rarely to condemn the innocent.[11]

The true judge avoids sentimentality, personal preference, and opinion, and is unafraid of carrying out both the unpopular and popular purposes of the law. The responsible judge is the equalizer, the bearer of proportionality, and the restorer of equilibrium. Judging is lawful only when consistent with the ends of justice itself, and to be proper its root power rests in the "sovereign as a master-virtue, commanding and prescribing what is just" [quidem est sicut virtus architectonica, quasi imperans et praecipiens quod justum est].[12]

Judges, when delivering judicial sentences such as death, imprisonment, or restitution, sin not against the person upon whom it is imposed, nor is its imposition, if varied according to circumstance, a sin against the respect of person.[13] Punishment responds to the sin itself. To the misfortune of the incarcerated or charged party, judges should focus on not only the individual dilemma but the need for a restoration of personal or communal equality. A judge's judgment is just if it is restorative to the individual harmed or beneficial to the common good.[14] Then, too, a judge may determine, according to the distributive philosophy of justice espoused in Chapter 4, that certain cases or situations are to be decided differently relative to circumstance, parties, or other mitigating factors. In this circumstance, Thomas urges jurists to weigh and evaluate cases on more than the pertinent statute or code, on more than the written language of the law, in order to avoid becoming wholly dependent on punishment as the sole basis for the judicial process. St. Thomas issues sound advice. "As stated above, judgment is an act of justice, in as much as the judge restores to the equality of justice, those things which may cause an opposite inequality. Now respect of persons involves a certain inequality, in so far as something is allotted to a person out of that proportion to him in which the equality of justice consists."[15]

This inequality entails neither an intentional injustice or harm, nor the wilful disregard for what is in equilibrium, but is a reflection of life's varying stations and degrees. For those empowered by money, political power, or social class, the quality of justice may differ from those less fortunate.

THE FORMAL REQUIREMENTS OF A JUDGESHIP

St. Thomas expends considerable time outlining the formalities of judicial qualification from diverse viewpoints: qualities and attributes, requirements and qualifications, and function and decision making. Thomas is very serious about the formal prerequisites for being a judge, since the authority of a judge is granted by the sovereign or the populace. Temporal authority, in addition to divine providence, empowers jurists. Judges effecting judgments do so by "authority from the ruler to do so."[16] As a result, judges do not operate in some individual domain, but from public authority.

The Judge as Public Official

Throughout his jurisprudence, Thomas makes plain that the task of judging is reserved to public officialdom. Judgment and judging resides in the individual endowed with some form of authority. Without formal sanction, a judge's act is nonbinding.[17] He goes out of his way to repeatedly deliberate on this aspect, one example referencing the book of *Deuteronomy*: "Thou shalt appoint judges and magistrates in all thy gates . . . that they may judge the people with just judgment."[18]

Judging, St. Thomas advances, is by its nature a public act, necessitating public position, even when dealing with "hidden" subject matter.[19] Judicial process itself, the operation of courts, evidence, witnesses, and testimony, represent a system built in the public domain. Private judicial process dismantles any notion of how a justice system should operate. Traditionally, judges publicly pronounce judgments. To further his argument, Thomas condemns any form of judging exerted by private individuals. He labels private adjudication a "usurpation" and a "perverse" judicial process.[20] Thomas's judge stands before not only the individual, but also the entire community. Judges interpret and enforce the law not according to individual demands alone, but, more appropriately, according to the collective intentionality of a political and social system. By focusing on the public side of a judgeship, Thomas emphasizes the social, political, and ethical relationships between individual and society. Moreover, this idea cautions jurists to remember their station and purpose and to be mindful of a judge's public, communal accountability. St. Thomas avidly portrays this public responsibility:

Now since it belongs to the same authority to interpret and to make a law, just as a law cannot be made save by public authority, so neither can a judgment be pronounced except by public authority, which extends over those who are subject to the community. Wherefore even as it would be unjust for one man to force another to observe a law that was not approved by public authority, so too it is unjust, if a man compels another to submit to a judgment that is pronounced by other than the public authority.[21]

Thomas is unflinchingly determined about the public nature of judicial office. While advocating the justness of the death penalty in select cases, he firmly forbids any private citizen the right to pronounce or carry it out. Public authority tends to weigh any issue in a greater collective sense, while the whims of the private citizen, whose disposition is less concerned with the general welfare than that of his or her own lot, will be unpredictable.[22] Thomas is reticent, almost nervous, about the prospect of a private citizenry entrusted with the power to inflict punishment. Those given charge of the whole can more faithfully judge its parts, Thomas finds. Individualized, vigilante justice is antagonistic to the common good.[23] One entrusted by political mandate or appointment perceives the responsibility on a grander scale.

That same reservation about privatized judges is quite clear in Thomas's objection to a cleric or churchman charged with orchestrating the death penalty. It belongs to a public official, whose views and perceptions emerge from a more comprehensive landscape, to deliver this type of sentence. Urging ecclesiastical prelates to "imitate their master," Jesus Christ, Thomas reserves the power of this penalty to those in the juridical realm.[24] The separation of ecclesiastical and juridical functions is an unequivocal requirement for the justice system, so much so that Thomas passionately "condemns" religious persons who utilize the formal judicial process to achieve particular aims.[25] As noted earlier, the law in human terms is incapable of addressing, advancing, or eradicating all that is wrong with the world, an ambition rightfully reserved to ecclesiastical powers, whose task is primarily the salvation of souls.[26] This salvation end game is not the province of the lawmaker, the jurist, or the judge.[27] Only by experience, training, and application will a judge be capable of issuing sound legal decisions. The private individual and the churchman has no such competency. Thomas declares, "It is unjust for anyone to be judged by one who has no public authority."[28]

The Judge as Legal Interpreter

Another facet of Thomas's jurisprudence worth a close look is his philosophy of judicial interpretation. What does a judge rely upon when interpreting law and facts? When deliberating, how much does the text of a law guide the arbiter? How dependent is the interpreter on external knowledge, principles of equity, and legislative history? How does a judge most accurately interpret and apply legal principles?

Generally, St. Thomas can be labeled a strict constructionist, that school of legal thought vigorously attentive to text, the written language of the law, when resolving a legal question. By contrast, a judicial activist uses the language of the law as an interpretive starting point, subsequently jumping off into other dimensions when ready to declare a decision or finding. An illustration is the activist asserting an identifiable, constitutional right to homosexual activity under the First Amendment's free exercise of religion or free press terminology. Aghast, the strict constructionist looks at the literal meaning of religion and press, while the activist imagines an abridged freedom tangentially tied to nonexistent language, whether by inference or imputation. As judicial activists are so prone to doing, they invent "penumbras" of privacy and zones of protection, none of which are explicitly enunciated in the Constitution, to further their goal of inclusivity.[29] The strict constructionist goes no further than the text on the table. The judicial activist will journey into other legal territory. Thomas's theory of interpretation is, by most measures, strict: "Hence it is necessary to judge according to the written law, else judgment would fall short either of the natural or of the positive right."[30]

For St. Thomas, written language, the substance of text, provides an anchor for law and its interpretation. "Judgment must be rendered according to the written law."[31] Without writings the interpreter could and would produce an endless array of interpretive results. Hence, from a practical perspective, judicial interpretation depends upon a consistent benchmark, that of the written law. But writings are not the sole grounds for legal principles of ideas. The wise interpreter can never forget that natural rights, granted to man by God and implanted by the natural law, are relevant to any legal interpretation. These natural rights may or may not take written form, but assuredly, no written law can contravene the purposes of these natural rights. Thomas suggests no allegiance to any written law contrary to the teleological principles so often announced, nor any adherence to the word of said laws, since such laws are "corruptions of law, . . . and consequently judgment should not be delivered according to them."[32] Laws inconsistent and contrary to the eternal, natural, and divine legal continuum are not laws at all, and a text enabling this type of law is not worthy of our interpretation. Such laws are "unjust" and have "no binding force."[33] When a Thomistic interpreter interprets, detachment from the ethical and moral dimensions infused in the law is impossible. Adherence to textual meaning depends upon adherence to the teleological and moral order of Thomism, as well as the words of the law.[34]

Evidence and Credibility

Continuing his discourse on legal interpretation, Thomas not only gauges his method of judicial interpretation, but also lays out sound suggestions on how a judge should weigh evidentiary quality. Since judges are expected to rule on evidentiary questions (e.g., admissibility, suppression, limitation, and exclusion), their rulings need adequate grounding. In general, Thomas admonishes the jurist to avoid any judgment that is grounded upon suspicion. Certainty is the mettle of evidentiary quality. Suspicion consists not of factual certitude, but "evil thinking based on slight inclinations."[35] Certainty insures credible judgment, which in turn assures justice. Certainty is not infallibility, but a significant evidentiary quality that is "not indeed the certainty of a demonstration, but such as is benefitting the matter in print."[36] A judge, as mediator between a plaintiff and a defendant, regularly issues rulings on evidentiary questions and is expected to provide an environment where the evidence submitted and admitted is of inherent credibility. Suspicion fails to meet the threshold of credibility. Addressing whether more than two or three witnesses are mandatory for credibility purposes, Thomas characterizes the numerical requirements of witnesses as artificial and unreliable: "For in human acts, on which judgments are passed and evidence required, it is impossible to have demonstrative certitude, because they are about things contingent and variable. Hence the certitude of probability suffices, such as may reach the truth in the greater number of cases, although it fail in the minority."[37]

Witness testimony that is contradictory on material matters can still be admitted into evidence, since the contrasts illuminate the dilemma at hand and allow a beneficial doubt to flourish on behalf of a particular party. Thomas analyzes these shifting burdens and presumptions with uncanny legal insight. In most cases, Thomas recommends the accused being given the "benefit of the doubt." Evidence is to be favorably construed for the defendant, rather than the plaintiff or prosecutor:

The evidence is not weakened if one witness says that he does not remember, while the other attests to a determinate time or place. And if on such points as these the witnesses for prosecution and defense disagree altogether, and if they be equal in number on either side, and of equal standing, the accused should have the benefit of the doubt, because the judge ought to be more inclined to acquit than to condemn, except perhaps in favorable suit, such as a pleading for liberty and the like.[38]

Amazingly, Thomas differentiates evidence and its content, quality, and contestability from the essence of the person offering it and, independently, by the truth or falsity of a particular allegation. Put another way, Thomas can scrutinize the defendant or the plaintiff from the very evidence before the trier of fact. In this fashion, an evidentiary record may be so insubstantial that it frees a guilty defendant, or it may appear so formidable as to award a disproportionate damage award to a feigning party. Theater may replace substantive legal truth. What is proffered into evidence may be true yet rejected, and practical wisdom demands that the judge and jury be capable of differentiating legal and factual truth. Evidence is "not infallible but probable; and consequently the evidence for one side is weakened by whatever strengthens the probability of the other."[39]

Like a seasoned judge, Thomas also categorizes testimonial evidence that is naturally suspect because of the party or circumstances involved in it. Credibility, therefore, depends on the message and the messenger. Those laboring under a defect of reason, the imbecile, the infant (and in an utterly sexist vein, "women"), or "persons united by family or household ties, or again owing to some external condition, as in the case of poor people, slaves, and those who are under authority, concerning whom it is to be presumed that they might easily be induced to give evidence against the truth" are other troublesome evidentiary categories for Thomas.[40] Modern-day experts in judicial process evaluate the credibility of witnesses and testimony using similar strategies.[41] "Saint Thomas would exclude from giving testimony men laboring under defect of bad character, as unbelievers and persons of evil repute, as well as those who are guilty of a public crime, and who are not allowed even to accuse."[42]

St. Thomas grants every witness a presumption of honesty and integrity and "good is to be presumed of everyone unless the contrary appear."[43] By presumption, Thomas recognizes the need for witnesses to be given the benefit of the doubt. Upon testimony, the court will construe the testimony as true unless a challenger overcomes this presumption with evidence in sufficient quantity to destroy the presumption. Doubt is weighed, not to benefit the prosecutorial attorney, but the beleaguered party being prosecuted. Doubts generate incredible, not credible, evidence in Thomas's eyes, and judges should avoid decision making on these shaky grounds: "He who interprets doubtful matters for the best, may happen to be deceived more often than not; yet it is better to err frequently through thinking well of a wicked man, than to err less frequently through having an evil opinion of a good man, because in the latter case an injury is inflicted, but not in the former."[44] Judges are required to preferentially weigh disputed and doubtful evidence on behalf of a defendant and to avoid an obsession to convict or condemn, always mindful of the possibility that inordinate zeal may lead to the condemnation of an innocent person.

At no place is the evidentiary genius of St. Thomas more apparent than in his discussion of evidence, truth, and the power of a judge to rule.[45] Here, Thomas integrates the role and occupation of a judge with that of the human person who dons the robes. Thomas vigorously corrects the advocate who thinks it possible for a judge to separate judicial decision making from the evidence presented. Cases of whatever sort or kind can be decided on a host of rationales that are bankrupt of evidentiary rigor, which is replaced by sentimental, racist, political, criminally corrupted, mindless, or angry decision making. Thomas scolds those who want justice without the evidentiary record to support it. In one case a judge, as a person, may know or feel something that has not been submitted by the advocates. In another, the formal record of evidence may be insubstantial and vacuous. How does the judge decide? It is the role as judicial information gatherer that provides the basis for judicial reasoning, not the private knowledge of the citizen who dons the robes. Judgment is "based on information acquired by him, not from his knowledge as a private individual, but from what he knows as a public person."[46]

If that same judge cannot pronounce evidentially, acquittal or dismissal is proper. So, Thomas suggests the real, indisputable truth may exist simultaneously with a legal truth, derived from either strong or weak evidence. In every case before the court, decisions have to be evidentially rooted. The judge may know after sifting through the evidentiary record that a decision soon to be rendered is contrary to the truth of the matter. Legal truth depends so heavily upon the court's evidentiary record that any judgment rendered will rest upon this legally suspect conclusion rather than the unsubstantiated, though true, allegation. For Thomas, the personal conscience of a judge is subject to the functionality of the judgeship: "In matters touching his own person, a man must form his conscience from his own knowledge, but in matters concerning the public authority, he must form his conscience in accordance with the knowledge attainable in the public judicial procedure."[47] Thomas respects the province of the jury and fact finder and cautions judges to show respect for deliberations even if he or she knows differently.

That Thomas affords significant respect to evidentiary matters is apparent at many points in his legal writings. The business of judgment, as delivered by judges and juries, is no small matter. Our efforts to judge rightly, humbly, and adequately pale before the divine judge who deliberates in perfect equilibrium, who accords proper weight and credibility in each class of evidence, and who knows when to convict and when to acquit. The human agent, as in every facet of existence, struggles to get it right. What is dead certain is the seriousness Thomas attributes to evidentiary credibility. The ramifications posed by Thomas for false testimony elucidate the centrality of evidential integrity in Thomas's jurisprudence. Terming falsehood in evidence a mortal sin, any judgment that arises from such testimony will be "unjust" and "not a judgment" in any sense.[48] False testimony is graphically described by St. Thomas as a "deformity."[49] Supportive of this condemnation is Thomas's description of perjury as a "contempt of God" that incurs the penalties pertinent to mortal sin.[50] In a court of law it is graver than infamy.[51]

A final suggestion from Thomas relating to quality of judicial interpretation involves experience and practical wisdom. Legal decision making is best when prudentially executed. Experienced judges are fortunate enough to predict impacts and ramifications, and to discover how singular rulings influence the communal whole. Judges and lawmakers, as Thomas recommends in his *Commentary on the Nicomachean Ethics*, are most effective when experienced: "But the inexperienced are understandably ignorant whether a work is done well or badly on the basis of what they read in books, for they do not know how to put into practice what is in the books. Now laws to be framed are, as it were, the results of the art of politics; they are framed as rules for activities of the state."[52]

So much of modern judicial activism lacks this perspective. Time and experience do much to advance judicial wisdom, Thomas determines, "but those who have not the habit acquired by practice and want to review written documents of this kind cannot properly judge them except by chance. However, they do become more capable of understanding such things by the fact that they have actually read through the written laws and constitutions."[53]

JUDICIAL PROCESS

In the area of courtroom and judicial processes, Thomas provides a remarkable series of procedural insights. Respect for person, in the roles of defendant and plaintiff, is a hallmark of Thomas's judicial process. Respect for authority, for ruler and state and for a judge as decision maker, is an equally important criteria in Thomas's justice machinery. Thomas's justice enterprise is developed not in the spur of the moment or as an afterthought, but as a well thought out, artfully devised system of legal checks and balances. Included are procedural and substantive protections for the litigating parties, caveats and restraints on judicial demeanor, and a dedication to the rule of law.

Judges are delegated the responsibility of assuring these procedural rights, the conduct of court, and the integrity of the litigants. Chapter 9 evaluates the conduct of lawyers and the tactics of the advocate. What remains here is a brief overview of rules and standards relevant to judicial conduct and courtroom expectations.

The Jurisdictional Mandate

Early in his discussion, Thomas cuts to the issue of jurisdiction. Jurisdiction, that right of a court to hear a case based on authority over person or particular subject matter, erects a procedural forum and locale. For example, jurisdiction over tax matters is reserved to the tax court, patents to the patent court, appeals to the appellate court. Thomas's admonition that only public authorities have the power to judge is also a jurisdictional question. Private parties lack both the power and the jurisdictional authority to hear or resolve a case, while public figures can declare the jurisdictional mandate. Thomas claims that a judge lacks jurisdiction to judge if the power to do so has not been delegated, nor will the judge be competent if devoid of any ordinary juridical authority.[54] Lacking power or authority to bind or oblige, Thomas would dismiss any proceedings in a case of faulty jurisdiction. As the general law has a coercive power or quality, the judgeship depends upon the same;

otherwise, proclamations from judicial authority would be of minimal effect. Thomas unreservedly connects the authority of law with the occupational efficacy of the law, since "A judge's sentence is like a particular law regarding some particular fact."[55] Further illustrating his procedural rigor, Thomas offers an advanced theory of pendant and/or ancillary jurisdiction whereby two courts (e.g., state and federal) have province over the same person or subject matter. In his example, dual jurisdiction of monk and monastery and monk and state would exist for religious infractions if the once exempted religious committed murder or theft.[56]

The Role of Accusation

No case should proceed to formal litigation without an accusation, says Thomas. To accuse is to trigger a systematic response. Accusation, according to Thomas, is the first maneuver in a series of moves in the typical criminal litigation. The judge and the justice system stand pat until a complaint and a complainant, a victim and a perpetrator, emerge. The crime victim is "bound" to accuse, not only for his or her good, but for the common interests and safety of the community.[57] The solid citizen reports and screams loudly of the injustice. Thomas's obligatory tone in the case of criminal activity does more than suggest the reporting of criminal conduct; it urges a full-scale public pronouncement. Individuals who idly sit by as criminality grows are injurious to the "commonwealth" [detrimentum reipublicae] and agents in the "bodily or spiritual corruption of the community" [in multitudinis corruptelam corporalem, seu spiritualem].[58]

Judges are not warranted or justified in proceeding with any case if lacking an accused or an accusation. In Thomas's world, the court insists on two parties to a criminal case; the state's allegation alone is not sufficient. Lacking either a plaintiff or defendant, a case is merely in expectancy. A judge is paralyzed until an accusation crystallizes, and Thomas sternly critiques any judge who decides, condemns, and penalizes a defendant without the existence of an accuser and an accusation. Thomas insists on the necessity of accusation: "Now, as stated above, justice is not between a man and himself but between one man and another. Hence a judge must needs judge between two parties, which is the case when one is the prosecutor, and the other the defendant. Therefore in criminal cases the judge cannot sentence a man unless the latter has an accuser."[59]

So convinced is he of the importance of accusation, that confrontational quality that apprizes defendants of what criminal acts are alleged or civil defendants of the civil actions to ensue, that St.

Thomas requires it be memorialized in a writing. The business of criminal litigation is so serious that Thomas wants the parties to be accurate in their assertions, to be confident of the facts and legal queries at hand, and to deliver to the court an initial record from which the conduct of trial can be governed. Verbal allegations transform into faded memories, and any judgment or sentencing drawn up without the aid and assistance of a memorialized record is likely to cause injustice. It is the judge that "stands between the accuser and the accused for the purpose of the trial of justice, wherein it behooves one to proceed on certainties, as far as possible."[60] Writings also may serve as a testimonial substitute, a permanent record for evidentiary purposes and as a basis or report for a judge's sentence. Accusations based on puffery, braggadocio, collusion, or evasion are unacceptable in any litigation.[61] During Thomas's time, as now, victims and witnesses were amply capable of inventing or devising less than credible accusations. To charge falsely is to *calumniate* the accused, to *collude* is to team up with others to invent an accusation, and to *evade* is to fail to report even though true.[62] Any defect in the accuser, the accused, or the accusation itself is declared by Thomas injurious to the person and the common good. The accuser "must eschew any total withdrawal of the accusation which would be in detriment to the common good."[63] False accusations must be harshly and swiftly dismissed and remedied. Mistakes or errors in process, charges, or loss of memory do not rise to the level of unjust accusation, and may be modified or corrected.

False accusations can justify retaliation by the wrongfully accused, suffering "like punishment."[64] To achieve equilibrium, Thomas suggests retaliation to cure the imbalance, and a "punishment of disgrace" [poena infamiae] is due those falsely accusing.[65]

The Power to Punish

Discussed in depth in Chapter 10 is the Thomistic theory of punishment and legal consequence. St. Thomas reserves the right to punish to public, legal officers and forbids imposition by private and ecclesiastical authorities. Punishment images his theory of justice and the virtues. Punishment is what is due. Judges are delegated the power to punish, to sentence, to initiate loss or forfeiture of rights, to imprison, to physically penalize, and to execute. With justice's mean as the centerpiece in a sentencing policy, the judge is attuned to proportionality and equality.

Thomistic jurisprudence affords wide-ranging judicial discretion in the application and enforcement of sentences, but admonishes the judge who exerts too much power, especially when unilaterally deciding that a lawful and just sentence should be remitted. Thomas does not forbid the demonstration of mercy and individualized case-by-case review. Part of his work dwells upon the nature of mitigation, examples being ignorance, accident, and involuntary acts. This form of judicial discretion is appropriate to the role of the judge.[66] In denying a judge the right to remit punishment, Thomas justifies his refusal on two fronts: First, the parties who have just litigated and adjudicated their cases would be left in an imbalanced, imperfect situation; second, to remit punishment, a judge would undermine the fundamental responsibility of a judge. Thomas imparts any right of remission to the ruler, the sovereign power whose acts "do not seem detrimental to the public good."[67]

NOTES

1. St. Thomas Aquinas, *Summa Theologica*, trans. English Dominican Friars, vol. 2 (New York: Benziger, 1947), II–II, Q. 57, a. 1.

2. Ibid., II–II, Q. 57, a. 1, ad 2. "Quod sicut eorum quae per artem exterius fiunt, quaedam ratio in mente artificis praeexistit, quae dicitur regula artis; ita etiam illius operis justi quod ratio determinat, quaedam ratio praeexistit in mente, quasi quaedam prudentiae regula."

3. St. Thomas Aquinas, "Summa Theologica," in *Basic Writings of St. Thomas Aquinas*, ed. Anton C. Pegis, vol. 2 (New York: Random House, 1945), I–II, Q. 93, a. 4, c.

4. Ibid., I–II, Q. 91, a. 2.

5. Aquinas, *Theologica*, vol. 2, II–II, Q. 60, a. 2, ad 3. "Quod illi qui sunt in gravibus peccatis, non debent judicare eos qui sunt in eisdem peccatis, vel minoribus."

6. One of the few close looks at Thomistic jurisprudence in contemporary legal practice is Michael Harding, "True Justice in Courts of Law," in St. Thomas Aquinas, *Summa Theologica*, trans. English Dominican Friars, vol. 3 (New York: Benziger, 1947), 3348–3349.

7. Joseph V. Dolan, "Natural Law and the Judicial Function," *Laval Theologique et Philosophique* 16 (1960): 107.

8. M. Gilson, *Law on the Human Level. Moral Values and Moral Life: The System of St. Thomas*, trans. L. Ward (St. Louis: B. Herder, 1931), 197.

9. Neil MacCormick, "Natural Law and the Separation of Law and Morals," in *Natural Law Theory*, ed. Robert P. George (Oxford: Clarendon Press, 1992), 107.

10. St. Thomas Aquinas, *Summa Contra Gentiles*, trans. Vernon J. Bourke, vol. 4 (Notre Dame: University of Notre Dame Press, 1975), bk. III, pt. II, ch. 121, 4.

11. Etienne Gilson, *The Christian Philosophy of St. Thomas Aquinas*, trans. L. K. Shook (New York: Random House, 1956), 311.

12. Aquinas, *Theologica*, vol. 2, II–II, Q. 60, a. 1, ad 4.

13. Ibid., II–II, Q. 63, a. 4; a. 1.

14. Ibid., II–II, Q. 64, a. 4.

15. Ibid., II–II, Q. 63, a. 4, c. "Sicut dictum est, judicium est actus justitiae, prout judex ad aequalitatem justitiae reducit ea quae inaequalitatem oppositam facere possunt. Personarum autem acceptio inaequalitatem quamdam habet, inquantum attribuitur alicui personae aliquid praeter proportionem suam, in qua consistit aequalitas justitiae."

16. Gilson, *Christian Philosophy*, 310.

17. See Aquinas, *Theologica*, vol. 2, II–II, Q. 67; George Quentin Friel, *Punishment in the Philosophy of Saint Thomas Aquinas and among Some Primitive Peoples* (Washington, D.C.: Catholic University of America Press, 1939), 126.

18. Deut. 16:18. Aquinas, *Theologica*, vol. 2, II–II, Q. 60, a. 2, c.

19. Ibid., II–II, Q. 60, a. 2.

20. Ibid., II–II, Q. 60, a. 6.

21. Ibid., II–II, Q. 60, a. 6, c. "Cum autem ejusdem auctoritatis sit legem interpretari (1), et legem condere; sicut lex condi non potest nisi publica auctoritate, ita nec judicium ferri potest nisi publica auctoritate; quae quidem se extendit ad eos qui communitati subduntur." See Dolan, "Natural Law," 109.

22. Aquinas, *Theologica*, vol. 2, II–II, Q. 64, a. 3.

23. Ibid., II–II, Q. 64, a. 3, ad 3.

24. Ibid., II–II, Q. 64, a. 4.

25. St. Thomas Aquinas, *An Apology for the Religious Orders*, ed. John Procter (St. Louis: B. Herder, 1902), bk. I, ch. 15.

26. Aquinas, *Theologica*, vol. 1, I–II, Q. 96, a. 2.

27. See Charles D. Skok, *Prudent Civil Legislation According to St. Thomas and Some Controversial American Law* (Rome: Catholic Book Agency, 1967), 123.

28. Aquinas, *Theologica*, vol. 2, II–II, Q. 60, a. 6.

29. *Griswold v. Connecticut*, 381 U.S. 479 (1965); *Roe v. Wade*, 410 U.S. 113 (1973).

30. Aquinas, *Theologica*, vol. 2, II–II, Q. 60, a. 5, c. "Quad lex scripta sicut non dat robur juri naturali, ita nec potest ejus robur minuere vel auferre, quia nec voluntas nominis potest immutare naturam."

31. Friel, *Punishment*, 127.

32. Aquinas, *Theologica*, vol. 2, II–II, Q. 60, a. 5, ad 1.

33. Ibid., II–II, Q. 60, a. 5.

34. Rommen's assessment of text and jurisprudence is worth reading. See Heinrich A. Rommen, *The Natural Law*, trans. T. Hanley (St. Louis: B. Herder, 1948), 188.

35. Aquinas, *Theologica*, vol. 2, II–II, Q. 60, a. 3.

36. Ibid.

37. Ibid., II–II, Q. 70, a. 2, c. "In actibus enim humanis, super quibus constituuntur judicia, et exiguntur testimonia, non potest haberi certitudo demonstrativa, eo quod sunt circa contingentia et variabilia; et ideo sufficit probabilis certitudo, quae ut in pluribus veritatem attingat, etsi in paucioribus a veritate deficiat."

38. Ibid., II–II, Q. 70, a. 2, ad 2. "Non tamen praejudicatur testimonio, si unus dicat se non recordari, et alius asserat determinatum tempus vel locum. Et si in talibus omnino discordaverint testes actoris et rei, si sint aequales numero, et pares dignitate, statur pro reo, quia facilior debet esse judex ad absolvendum quam ad condemnandum; nisi forte in causis favorabilibus, sicut est causa libertatis, et hujusmodi."

39. Ibid., II–II, Q. 70, a. 3, c. "Non habet infallibilem certitudinem, sed probabilem. Et ideo quidquid est quod probabilitatem afferat in contrarium, reddit testimonium inefficax."

40. Ibid.

41. See Charles P. Nemeth, *Litigation, Pleadings and Arbitration*, 2d ed. (Cincinnati: Anderson, 1997); Lawrence S. Charfoos and David W. Christensen, *Personal Injury Practice: Technique and Technology* (Rochester, N.Y.: Lawyer's Cooperative Publishing, 1988); Charles P. Nemeth, *Law and Evidence: A Primer for Criminal Justice, Criminology, Law and Legal Studies* (Upper Saddle River, N.J.: Prentice Hall, 2001).

42. Friel, *Punishment*, 136.

43. Aquinas, *Theologica*, vol. 2, II–II, Q. 70, a. 3, ad 2.

44. Ibid., II–II, Q. 60, a. 4, ad 1. "Ille qui in meliorem partem interpretatur, frequentius fallitur; sed melior est quod aliquis frequenter fallatur, habens bonam opinionem de aliquo malo homine, quam quod rarius fallatur, habens malam opinionem de aliquo homine bono; quia ex hoc fit injuria alicui, non autem ex primo."

45. Ibid., II–II, Q. 67, a. 2.

46. Ibid., II–II, Q. 67, a. 2, c. "Et ideo informari debet in judicando non secundum id quod ipse novit tanquam privata persona, sed secundum id quod sibi innotescit tanquam personae publicae."

47. Ibid., II–II, Q. 67, a. 2, ad 4. "Quod homo in his quae ad propriam personam pertinent, debet informare conscientiam suam ex propria scientia; sed in his, quae pertinent ad publicam potestatem, debet informare conscientiam suam secundum ea quae in publico judicio sciri possunt, etc."

48. Ibid., II–II, Q.. 70, a. 4.

49. Ibid., II–II, Q. 70, a. 4, c.

50. Ibid., II–II, Q. 98, a. 3, c.

51. Ibid., II–II, Q. 98, a. 3, ad 3.

52. St. Thomas Aquinas, *Commentary on the Nicomachean Ethics*, trans. C. I. Litzinger (Chicago: Henry Regnery, 1964), X. L.XVI:C 2176.

53. Ibid., X. L.XVI:C 2178.

54. Aquinas, *Theologica*, vol. 2, II–II, Q. 67, a. 1.

55. Ibid., II–II, Q. 67, a. 1, c. "Quod sententia judicis est quasi quaedam particularis lex in aliquo particulari facto."

56. Ibid., II–II, Q. 67, a. 1, ad 3.

57. Ibid., II–II, Q. 68, a. 1, c.

58. Ibid.

59. Ibid., II–II, Q. 67, a. 3, c. "Justitia autem, sicut supra dictum est, non est ad seipsum, sed ad alterum. Et ideo oportet quod judex inter aliquos duos dijudicet; quod quidem fit, cum unus est actor, et alius est reus. Et ideo in criminibus non potest aliquem judicio condemnare judex, nisi habeat accusatorem."

60. Ibid., II–II, Q. 68, a. 2, c. "Ita quod judex inter accusatorem et eum qui accusatur medius constituitur ad examen justitiae; in quo oportet, quantum possibile est, secundum certitudinem procedere."

61. Ibid., II–II, Q. 68, a. 3.

62. Ibid., II–II, Q. 68, a. 3, c.

63. Friel, *Punishment*, 131.

64. Aquinas, *Theologica*, vol. 2, II–II, Q. 68, a. 4.

65. Ibid., II–II, Q. 68, a. 4, ad 3.

66. Ibid., II–II, Q. 67, a. 4, ad 1.

67. Ibid., II–II, Q. 67, a. 4, c.

CHAPTER 9

Law, Justice, Lawyers, and Advocates

Central to any lawyer's vocation is truth. Legal advocates are cautioned that falsehoods are not only destructive to the justice system, but also to the soul. Acceptable legal advocacy can be tenacious, innovative, and creative, but not at the expense of justice and truth. Falsehoods of every sort are vociferously condemned by St. Thomas. Lawyers are not to be party to any unjust law, for to advocate the merits of an unjust law is to advance injustice. Unjust laws bind neither lawyer nor client.

At trial or other legal proceeding, the lawyer needs to refrain from all falsehood, suspicion, rumor, calumny, collusion, and evasion. Those who engage in such tactics should be barred from the practice of law. If meritorious and factually grounded, Thomas insists the lawyer aggressively pursue defense and prosecution using the wits given to him or her by God. These general insights extend to witnesses, the presentation of evidence, and candor toward the tribunal. In sum, Thomas's portrait of a lawyer contains professional competencies, but more compellingly, a picture of a moral agent dedicated to virtue and truth.

THE LAWYER IN THOMISTIC JURISPRUDENCE

Lawyers do not escape Thomistic scrutiny, and in fact, are a topic of enormous importance in the legal theory of St. Thomas. Just as human law is necessary, laudatory, and foundational to civilization, so too is the lawyer, who interprets, advocates, or challenges the legitimacy of any law. Lawyers specialize in the law as an instrument in procedural and substantive legal settings. Employing the law as promulgation or act is only the starting point. A law, aside from being a juridical act, is by its proper nature an ordination of reason and directed to and the subject of virtuous conduct, the foremost being the virtue of justice itself. Lawyers clamoring for justice do so in a holistic sense, rather than upon the urging of individual clients. Lawyers, if carrying out their tasks correctly, remember the comprehensive definition Thomas attributes to law, avoiding the muddle of individual preference and retaining a rational prescription for the whole, for the good, and for the universe.

Thomas perceives the practice of law in both secular and spiritual terms. When deciding whether a lawyer should take or charge a fee for his or her advocacy, Thomas states, "Though knowledge of law is something spiritual, the use of that knowledge is accomplished by the work of the body: hence it is lawful to take money in payment of that use, else no craftsman would be allowed to make profit by his art."[1]

In this framework, lawyering is more than a series of mechanical steps, it is a spiritual undertaking, entwined and entangled in the mesh of man's intellect, reason, ends and goals, natural-law imprints, and the image of God's creation. Spouting off legal maxims and principles and being slavishly attendant to legal promulgations without the broader perspective offered by Thomas is not the practice of law in the truest sense. The practice of law and lawyering itself is a sojourn in the just and unjust world of human existence.[2] Good lawyers use the cerebral skills of the intelligent being, and are mindful of their spiritual and rational makeup. Certainly, the truly proficient lawyer develops superlative analytical talents, becomes a sterling orator and rhetorician, excels in the tactics and techniques of the litigator, and aggressively pursues the client's victory or position though these competencies.

More germane for St. Thomas is the permanent remembrance of the hierarchical structure of law, descending down from the divine exemplar, inherent and burned into our natural beings, aided by divine revelation, and dependent upon the order that emanates from nature and the positive laws enacted for the common good. Lawyers, like all human agents, are subject to this plan and need to submit their persons and occupation to this teleological approach. The state cannot neglect the purposes and effects of the natural law, since the natural law is given to us "by the mercy and wisdom of the truly Supreme Legislator."[3]

Lawyers, in St. Thomas's eyes, are more than dockyard bullies who if screaming loud enough, antagonizing opponents enough, and representing clients zealously enough are aggressive victors. In the contemporary courtroom, the search for truth is often replaced and unfortunately vanquished by those whose message rests on drama more than truth. Form over substance, fair over right, replaces the true and the good in law and lawyering. A client's rights or protections, just as a lawyer's vocation, are not singularly grounded in the promulgative reality, but in a law "that ought to be."[4] The lawyer as "role" is, at best, an amoral functionary. Thomas insists on much more.

To the dismay of the justice system, modern legal practice repeatedly witnesses lawyers who advocate claims knowing of their falsity, represent cases thoroughly vacant in merit, adopt litigation strategies that wear down opponents by the exhaustion of the opponent's resources, and orally argue avant garde, even bizarre, legal arguments. And why not? For most contemporary legal professionals, lawyering is about gamesmanship, tactics, and victory for client and cause, with little care for means. Modern law schools speak of ethics in regulatory provisions or case-law determinations, not the Thomistic ideals of truth, teleology, and justice. Justice is about what is *right*. Justice concerns itself solely with right reason, virtue, and human and communal goods. Justice is not primarily about results tabulated in a win–loss column. Lawyers, for St. Thomas, are in the business of truth, not in a war of combatants or deceptive theatrical performances. Thomas's comparison of a soldier to a legal practitioner is instructive. The soldier he allows to be deceptive while in the midst of battle, though similar tactics of the lawyer–advocate are rejected:

As stated above, it is lawful for a soldier, or a general to lay ambushes in a just war, by prudently concealing what he has a mind to do, but not by means of fraudulent falsehoods, since we should keep faith even with a foe, as Tully says (*De Offic.* 29). Hence it is lawful for an advocate, in defending his case, prudently to conceal whatever might hinder its happy issue, but it is unlawful for him to employ any kind of falsehood.[5]

This sketch of the lawyer–advocate is consistent with Thomas's overall view of human operations, inclinations, and dispositions. Lawyers are no different from other actors on the world stage.

This generality, however, does not cause Thomas to hesitate in laying out a blueprint for the legal profession. Eruditely, Thomas addresses the practice of law from various vantage points. Exactly how does a lawyer morally and ethically advocate? How does truth serve as an ethical guidepost for the lawyer? Does the virtue of justice guide the lawyer? Do acts of injustice eventually transform the just lawyer into an unjust person? Is there a relationship between injustice, falsehood, immorality, and the condition of a lawyer's soul, or are these injustices manifestations of a profession and not the lawyer's personhood? Is there a difference in professional and ethical parameters for those representing defendants or plaintiffs? How effective are lawyers in meting out justice by giving what is due to others and equalizing the imbalances that are inherent in civil harms and criminal wrongs? Not surprising, Thomas's job description for "lawyer" comprises more than professional obligations and proficiencies, but also includes the rich formula for the good life, since to justice "is annexed truth."[6]

THE LAWYER AS ADVOCATE

Delivering a legal argument, arguing for or against a particular law, precedent, or statute, or urging the adoption of a specific principle in law or equity is the sum and substance of the advocate. Lawyers perform a myriad of functions, and throughout their professional careers this will most assuredly include legal argument. It is the business of the advocate to vigorously represent cases or clients in their respective conditions and circumstances. Vigor of representation, however, is not a license to act without moral parameters. "Zealous representation," a "vigorous defense," "unfailing loyalty to client and case," and being "a hired gun" for defense or prosecution are the standard "shop" descriptions for the lawyer–advocate. These depictions primarily portray a role or occupation of touting or toeing the line or case argument and advocacy. Such bantering is an incomplete inquiry into the nature of advocacy, since the advocate need delve into other underlying issues, such as the meritorious basis for claim or charge and the justness and justice in the claim or charge. In other words, the advocate, before tuning up the vocal cords, assesses the morality, the virtue, and the end result of the case to be advocated. Lawyers, in Thomas's moral setting, cringe at false factual averments and avoid any type of deliberate or selective ignorance of facts. Lawyers are in the business of justice, and Thomistic justice, as has been articulated, is not the province of victories and legal scorecards. Adopting a tone of condemnation, Thomas chides the lawyer who advocates the unjust cause: "It is unlawful to co-operate in an evil deed, by counseling, helping, or in any way consenting, because to counsel or assist an action is, in a way, to do it."[7]

Imagine this view in the modern-day courtroom, where lawyers march in lockstep with criminals known to be guilty or with litigants whose cases are disingenuous in the best light. Preferring the comfort of ignorance about client and case is unacceptable for those attuned to Thomas's jurisprudence. Thomas's legal advocate is aggressive about both the profession and those represented, as symbolized by his characterization of those advocating an unjust cause as "ungodly."[8] The ungodly operate by means of chicanery, "fraudulent falsehoods," and engaging in a perversion of "his art for an evil end."[9] George Friel interprets Thomas correctly:

> If in the course of a suit, the advocate finds that his case is unjust, he must give up the case, or induce his client to give way, or make some compromise without prejudice to the other side. In the course of a suit he may make use of all prudent and honest means, e.g., by not revealing all the truth, etc. On the other hand, he may never commit a crime to save his client. In criminal cases he may defend the criminal always, provided that he uses neither fraudulency nor lies.[10]

For those laboring in the muck of institutionalized legal practice, a policy of honesty and disclosure appears both naïve and incomprehensible. For many, the legal system has institutionalized, and thereby legitimized, a selectively disclosed type of legal advocacy. It is a business not interested in putting all the cards on the table, but instead hides behind a lax occupational positivism. Cases and claims docketed in the prothonotary's office rarely press the advocate's conscience. For the most part, today's attorneys are not mindful of the moral or metaphysical connotations of law; nor is the justice system itself. The consequences of a legal culture and infrastructure dominated by the positivist's ideal is far-reaching and has invaded law school classrooms and courtrooms.[11] A lawyer's model gutted of moral demands entices the bulk of advocates. Why should the advocate care when legal pundits creatively cook up new and untested theories of injury and defense? Who can resist criminal defenses of the sort invented in the last three decades (e.g., television addiction, postpartum blues, junk food compulsions, astrological imbalances, and sexual addiction)? Advocacy without moral consequences is nothing more than a mindless series of movements and rationalizations. Thomas recoils at this narrow view of lawyering, since a lawyer's function must be "seen in its full light, must be seen against the background of his teleological conception of man and the universe . . . to the rule or domain of that higher law that leads all things to their final end or goal."[12]

Just as an unjust law is really not a law in the truest sense and therefore not obligatory, it is contrary to justice itself, to the very idea of law as an ordination, to advocate an unjust cause. Law "is binding in conscience only if it is law in the truest or most essential sense, and, it is binding in conscience if it is law in the essential sense because the essence or nature of law is intimately bound up with justice."[13] For St. Thomas's part, the unjust advocate is an accomplice who sins so grievously that he or she is "bound to restitution of the loss unjustly incurred by the other party by reason of the assistance he has provided."[14] Honesty toward and in the tribunal, a moral basis for case and cause, and a rejection of unmeritorious cases in these times seems almost surreal. Gilson's remarks would fall on deaf ears in today's legal community: "But a lawyer lacking morality ought to be even more unthinkable, because no lawyer is allowed to plead an unjust cause. If he does so in error and good faith, he commits no fault. But if he knows that the cause he is defending is unjust, he gravely offends against justice."[15]

For the positivist attorney, there is little to hold onto: only the cause, good or bad. Lawyers need more than the artificiality and insubstantiality of promulgation and enactment.[16] A just lawyer acts compatibly with reason, operates in conformity with the natural law, strives for the life of virtue, and perpetually seeks the perfect good of all existence. These ingredients for the good and happy man or woman are applicable to the good and happy lawyer.[17]

To the advocate, then, is the heady responsibility of advocating in conformity with this plan, advocating not as an automaton, but as a moral agent. Thomas labels this power unique to rational creatures alone, since the "rational creature holds dominion over his acts, moving himself freely in order to perform his actions."[18] Only then will the advocacy bring about what is due, what is right, assuring a "certain rectitude, . . . an equality between things and persons."[19]

Thomas is realistic enough to forgive or excuse the advocate who has been misled. As any lawyer discovers, a client's word is often an abridged or slanted story line. The correctional population of America, numbering in the millions, is uniformly innocent, the inmates declare. While blind acceptance of a client's vision of truth is unwise, Thomas withholds judgment from those advocating a claim in good faith. This lack of knowledge, or the client's delivery of inaccurate knowledge, may be the foundation upon which the advocate develops a case theory. Thomas excuses this to some extent: "If, however, he defends an unjust cause unknowingly, thinking it just, he is to be excused according to the measure in which ignorance is excusable."[20] This toleration melts away when and if the advocate determines that the theory of his or her advocacy is fraudulent or false. Continued advocacy in the fraudulent cause is inexcusable and is assuredly a systematic attack against "commutative justice, legal justice, or at least against truth."[21] St. Thomas recognizes that discovery of client or case falsehood exacts a series of dilemmas on the practitioner and cautions the advocate against the radical implications of immediate withdrawal from representation. He also reinforces the need for continued discretion in matters of privilege and confidentiality. The advocate need not help the opposition, even though the basis of the advocacy has been altered by subsequent discovery of its injustice. Thomas shows keen sensitivity to the due process implications of withdrawn or substitute counsel: "He ought not to throw up his brief in such a way as to help the other side, or so as to reveal the secrets of his client to the other party. But he can and must give up the case, or induce his client to give way, or make some compromise without prejudice to the opposing party."[22]

As an officer of the court, the advocate, as described in current parlance, should not advocate a case lacking in merit, nor that which is injurious to the profession as a whole.[23] Thomas's benchmark for the just or unjust cause certainly assures both the quality and integrity of both case and advocate.

THE LAWYER, TRUTH, AND FALSEHOOD

Since justice is concerned with the right, is an "expression of right,"[24] is defined in terms of what is due and what is in balance and equilibrium, is an expression and reflection of the virtuous ordination of the human person, emanates from the Creator, and impresses itself in the form of primary and secondary principles of the natural law, truth is at its core. For the lawyer, truth is fittingly attributed to every aspect of law and its practice. At various places in the *Summa Theologica*, Thomas treats the opposite of truth telling, including dwelling upon falsehood, cheating in buying and selling, wilful deceit in the transfer of goods and services, overstatement and unconscionability in the value of a thing, violation of vows and oaths, perjury, and lying.[25] Lying and falsehood is opposed to truth, St. Thomas states, except in accidental cases. Lying, (*mendacium*) is neither the product of negligence nor involuntariness, but a formal declaration of falsity in "opposition to the mind" [*contra mentem*].[26] A lie is contrary to charity, in confrontation with justice, and an inequity.[27] Dissimulation and hypocrisy are as vigorously condemned by St. Thomas. Words, the sum and substance of lies and falsehoods, represent one of many means to falsehood. Signs, acts, and deeds that are disingenuous encompass falsity:

Accordingly just as it is contrary to truth to signify by words something different from that which is in one's mind, so also is it contrary to truth to employ signs of deeds or things to signify the contrary of what is in oneself, and this is what is properly denoted by dissimulation. Consequently dissimulation is properly a lie told by the signs of outward deeds. Now it matters not whether one lie in word or in any other way, as stated above. Wherefore, since every lie is a sin, as stated above, it follows that also all dissimulation is a sin.[28]

St. Thomas's legal system depends on hard evidence, not suspicion, rumor, and doubt.[29] Suspicion, for example, is nothing more than a "perversity of the affections" that cannot lead to the type of legal truth necessary for acquittal or conviction.[30] Dubious ideas should not control legal reasoning, because lawyers "strive to make [judgments] in accord with things as they are."[31] Truth has a hardness to it, be it the truth of temporality or universality. Falsehood, deceit, and deception have no place in Thomas's legal system, nor in his profile of the legal professional. Falsehood implies an internal secrecy that is corrosive and corruptive to both lawyers and individuals, since "secrecy is sometimes a cause of sin."[32] Falsehood in accusation in any form, already covered in Chapter 8, such as calumny, collusion, and evasion, are just as difficult for Thomas to tolerate, for each of these guiles "deceitfully hides" the truth.[33] Thomas actually screens a candidate for admission into legal practice by assessing the candidate's character in relation to truth or falsity. Personal defects of the soul should be a basis for exclusion from the legal profession. Those already in the profession will be "debarred" if found dishonest.[34] "Persons of ill-repute, unbelievers, and those who have been convicted of grievous crimes" are unbecoming candidates for the lawyerly arts.[35] Thomas's lawyer is the completely virtuous person who possesses the functional skills necessary to advocate legal claims, and "those who are defective in these points, are altogether debarred from being advocates either in their own or in another's cause."[36] Labeling certain falsehoods as "sins committed against justice," Thomas identifies various strategies in plaintiff and defense litigation, diverse approaches in the delivery of witness testimony, and the means adopted to save one's life or freedom.[37] In each of these contexts, truth is the standard bearer and falsehood is scathingly critiqued.

Defense Counsel and Defendants

At no place in the justice process do lawyers confront the horrid landscape of falsehoods more than in criminal defense work. In criminal cases, defendants are on the block for fines, incarceration, restitution, or other restriction. Counsel is hired or assigned, as Gilson points out, to "defend them as skillfully as he can, never resorting to falsehoods but allowing himself those ruses and reservations necessary for the triumph of justice."[38] Intentional falsehoods are never tolerated by Thomas, but a masterful defense is integral to the aims of justice. As a defendant, Thomas ascribes no quality of falsehood in silence, in a refusal to incriminate oneself, and in a defense strategy that employs "lawful means, and such as are adapted to the end in view, which belongs to prudence," nor to give testimony on questions the defendant has no obligation to answer.[39] "St. Thomas wisely concludes that a good defendant, while he may prudently hide impeding evidence, should not resort to falsehood."[40] Lawyers advising caution in defense testimony, a lack of cooperation regarding a confession, or a lawful nondelivery of incriminating evidence are not engaged in falsehood. Instead, St. Thomas perceives this conduct as "praiseworthy," for the defense is not based upon "calumnies," but prudence.[41] Western legal tradition, culminating in the constitutionalism of the American colonies, specifically at the Fifth Amendment's prohibition on self-incrimination, rests side by side with Thomistic legal theory.

On the other hand, the line to aggressive defense can transform into patent falsehood, a situation never pleasing to St. Thomas: "But it is unlawful for him, either to utter a falsehood, or to withhold a truth that he is bound to avow, or to employ guile or fraud, because fraud and guile have the force of a lie, and so to use them would be to defend oneself with calumnies."[42]

The terminal nature of the death penalty would lead most to the conclusion that the lie, or any other legal defense tactic, would be an exception to St. Thomas's resistance to falsehood. Even here, Thomas does not tolerate the falsehood to save the bodily flesh, but condemns that body to death in order to assure the salvation of the soul. It is justice's reciprocity that can only come to fruition upon execution, and to prevent its imposition in a defense tactic achieves the status of a "sin." God ordains "the punishment of evil-doers" [in quo est divinitus instituta ad vindictam malefactorum].[43] The man at the gallows cannot fight or lie or defend himself with calumny or other deception. Lies and falsehoods cause injury to the judicial process, according to St. Thomas: "To lie, with injury to another person, in order to rescue a man from death is not a purely officious lie, for it has an ad-mixture of the pernicious lie: and when a man lies in court in order to exculpate himself, he does an injury to one whom he is bound to obey, since he refuses him his due, namely an avowal of the truth."[44]

Using the judicial process to every advantage is not a falsehood in any sense. A lawyer's conduct as advocate is typically constrained by the rules of civil and criminal procedure, evidence, and appellate process. These types of rules set forth professional parameters. To argue within them in the most vigorous of styles would not be surreptitious, but prudential. At one locus in the *Summa Theologica*, Thomas refers to appeals from judgments. At issue is whether this type of juridical process is, or has the potential to be, filed from false motives. Surely, if an appeal is filed for purposes of delay and contentiousness, the appeal merely compounds injustice, but if it is for a legitimate cause, the appeal is characterized by Thomas as a "prudent means of escape."[45] The lawfulness of the process, whether appeal or otherwise, is imputed in the motive. Appeals also serve as a potential remedy or bulwark against unjust oppression or arbitrary decision making.[46]

In the final analysis, the fraudulent will reap the fruits of their deception and simultaneously deliver an injustice to the client and the justice system as a whole. Thomas dramatically conveys that "Those who commit frauds, do not design anything against themselves or their own souls; it is through God's just judgment that what they plot against others, recoils on themselves, according to Ps. vii. 16, *He is fallen into the hole he made.*"[47]

Counsel and Witnesses

The delivery of testimony by witnesses is another critical junction for lawyers advocating cases. Witnesses, while independent of counsel are closely tied to the advice of counsel, and intently listen to their commands and exhortations. Litigation manuals and advocacy treatises spend considerable time examining the role, function, and scope of witness testimony and how lawyers lead in its preparation.[48] That preparation consists of a factual review determining the breadth and depth of testimonial subject matter, tactics for fielding the onslaught of direct or cross-examination, and generic suggestions on truth telling and obligations to the court. Universally evident in the witness–lawyer relationship is a witness's deep dependence upon the instruction of counsel and the need for advice on how to proceed testimonially. For this reason, the deception of a witness can possibly be imputed to counsel's preparation. At a minimum, a deceptive witness should be ferreted out by counsel, since candor before the tribunal is required.

Thomas understands the interplay between lawyer and client, lawyer and court, and client and court when dealing with matters of testimonial disclosure. Already noted is the right of the criminal not be compulsed as a witness, and that the lack of testimony by a nonparticipatory silence cannot be declared unlawful.[49] "Withholding the truth," Thomas writes, the witness "is not bound to avow," is not falsehood or calumny.[50] Counsel may instruct a witness that testimony is not required, despite the witness knowing what the truth or falsity of the subject matter is. This litigation tactic is termed "prudential" by Thomas.[51] Also instructive is Thomas's suggestion that a witness "not lay bare his own guilt," nor be subject to compulsed testimony by a judge not granted the power to examine or "unmasked by another."[52] It is only when that witness stands upright, announcing to the world his or her innocence when the truth is otherwise, that a legal falsehood is born. There are and will be cases when the "accused is not bound to satisfy" the judge or other authority.[53] Counsel who recommends nonincriminatory silence is attentive to Thomas's distinction between the substantive, affirmative falsehood, which is categorically wrong, and the legitimate reason to not testify under questioning. It appears upon a closer reading that Thomas holds a judge incapable if examining a criminal defendant witness, since it is not a matter "to which the rights of his authority extend."[54]

The relationship between a witness and a lawyer–advocate is a cumbersome and complicated one. In one way, Thomas exhorts truth; in another way, he respects the processes of adjudication as either limiting, expanding, or nullifying testimonial evidence. With wit and foresight, Thomas expects the witness, the client, and his or her lawyer to test the legal waters with an aggressive professional posture coupled with moral virtue. Witnesses are not empty shells spouting off whatever is fed their psyches. Witnesses, particularly those in peril of life and limb, should be more than lambs to the slaughter, resigned and pessimistic, showing no resistance. In the ebb and flow of litigation and the dynamic of judges, lawyers, and parties, truth is not a rubber stamp, but a blend of both facts and law, of both substance and process. Thomas challenges the witness, the defendant especially, to use his or her intellectual arsenal. Thomas, when dealing with the acceptable means to avoid the death penalty, urges the human actor to utilize his or her wits and tactical insight to defend against death, "but only such as is accomplished with due moderation" [sed solum quae fit cum debito moderamine].[55]

St. Thomas's analysis of witnesses extends to questions of quality, the reliability and credibility of the purported testimony. Counsel's review of prospective testimony is a search for reliability of what will be said and credibility, that quality of truth and falsity that renders or devalues testimonial evidence. Counsel filters the evidence in initial interview, cross-checking, corroborative fact finding, and other scrutiny. The lawyer who accepts testimony at face value is not performing this basic task. Even a story that is inno-

cently offered, without malicious or sinister motives, may lack credibility. Lawyers who utilize testimony that results from faulty
memory, defect of reason, or confused perceptions are also failing
in their primary duties. Thomas stresses the need for this type of
testimonial quality control, resisting every level of doubt in the
evaluation of a witness's presentation, but mindful that human
beings have certain faults or inconsistencies in recollection. Only
false testimony "directly and intentionally" [per se et ex intentione]
delivered is condemned.[56]

The concern for testimonial quality can be detected in his discussion of evidentiary sufficiency. When is testimonial evidence to be
believed? What should counsel do to assure the believability and
integrity of witness testimony? A witness who contradicts his or
her testimony over a central, material matter necessitates the need
for a greater number of witnesses. Otherwise, the evidence is to be
deemed unworthy of belief. On most material issues or facts, Thomas urges the examiner to pay strict attention to overall credibility. On the other hand, witnesses, Thomas asserts, can and do forget
certain things. The materiality of evidence gauges the seriousness,
or lack thereof, of the falsehood. Credibility is measured by essential, material questions of fact, not "whether the weather were cloudy
or fine, whether the house were painted or not, or such like matters, such discrepancy does not weaken the evidence, because men
are not wont to take much notice of such things, wherefore they
easily forget them."[57] Inaccuracy relating to minor, immaterial details does not make the witness's testimony inadmissable. This distinction between material evidence and irrelevant or immaterial
subject matter is a perpetual caveat to counselors-at-law who weigh
and evaluate the quality and content of testimony. Witnesses, de-
plorably inconsistent in their recitations, should not be the basis
for any action in law. Punishments, findings of guilt or innocence,
damage awards, and requests for legal or equitable remedies should
stand on a foundation of evidentiary reliability, testimonial or not.
Lawyers are obliged to sift through the evidentiary deposit, to assure justice in the legal marketplace, and, even more poignant, to
heed the call of salvation of those testifying. Giving testimony is
not purely a functional exercise, but a guarantee that due process
and a substantive grounding exist in the case.[58] To allow witnesses
to testify, either knowing or reliably suspecting their lack of integrity, is to advance an injustice. Corrupt testimony is a "deformity"
in three ways.[59] First, it affronts the oath of the testifier and causes
perjury in the courtroom. Second, since every falsehood is a violation of justice, it is a "mortal sin generically" [peccatum mortale].[60]

Last, even if not mortal in design, Thomas characterizes each and every lie a sin [quod omne mendacium est peccatum].[61]

Falsehood, at every juncture in law and life itself, is contrary to justice, and it behooves the lawyer to screen and test the testimony witnesses are to relay. For all falsehood, lying, and perjury is a mockery and slander to the judicial process, an infamy, an irreverence to God, and in contempt of God.[62]

SPECIAL OBLIGATIONS OF THE LAWYER–ADVOCATE

Aside from these general prescriptions of truth that mold both person and counselor, St. Thomas perceives certain unique obligations in the legal profession. As in the defense or prosecution of a case, it is not enough to be functional as a lawyer–advocate. More relevant to Thomas is the law's proper ends and the means chosen by a lawyer to meet those ends. Throughout this work we have repeatedly witnessed the melding of the law as human enactment and the law in a teleological sense. Being a lawyer has special demands beyond the grind and battles of daily practice because of the profession's subject matter. To be in law mandates the lawyer to engage in just activities in the courtroom and outside its hallowed halls. Thomas, displaying his prophetic foresight, preempts the twentieth century's concept of social justice and pro bono legal practice.

Legal Practice as a Work of Mercy

Responding to whether a lawyer is obligated to represent the poor, Thomas pragmatically integrates the corporal works of mercy into legal practice. Suits of the poor do not mandatorily oblige the legal professional, but a lawyer cannot in every instance shun this need.[63] Realizing that human needs are not exclusively physical, in the sense of nourishment or clothing, Thomas perceives a parallel need in bodily sustenance and the imperative of the advocate.[64] Further on, Thomas intimates that those of talent and blessings and in life's better station should not forget those in graver conditions, since every man and woman is "bound to make good use of the talent bestowed on him, according to the opportunities afforded by time, place, and other circumstances, as stated above."[65] Recognizing that Christian charity is balanced with occupational capacity, economic realities, familial demands, and a never-ending, perpetual stream of those in need, Thomas demands a contribution, not a lifelong obligation, "else he would have to put aside all other business, and occupy himself entirely in defending the suits of poor people. The same applies to a physician with regard to attendance on the sick."[66] No one lawyer can be encumbered with all of life's misery. To take on every suit of the poor would be a recipe for professional and personal destruction.

The lawyer, however, cannot escape the charitable responsibilities of the good life, and while circumstances amongst lawyers may differ, each advocate is capable of making a contribution to less-fortunate litigants. When evaluating the propriety of lawyers' fees, Thomas again reminds the practitioner that compensation earned and the lawyer who earns it cannot be aloof to human misery and its costs. Doing merciful things for others reaps not a monetary reward, but divine applause, suggests St. Thomas: "But when a man does give a thing out of mercy, he should seek, not a human, but a divine reward. In like manner an advocate, when he mercifully pleads the cause of a poor man, should have in view not a human but a Divine need; and yet he is not always bound to give his services gratuitously."[67] At the same time, the merciful lawyer looks at his or her accounts, to his or her business ledger, so that legal charity will not dissipate the lawyer's livelihood. Gilson speaks rightly of this balance between charitable delivery of legal service and the maintenance of a legal practice: "A lawyer or doctor who spent their time looking for indigents would find their clientele growing too rapidly for their income."[68]

Confidentiality

In confidentiality analysis, a privilege exists, a protection against divulsion of certain evidence, whether it is testimonial or of other form. Reviewed thus far is the right not to be compulsed against onself or forcibly made to give testimony. During Thomas's era there was, and there still is, an understanding of the privileges that existed between a priest and penitent and, to some extent, a lawyer and client. Privileges exist because of a general interest in fostering truth and honest discussion between the parties. Secrecy, for St. Thomas, has dual qualities, of fidelity and guile. In fidelity, that loyalty to another not to divulge what has been conditionally spoken with the implied and express promise not to disclose its content, we see the essence of human honor. Thomas briefly comments that "it is contrary to fidelity to make known secrets to the injury of a person."[69] Fidelity embraces loyalty of one to another, not only in a professional sense, but in friendship and familial bonds. Thomas labels fidelity as a basis for being not bound to give evidence.[70] "Against such a duty a man cannot be obliged to act on the plea that the matter is committed to him under secrecy, for he would break the faith he owes another."[71]

Privilege in the confessional is sanctimoniously and unreservedly protected by St. Thomas, since the sacrament of confession "is more binding than any human precept."[72] In this instance, the truth of the conversation between the privileged parties can be withheld from legal authority, since the protection and content of the privilege outweighs the need for the evidence. Hiding information under the guise of privilege does not always infer guile, except when the party asserting the privilege "deceitfully hides the matter about which he makes the accusation."[73]

CONCLUSION

Consistent with Thomas's worldview of human activity and law, lawyers are expected to act in accordance with their essential nature, with reason being their rule and measure. Thomas's lawyer is implanted with self-evident propositions, the primary tenet of the natural law—doing good and avoiding evil—and its *per se nota* first principles, from self-preservation to procreation, as well as a panoply of secondary precepts. The Thomistic lawyer acts justly, gives everyone his or her due, searches for equality amongst people and things, and focuses on truth.

The Thomistic advocate engages in a sort of microscopic inquiry most present-day lawyers would find arcane and irrelevant. Today's lawyer treads water in a sea of positivism, with billable hours being the prime incentive, instead of Thomas's admonition to take only the just case and avoid falsehoods of every form, whether personal or that of a client or witness. To be sure, the practice of law consists of professional function and a series of job competencies. Side by side with function is the urgent reminder to do just things, to advocate truth, to shun falsehood, craftiness, guile, and deceit, and to frown upon litigation techniques that Thomas terms calumny, collusion, and evasion. The lawyer is justice personified, intricately inspecting evidence and testimonial storylines, and fashioning accusations and defenses that are supportable by law and fact.

Add to this the lawyer's obligation to self, to court, to colleague, and, most important, to God. Offer the advocate's skill of representation to the poor, but not as a sole occupation, lest the lawyer not remain professionally viable. Latch onto the law, from its written anchor, and proffer arguments zealously. Prudentially defend, prosecute, and appeal, examine the case and its parties, never apologizing for the tenacity of your approach, always mindful of its integrity and goodness.

Thomas's lawyer is far more complicated than the prototype molded and produced by twentieth-century America's legal education system. If the trend continues into the twenty-first century, we will continue to observe a lawyer product that takes on the armor of a social worker, one who helps others, cares mostly in an individualistic sense, and is chiefly, almost obsessively, governed by the language of individual rights. It is a safe bet that most law schools will care little about the moral life and more about the sensitive and caring lawyer, who labors to right all the wrongs the world suffers from, who perceives law not as an ordination of reason and an expression of virtue, but as an instrument for positive, corrective humanism. Today, lawyers toy with law in a promulgative sense, finding laws already on the books or those soon to be invented in the legal laboratory to be a panacea for life's ills. Thomas places human enactments at the bottom of his continuum of laws. Its last-place finish doesn't imply a shortage of value. To the contrary, Thomas integrates and necessitates human law into his entire schema.[74] But the temptation when working with these temporal inventions (e.g., regulations, ordinances, statutes, and so on) is mesmerizing. Within the modern judicial perspective, lawyers truly believe that the legal enactment is power itself, has force inherently, and is inherently coercive. It is only a matter of time before this same lawyer, believing in the false gods of positivism, elevates his or her own role into a mightier, supernatural dimension. Lawyers, like laws themselves, are not the architects of justice, but servants to it, St. Thomas argues. The impotence of human law and the abject frailty of lawyers who advocate its content is obvious to St. Thomas. We can only "fall short of just due," since our efforts restore only a portion of paradise lost.[75] St. Thomas never loses sight of his place, the place of law and that of lawyers advocating in the temples of justice: "To judge belongs to God in virtue of His own power: wherefore His judgment is based on the truth which He Himself knows, and not on knowledge imparted by others: the same is to be said of Christ, Who is true God and true man: whereas other judges do not judge in virtue of their own power, so that there is no comparison."[76]

NOTES

1. St. Thomas Aquinas, *Summa Theologica*, trans. English Dominican Friars, vol. 2 (New York: Benziger, 1947), II–II, Q. 71, a. 4, ad 2. "Quod etsi scientia juris sit quoddam spirituale, tamen usus ejus fit opere corp-

orali; et ideo pro ejus recompensatione licet pecuniam accipere; alioquin nulli artifici liceret de arte sua lucrari." As Joseph V. Dolan, "Natural Law and the Judicial Function," *Laval Theologique et Philosophique* 16 (1960): 96, points out, lawyers and their laws are meaningful when the law retains "a certain universality and remain[s] at some distance from the contingent singulars. It cannot become so completely configured to any individual action as to destroy its usefulness as a measure for the others."

2. For an interesting analysis of lawyering being more than mere practice, see Louis M. Brown and Thomas L. Shaffer, "Toward a Jurisprudence for the Law Office," *American Journal of Jurisprudence* 17 (1972): 125–152.

3. Igor Grazin, "Natural Law as a Form of Legal Studies," *American Journal of Jurisprudence* (37, 1992): 16.

4. Joseph V. Dolan, "Natural Law and Modern Jurisprudence," *Laval Theologique et Philosophique* 16 (1990): 44.

5. Aquinas, *Theologica*, vol. 2, II–II, Q. 71, a. 3, ad 3. "Quod, sicut supra dictum est, militi vel duci exercitus licet in bello justo ex insidiis agere, ea quae facere debet prudentur occultando, non autem falsitatem fraudulenter faciendo, quia etiam hosti fidem servare oportet, sicut Tullius dicit (in De offic. lib. I, in tit. De bellicis offic. a med. et De fortitud. lib. III, circ. med.) Unde et advocato defendenti causam justam licet prudenter occultare ea quibus impediri posset processus ejus; non autem licet ei aliqua falsitate uti."

6. Ibid., II–II, Q. 80, a. 1, c.

7. Ibid., II–II, Q. 71, a. 3, c. "Quod illicitum est alicui cooperari ad malum faciendum, sive consulendo, sive adjuvando, sive qualitercumque consentiendo, quia consilians et coadjuvans quodammodo est faciens."

8. Ibid., II–II, Q. 71, a. 3, c.

9. Ibid., II–II, Q. 71, a. 3, ad. 3; ad. 1.

10. George Quentin Friel, *Punishment in the Philosophy of Saint Thomas Aquinas and among Some Primitive Peoples* (Washington, D.C.: Catholic University of America Press, 1939), 138.

11. Dolan, "Natural Law and Modern Jurisprudence," 40.

12. Robert J. Kreyche, "Virtue and Law in Aquinas: Some Modern Implications," *Southwestern Journal of Philosophy* 5 (1974): 113.

13. Edward J. Damich, "The Essence of Law According to Thomas Aquinas," *American Journal of Jurisprudence* 30 (1985): 81.

14. Aquinas, *Theologica*, vol. 2, II–II, Q. 71, a. 3, c.

15. Etienne Gilson, *The Christian Philosophy of St. Thomas Aquinas*, trans. L. K. Shook (New York: Random House, 1956), 320.

16. For a persuasive discussion of how legal activity inevitably depends upon moral certitude, see Henry Mather, "Natural Law and Right Answers," *American Journal of Jurisprudence* 38 (1993): 297–334.

17. James V. Schall, "The Natural Law Bibliography," *American Journal of Jurisprudence* 40 (1995): 160.

18. St. Thomas Aquinas, *Summa Contra Gentiles*, trans. Vernon J. Bourke, vol. 4 (Notre Dame: University of Notre Dame Press, 1975), bk. III, pt. II, ch. 111, 1.

19. E. T. Gelinas, "Right and Law in Thomas Aquinas," in *Myth and Philosophy*, ed. George F. McLean, vol. 45 (Washington, D.C.: American Catholic Philosophical Association, 1971), 131.

20. Aquinas, *Theologica*, vol. 2, II–II, Q. 71, a. 3, c. "Si autem ignoranter injustam causam defendit, putans esse justam, excusatur secundum modum quo ignorantia excusari potest."

21. Michael Harding, "True Justice in Courts of Law," in Aquinas, *Theologica*, vol. 3, 3356.

22. Aquinas, *Theologica*, vol. 2, II–II, Q. 71, a. 3, ad 2. "Non debet eam prodere, ut scilicet aliam partem juvet, vel secreta suae causae alteri parti revelet. Potest tamen et debet causam deserere, vel eum cujus causam agit, ad cedendum inducere, sive ad componendum sine adversarii damno."

23. See American Bar Association, *Model Rules of Professional Conduct* (1995).

24. Aquinas, *Theologica*, vol. 2, II–II, Q. 57, a. 1, ad. 3.

25. Ibid., II–II, Q. 77; Q. 77, a. 3; Q. 77, a. 4; Q. 88, a. 6; Q. 89; Q. 98; Q. 110.

26. Ibid., II–II, Q. 110, a. 1, c.

27. Ibid., II–II, Q. 110, a. 4.

28. Ibid., II–II, Q. 111, a. 1, c. "Ita etiam opponitur veritati quod aliquis per aliqua signa factorum vel rerum aliquid significet contrarium ejus quod in eo est, quod proprie simulatio dicitur. Unde simulatio proprie est mendacium quoddam in exteriorum signis factorum consistens. Non refert autem utrum aliquis mentiatur verbo, vel quocumque alio facto, ut supra habitum est. Unde cum omne mendacium sit peccatum, ut supra dictum est, consequens est etiam quod omnis simulatio est peccatum."

29. Ibid., II–II, Q. 60, a. 3.

30. Ibid., II–II, Q. 60, a. 3, c.

31. Ibid., II–II, Q. 60, a. 4, ad. 2.

32. Ibid., II–II, Q. 66, a. 3, ad. 1.

33. Ibid., II–II, Q. 68, a. 3, ad. 2.

34. Ibid., II–II, Q. 71, a. 2, c.

35. Ibid.

36. Ibid. "Qui in his defectum patiuntur, omnino prohibentur ne sint advocati nec pro se, nec pro aliis."

37. Ibid., II–II, Q. 69.

38. Gilson, *Christian Philosophy*, 320.

39. Aquinas, *Theologica*, vol. 2, II–II, Q. 69, a. 2, c.

40. E. K. Rand, *Cicero in the Courtroom of St. Thomas Aquinas* (Milwaukee: Marquette University Press, 1946), 48–49.

41. Aquinas, *Theologica*, vol. 2, II–II, Q. 69, a. 2, c.

42. Ibid. "Non autem licet ei vel falsitatem dicere, vel veritatem tacere quam confiteri tenetur, neque etiam aliquem dolum vel fraudem adhibere, quia fraus et dolus vim mendacii habent; et hoc est calumniose se defendere."

43. Ibid., II–II, Q. 69, a. 4, sed contra.

44. Ibid., II–II, Q. 69, a. 1, ad 2. "Quod mentiri, ad liberandum aliquem a morte cum injuria alterius, non est mendacium simpliciter officiosum, sed habet aliquid de pernicioso admixtum. Cum autem aliquis mentitur in

judicio ad excusationem sui, injuriam facit ei cui obedire tenetur, dum ipsi denegat quod ei debet, scilicet confessionem veritatis."

45. Ibid., II–II, Q. 69, a. 3, c.

46. Ibid., II–II, Q. 69, a. 3.

47. Ibid., II–II, Q. 55, a. 5, ad 3. "Quod illi qui fraudes faciunt, ex eorum intentione non moliuntur aliquid contra seipsos, vel contra animas suas: sed ex justo Dei judicio provenit ut id quod contra alios moliuntur, contra eos retorqueatur, secundum illud (Psalm. VII, 16): Incidit in foveam quam fecit."

48. See Charles P. Nemeth, *Litigation, Pleadings and Arbitration*, 2d ed. (Cincinnati: Anderson, 1997); Charles P. Nemeth, *Law and Evidence: A Primer for Criminal Justice, Criminology, Law and Legal Studies* (Upper Saddle River, N.J.: Prentice Hall, 2001); Lawrence S. Charfoos and David W. Christensen, *Personal Injury Practice: Technique and Technology* (Rochester, N.Y.: Lawyers Cooperative, 1995).

49. Aquinas, *Theologica*, vol. 2, II–II, Q. 69, a. 2.

50. Ibid., II–II, Q. 69, a. 2, c.

51. Ibid., II–II, Q. 69, a. 2.

52. Ibid., II–II, Q. 69, a. 1, ad. 1.

53. Ibid., II–II, Q. 69, a. 1, c.

54. Ibid.

55. Ibid., II–II, Q. 69, a. 4, ad 1.

56. Ibid., II–II, Q. 70, a. 4, ad 1.

57. Ibid., II–II, Q. 70, a. 2, ad 2. "Si tempus fuerit nubilosum vel serenum, vel si domus fuerit picta, aut non, aut aliquid hujusmodi; talis discordia non praejudicat testimonio; quia homines non consueverunt circa talia multum sollicitari, unde facile a memoria elabuntur."

58. Ibid., II–II, Q. 70, a, 3, ad 3. "To give evidence is necessary for salvation, provided the witness be competent, and the order of justice observed" [Quod testificari est de necessitate salutis, supposita testis idoneitate, et ordine juris].

59. Ibid., II–II, Q. 70, a. 4, c.

60. Ibid.

61. Ibid.

62. Ibid., II–II, Q. 98, a. 3, c.

63. Ibid., II–II, Q. 71, a. 1.

64. Ibid., II–II, Q. 71, a. 1, sed contra. "He that lacks food is no less in need than he that lacks an advocate" [Non minor necessitas est indigentis cibo quam indigentis advocato].

65. Ibid., II–II, Q. 71, a. 1, ad 2. "Quod homo talentum sibi creditum tenetur utiliter dispensare, servata opportunitate locorum et temporum, et aliarum rerum, ut dictum est."

66. Ibid., II–II, Q. 71, a. 1, c. "Alioquin oporteret eum omnia alia negotia praetermittere, et solis causis pauperum juvandis intendere. Et idem dicendum est de medico quantum ad curationem pauperum."

67. Ibid., II–II, Q. 71, a. 4, ad 1. "Sed quando eam misericorditer impendit, non humanam, sed divinam remunerationem quaerere debet. Et similiter advocatus quando causae pauperum misericorditer patrocin-

atur, non debet intendere remunerationem humanam sed divinam; non tamen semper tenetur gratis patrocinium impendere."

68. Gilson, *Christian Philosophy*, 320.

69. Aquinas, *Theologica*, vol. 2, II–II, Q. 68, a. 1, ad 3. "Quod revelare secreta in malum personae, est contra fidelitatem."

70. Ibid., II–II, Q. 70, a. 1.

71. Ibid., II–II, Q. 70, a. 1, ad 2. "Et contra hoc debitum obligari non potest per secreti commissum, qua in hoc frangeret fidem quam alteri debet."

72. Ibid.

73. Ibid., II–II, Q. 68, a. 3, ad 2.

74. St. Thomas Aquinas, "Summa Theologica," in *Basic Writings of St. Thomas Aquinas*, ed. Anton C. Pegis, vol. 2 (New York: Random House, 1945), I–II, Q. 95, a. 1.

75. Aquinas, *Theologica*, vol. 2, II–II, Q. 80, a. 1, c.

76. Ibid., II–II, Q. 67, a. 2, ad 2. "Quod Deo competit judicare secundum propriam potestatem; et ideo in judicando informatur secundum veritatem quam ipse cognoscit, non secundum hoc quod ab aliis accipit; et eadem ratio est de Christo, qui est verus Deus et homo."

CHAPTER 10

Law, Justice, Sentencing, and Punishment

A penology with consequence aptly describes the Thomistic idea of punishment. To restore equilibrium and balance caused by unjust activities, such as criminal behavior, St. Thomas legitimizes a penology of punishment. Punishment restores the imbalance in both temporal and eternal affairs. Punishment is what is due another. For most contemporary penologists, Thomas's methods of punishment seem out of the mainstream. Corporal punishment, dismemberment, and the death penalty are labeled acceptable reactions to injustice. Each of these practices either delivers a message of deterrence or removes a corrupted, infected member from the body politic. Thomas's insistence on restoration of the whole is quickly evident in his analysis of restitution, and he shows a keen awareness of victims' rights.

PUNISHMENT AS RECIPROCITY

St. Thomas insists on corrective measures in any plan of systematic criminal justice. Despite the inherent goodness of the human species, admitting certain natural inclinations, and granting God's divine impression in creation, human beings still need correction and consequences in the event of doing wrong. Correction implies a soft or hard coercion and a series of guiding influences to keep the citizen morally erect. Punishment is "especially necessary against those who are prone to evil."[1] Rewards as well as punishments,

Thomas indicates, are devised "so that men may be drawn away from evil things and toward good things."[2] Laws not backed by correction would be hollow admonitions. Laws, to be effective and binding, "must be obligatory, must have coercive power, and the coercive force of the law consists essentially in the fear of punishment."[3]

By their nature, corrective measures are consequences for activity injurious to both individual and society, and their imposition seeks to correct an imbalance. Commutatively, punishment directs itself to a restoration of things and people, equalizing and correcting imbalances. In the legal system, punishment is commutative and corrective. Corrective justice is, by nature, a corrective measure, and a form of justice "which guides the judge not in determining whether a defendant has unjustly impinged in some way upon the interests of a plaintiff," but as a response to a particular injustice.[4]

Aside from this commutative quality, others assert that Thomas's theory of punishment is grounded in its distributive counterpart (allocating justice according to circumstance and individual characteristics).[5] Thomas's depiction of legal justice deals with individual interrelationships and consequences in relation to others ("ad bonum alterius singularis personae").[6] Punishment, therefore, not only restores the equilibrium in a commutative sense; it assures or maintains the present order of economic, political, and social classes, and hence displays both commutative and distributive qualities.

In both civil and criminal cases, punishment and consequence seek to restore individual and community balance. Case by case, fact by fact, Thomas engages a penological theory of reaction to activity in a holistic sense in which individual acts multiply to corrupt the common good. The entire justice system maintains its autonomy by meting out consequence, both individually and collectively.

Courtrooms are the perfect place to witness the experiment. The judge's very office expressly delineates "punishment" and other forms of correction as a judicial function. Punishment gives "the law its proper effect."[7] Thomas forcefully bolsters the legitimacy of judicial punishment in the *Summa Contra Gentiles*: "It is obvious that these men do not sin when they punish the wicked, for no one sins by working for justice. Now, it is just for the wicked to be punished, since by punishment the fault is restored to order, as is clear from our statements above. Therefore, judges do no wrong in punishing the wicked."[8]

Whether in a criminal or civil case, harm to both person and state is injustice to be responded to. Silence and inactivity will not remedy the injustice. More particularly, judges cannot turn their heads or shy away from injustice. The task of the judge "is justice" [Judex dicitur quasi jus dicens].[9] If justice is rendering to each what is due, justice's formula compels negative consequences.[10] Those who do wrong are due something. Civilized societies and individuals attuned to virtue, the fundamental purposes of law, and the importance of the common good find corrective measures essential for survival. Punishment is a form of lawful restraint, St. Thomas suggests, for its imposition restrains men from "wickedness," inducing them "to virtuous deed[s]."[11] Without punishment injustice would go unchecked and its effects would multiply.[12]

Since justice is reciprocity and balance, those refusing its virtuous content, bypassing its virtuous instruction, and snubbing its content need to suffer correctional consequences. Punishment is the debt that is due from one who owes another. Thomas terms debt a loss, a "detriment" that needs elimination.[13] In criminal cases, punishment responds to the sin of commission, Thomas concludes. Inherently, punishment is not wrong, but the inevitable by-product of wrongdoing. As such, punishment is "the effect of sin, not directly, but dispositively."[14] The debt of punishment only exists because of some malevolent act or disposition, some defect or excess of reason, or some "inordinate affection."[15] Punishment desires the settling of debts, the reestablishment of order, both to individual and community, and the quelling of chaos and disturbance. Thomas emphasizes its crucial role in legal or social systems: "As we have stated above, sin incurs a debt of punishment through disturbing an order. But the effect remains so long as the cause remains. Therefore, so long as the disturbance of the order remains, the debt of punishment must needs remain also."[16]

Punishment, even the severe variety, is legitimately inflicted for four reasons. First, punishment relates to the severity and gravity of the sin causing its imposition. A "greater sin, other things being equal, deserves a greater punishment."[17] Second, without punishment the human species would habituate to sin and misconduct, and because of this negative reality, St. Thomas deems punishment a "cure" and a message for those who stray. Third, punishment serves a deterrent function also, both for the individual actor and those who learn from the punishment of others. Last, allowing evil and error to go unchecked is a sure recipe for cultural disaster, according to Thomas. Punishment is the bulwark fending off the madness in individual activity and, as an added benefit, ensures tranquility and deters unacceptable behaviors. Punishment is inexorably tied to the goods integral to Thomistic thinking since a consequence is personal improvement.[18]

Communally, punishment screams its message loud and clear. Thomas's visual imagery of the "hanged thief" is graphic and instructional. "Even the punishment that is inflicted according to human laws is not always intended as a remedy for the one who is punished, but sometimes only for others. Thus when a thief is hanged, this is not for his own amendment, but for the sake of others, who at least may be deterred from crime through fear of the punishment."[19]

Individually, punishment may sting enough, may prod enough to redirect, and may even rehabilitate the individual offender. In teleological jurisprudence, the individual's goodness will surely lead to communitarian goodness. Punishment plays a significant role in the promotion of the common good. In select cases, punishment as disclosed by Thomas demonstrates a more global perspective than an unconditional concern for individual need. Human laws and their corresponding punishments sensibly include that "people are punished with death, not, of course, for their own improvement, but for that of others."[20] The reciprocal quality of punishment is one of Thomas's most attractive insights, as poignant today as at the time he uttered it. A culture without consequence, without behavioral yardsticks, without moral and legal standards and judgments, is ultimately short on justice.

Punishment, says St. Thomas, extends even beyond our temporal lifetime, as long as eternity. The "punishment of evildoers promotes the common good" and produces consequences that foster shared goals, stability, and general good (*bonum commune*) of the community.[21] Punishment in the right dosage can make men abhor wrong.[22]

God, according to St. Thomas, is both the ultimate lawgiver and issuer of just punishment. In the *Summa Contra Gentiles*, punishment is always reserved for those erring, while happiness is reserved for those living the good life. "Moreover, as good things are owed to those who act rightly, so bad things are due to those who act perversely. But those who act rightly, at the end intended by them, receive perfection and joy. So, on the contrary, this punishment is due to sinners, that from those things in which they set their end they receive affliction and injury."[23]

The legitimacy of punishment, with regard to the individual and the community, is not adjudged independently of its root philosophy. A corrupt philosophy is sure to foster a corrupt punishment ideology. Thomas's jurisprudence integrates his philosophical perspective into his penal justification. As such, punishment rectifies and repairs the injustice, promoting a reciprocity where all things are again in balance.

TYPES OF PUNISHMENT AND PENALTIES
IN THOMISTIC JURISPRUDENCE

Thomas's analysis of punishment, its justification, its type, and its form is an erudite penological theory, and includes relationship of punishment to offender, society, and victim; a critique of the quality of criminal activity and criminal agency; theories of retribution; and retaliation, vengeance, remediation, and rehabilitation. Thomas has unequivocal ends in mind, and his discussion of the diverse forms or types of punishment elucidates his correctional ideals.

Corporal Punishment

Contemporary perspectives on the role of corporal punishment are vastly different from those prevalent in Thomas's time. Modern thinkers, whether issuing opinions on child discipline, physical beatings in correctional facilities, whipping, flogging, and other physical assaults, even when emanating from proper authority, generally frown upon these practices. Invariably, these measures are labeled cruel, unusual, ruthlessly unnecessary, and barbaric. To physically injure another, a behavioral scientist would argue, is to admit an inadequacy, not the inadequacy of the perpetrator of a crime, but the inadequacy of the party charged with rehabilitation, especially in correctional facilities where the perpetrator resides. While remedial, resurrective change in the person is desirable, such optimism cannot preclude the application and imposition of physical force. Thomas even suggests that maiming is an acceptable reaction to criminality. Cutting off members of the human body—the legs, the arms, the hands, and so on—is both lawful and penologically sound. Thomas explains that dismemberment can be a wise application of judicial power, an exercise that Thomas reserves solely and exclusively to public authority: "If, however, the member be decayed and therefore a source of corruption to the whole body then it is lawful with the consent of the owner of the member, to cut away the member for the welfare of the whole body, since each one is entrusted with the care of his own welfare."[24]

To illustrate, castration has, at times, been a punishment option in the Western, Eastern, and Islamic worlds. This cutting away of the sexual organ, the physical removal of the member of the body, would readily be lawful in a case of rape, pedophila, incest, sodomy, or other brutal crime. Without the sexual organ, the perpetrator will not again perpetrate, and for St. Thomas, excision of the organ benefits the common good. Even though contrary to the natural order and function of the body, the excision in select cases "is nevertheless in keeping with natural reason in relation to the common good."[25]

Thomas confirms the suitability of physical, corporal punishment in his discussion of vengeance. Whether punishments are an acceptable expression of vengeance will depend upon the motives for the vengeance. If the vengeance is born of hatred, it will be an illegitimate exercise. If born for a concern for the common good, vengeance justifies punishments involving "bodily safety," including the "loss of eye for eye whereby man forfeits his bodily safety."[26] Thomas's affirmation of physical, corporal punishment is further buttressed in his analysis of parents and children. Present theories of child rearing suggest an aversion to the use of physical control as a disciplinary response. Popular media and psychological punditry has made the practice all but anathema. To St. Thomas, the power of the parent is equated with the lawfulness of physical correction. Spare not the rod, but do not inflict "blows on them without moderation."[27] Insensible, unwarranted, disproportionate physical correction is not tolerated by Thomas, but for the maintenance of the household and the corrective training of children, physical correction is expected. This power dimension, the authoritative justification, unfortunately also allows the master to physically correct the slave in Thomas's world. This anomaly of justice is not based on a racist ideology or a eugenic theory of mastery, but one of political, militaristic, and social authority. In this fashion, the slave is childlike, not as an inferior being, but as subordinate to authority. Children need training, while, as harsh as it sounds, slaves need control. In both cases, physical control is an option. Extending these principles to a penal setting, and accepting the legitimacy of a judicial sentence that imposes a physical punishment in place of incarceration, is consistent with Thomas's theory of punishment.

Imprisonment

The penological theory of St. Thomas generously allows the penalty of incarceration. The body of literature he provides on this topic is meager, but rich in justification. In responding to the question of whether it is lawful to imprison a man, he raises the dichotomy of free will and incarceration. How could a free-willing, freely moving human agent be confined in space and time? Isn't imprisonment "inconsistent with free will?"[28] In ideal terms, Thomas agrees with the inconsistency, but quickly talks of the criminal's activity extinguishing the claim of freedom. Once the criminal perpetrates a crime, he argues, any natural claims based on freedom are forfeited: "A man who abuses the power entrusted to him deserves to lose it, and therefore when a man by sinning abuses the free use of his members, he becomes a fitting matter for imprisonment."[29]

Forfeiture, that loss of claim or right, is at odds with present criminological thinking, replaced with the talk of prisoners' rights, the right of rehabilitation, and the proliferation of correctional and constitutional law protections. This state of affairs is markedly opposite Thomas's correctional philosophy. Prisons are good for two reasons: individual punishment and precaution against evil.[30] Prisons represent a twofold rationale for incarceration: deterrence and the infliction of punishment. Both objectives are compatible with Thomas's view on why incarceration can and is a sound penal practice.

Imprisonment is another venue for paying one's debt. Public authority has every right to imprison, St. Thomas says, as long as it is to "be done according to the order of justice, either in punishment or as a measure of precaution against some evil."[31] Imprisonment without fault or the existence of morally evil action would be disproportionate and unjust. Culpability is a prerequisite to its legitimacy, and the severity of the criminal act is pertinent to its duration. Thomas persistently condemns the lawmaker, the judge, or other lawful authority who imposes unreasonable sentences or other penalties.[32] Penalties disproportionately imposed, including that of imprisonment, are unjust if they are unreasonably related to the common good, are an excessive burden, or are beyond the power of the judge or lawmaker.[33]

Mandatory prison terms for driving under the influence and drug-possession cases, habitual-offender statutes, and the extraordinarily harsh terms of imprisonment for domestic violence would not be favored by St. Thomas. The term of imprisonment must correlate to the severity of the act. Novel or faddish criminalities, and of recent note, hate crimes, tend to exaggerate their seriousness, and as a result, oversell the punishment. Proportionality, that union of act and reaction, is always relevant in a penal context.

No doubt, talk of prisons and incarceration would be unnecessary if man were always virtuous. Humankind is predictably frail and the nation and state need a consequence that promotes order. Imprisonment is a justifiable and lawful act that achieves this aim.

The Death Penalty

The Thomist resolve in matching consequences with particular criminal acts is markedly evident in the examination of the death penalty. Thomas is an unreserved, unequivocal supporter of the death penalty in certain cases. His words and arguments rarely manifest hesitation, and, in fact, there is a sort of ardent, passionate conviction typically found in the office of the district attorney.[34] In his *Commentary on the Nicomachean Ethics*, Thomas exhibits no trepidation in the infliction of severe punishments: "The insubordinate and the degenerate are allotted physical punishments like beatings and other chastisements, censure and loss of their possessions. However, the absolutely incurable are exterminated—the bandit, for instance, is hanged."[35]

At the same time, he employs the language of a surgeon who saves the whole body from the corruption of its infected members.[36] The legitimacy of this form of punishment is grounded in both theology and jurisprudence. Justifying the death of sinners to the betterment of the common good, Thomas proclaims, "When, however, the good incur no danger, but rather are protected and saved by the slaying of the wicked, then the latter may be lawfully put to death."[37]

Sinners and criminals are injurious to the whole and an imperfection eating away at the community and culture, distracting us in our imperfect journey to the perfect God. The death penalty simply "puts to death those who are dangerous to others."[38] Writing from a medical slant, Thomas urges the cutting away of infected members, the removal of rotted appendages and diseased bodily components whose infectiousness is sure to spread amongst the remaining healthy parts. Bad individuals infect the whole in a similar way. An example of the Thomistic method is evident when he states, "For this reason we observe that if the health of the whole body demands the excision of a member, through its being decayed or infectious to the other members, it will be both praiseworthy and advantageous to have it cut away."[39]

To justify the infliction, Thomas argues that the common good replaces the individual need for self-preservation, and even though self-preservation is an inherent, natural-law precept, forfeiture of that right occurs by the conduct committed. St. Thomas tempers this rigid approach by negating the possibility of the death penalty in a host of other circumstances. Clerics and religious authorities are forbidden to kill the sinner or criminal, for it is not within their competence to deal with human justice, only matters of the spiritual, since clerics are unqualified "to meddle with minor matters" [quod minoribus se ingerant].[40]

Also instructive is Thomas's admonition that people should not be executed by private individuals, since the act of the death penalty is one of public authority and public justice. The care of the common good "is entrusted to persons of rank having public authority."[41] Only public officers may slay legitimately. The power of punishment belongs to those in whose "office it is to impose the law; indeed, lawmakers enforce observance of the law by means of rewards and punishments."[42]

Mitigation, defensible conduct, and exculpatory rationales should not be disregarded when weighing the suitability of the death penalty.[43] Thomas's keen understanding of intentionality—the *mens rea* of a criminal act—is evident in his analysis of proportionate punishments. Chance events, accidents, negligent acts, or carelessness that cause the death of another mitigate the necessary level of intent to justify the death penalty.[44] Voluntary, wilful acts incurs the severity of death, and "chance happenings, strictly speaking, are neither intended nor voluntary. And since every sin is voluntary, according to Augustine (*De Vera Relig.* xiv) it follows that chance happenings, as such, are not sins."[45]

While a staunch supporter of the death penalty, Thomas passionately denies its applicability in cases of innocence, doubtful facts, or insubstantial criminality. Levels of criminal victimization instruct the sentencing authority on the suitability of this extreme punishment. Thomas never ceases discussing the equitable quality of justice, since the judgment of the death penalty should be "in accordance with the conditions of commutative justice, in so far as rewards are apportioned to merits, and punishments to sins."[46] In cases of innocent defendants, Thomas tolerates no death penalty application. Not even the fact that the whole society can benefit from the loss of one innocent being, as a sort of constructive message, impresses Thomas. Death penalty imposition is exclusively reserved for the culpable. The death of an innocent and just person is a gross injustice. The death of any just man robs the community of a meaningful member, but the execution of the unjust man, who "despises God more" [quia magis Deum contemnit] aids communal tranquility.[47] Thomas reserves acrid criticism for the judge who allows the innocent man to perish: "If the judge knows that a man who has been convicted by false witnesses, is innocent he must, like Daniel, examine the witnesses with great care, so as to find a motive for acquitting the innocent: but if he cannot do this he should remit him for judgment by a higher tribunal."[48]

If the evidence supports the death penalty conclusion, the judge, even though he or she may personally believe otherwise, lacks discretion to alter the sentence, because it is not "he that puts the innocent man to death, but they who stated him to be guilty."[49] The lack of hesitancy in Thomas to enforce and impose death penalty punishments does not imply a cavalier attitude toward its severity nor a lack of deliberation on its applicability to varied circumstances. Few thinkers in history have as precisely forged and formulated a basis for its legitimacy. Thomas determines that freely choosing beings socially exist with others, in communal settings, impacting one another whether conscious of it or not.[50] Just as telling is our own character, that which constitutes our good or evil, either living in accordance with the law or not. For those who choose to undermine and undercut the collective whole, to infect it, or to riddle it with disease, there is a penalty of both punishment and forfeiture.

Those deliberately choosing a life of criminality lose more than the freedom of movement or the freedom of life as usually understood: They lose their essential dignity, the fundamental attributes that compose and construct the human species. Criminals forfeit rights not only because of their deeds, but because their deeds transform them into beasts.[51] By departing from the order of reason, Thomas paints man as falling "away from the dignity of his manhood, in so far as he is naturally free, and exists for himself, and he falls into the slavish state of the beasts, by being disposed of according as he is useful to others. . . . For a bad man is worse than a beast, and is more harmful, as the Philosopher states (*Polit.* i.1 and *Ethic.* vii.6)."[52] In correctional parlance, one often hears the prison rank and file speak of the prisoners being animals, acting like apes, and having no sense of humanity. The registry of criminal deeds committed by the prison populace more often describes beasts than men.

Restitution

Another facet of Thomas's punishment and sentencing continuum is impressively ahead of its time: restitution. So often criminals serve time and incur punishments, but never recompense to the victim. Victims are a necessary component in the Thomistic criminal process. In restitution, the perpetrator is ordered to make the victim whole by paying for losses, compensating for damages, or returning what was stolen or converted. It is the quintessential act of commutative justice. Equilibrium is restored when property of equal or identical value is returned, when payment for limb or loss of function compensates, or when correction of a defamation or slander to name is publicized.[53] It is a wonderfully rich conception of making whole, of causing a restoration or reestablishing equality from inequality.[54] In the criminal court, the judge has the power to effect restitution by a wide array of means. Restitution reestablishes equality, since in every criminal case the perpetrator is obliged to "restore just so much as he has belonging to another" [ad quod sufficit quod restituat tantum quantum habuerit de alieno].[55]

State legislature after state legislature has enacted victims' compensation programs that promote restitution in a manner that would cause Thomas joy.[56] Forcefully, Thomas forbids the criminal actor to be unaccountable, to hide behind mechanical, judicial processes that isolate victims of crime from the criminal's accountability. In Thomas's eyes, the victim deserves an apology by either word or deed, by compensation or substitute, and, most important, by the system's effort to recast the loss in the closest, most complete sense. Victims are always, perennially, owed this debt, this restitution, even for eternity. Thomas could not be clearer when he comments that "he that has sinned is bound to satisfaction. Now restitution belongs to satisfaction. Therefore he that has taken a thing is bound to restore it."[57] Putting off, excusing or delaying restitution is frowned upon too. To delay is merely to compound the sin already committed.[58]

PUNISHMENT AND SALVATION

Thomas blends, in a theological flavor, punishment, forgiveness, recompense, and salvation. A spiritual balance must be rectified, for those in sin, those who need to right their own injustices, are in need of a mechanism to correct personal harm or injustice. Punishment lends itself well to this rectification. In general, punishment expresses a contrition of the soul, while the punished party simultaneously serves out the terms and conditions of the confinement. Every punishment ties itself to the spiritual health of the soul and is an opportunity to repent and begin anew. It is a chance to live like the rational man God intended in His exemplar, to cast aside the slavish, brutish habits that dominate both intellect and will. If not, the eternity of the afterlife will not in the ultimate end be the joy and wonder of the beatific vision of God, but the misery and agony of damnation.

St. Thomas is forever vigilant about the state of the perpetrator's soul. In response to whether mortal sin punishes forever, Thomas states that "he who is punished by this punishment, so that he is deprived of the ultimate end, must remain deprived of it throughout eternity."[59] Here is where Thomas's teleology gives brilliance to his criminology. Salvation should be the ultimate end of any penology. The penology proposed by St. Thomas doesn't debate the varied inherencies in the human condition, but is more than willing to perceive the human being as malleable, correctable, and changeable. The richness of St. Thomas's thought leads not to an intractable portrait of man, but one most capable of alteration and reform. It is optimistic because it believes in the power of reason and will, the strength derived from freedom itself. Any system of rewards and punishments cannot conclude otherwise. Thomas's penology ends its journey with the reminder that the most tragic of punishments is a lost felicity, the hopeless deprivation that comes from estrangement from God. The criminal's most pressing loss is in being "cut off from happiness."[60] The assurance of salvation is the ultimate aim of restitution and any other method of punishment.[61]

NOTES

1. St. Thomas Aquinas, "Summa Theologica," in *Basic Writings of St. Thomas Aquinas*, ed. Anton C. Pegis, vol. 2 (New York: Random House, 1945), I–II, Q. 100, a. 7, ad 4.

2. St. Thomas Aquinas, *Summa Contra Gentiles*, trans. Vernon J. Bourke, vol. 4 (Notre Dame: University of Notre Dame Press, 1975), bk. III, pt. II, ch. 142, 3.

3. George Quentin Friel, *Punishment in the Philosophy of Saint Thomas Aquinas and among Some Primitive Peoples* (Washington, D.C.: Catholic University of America Press, 1939), 123.

4. See W. J. Waluchow, "Professor Weinreb on Corrective Justice," in *Justice, Law and Method in Plato and Aristotle*, ed. Spiro Panagiotou (Alberta: Academic, 1987), 155.

5. For an insightful examination, see Vernon J. Bourke, "Justice as Equitable Reciprocity: Aquinas Updated," *American Journal of Jurisprudence* 27 (1982): 21.

6. Ibid., 19.

7. Joseph V. Dolan, "Natural Law and the Judicial Function," *Laval Theologique et Philosophique* 16 (1960): 107.

8. Aquinas, *Gentiles*, III–II, ch. 146, 1.

9. Dolan, "Natural Law," 107.

10. St. Thomas Aquinas, *Summa Theologica*, trans. English Dominican Friars, vol. 2 (New York: Benziger, 1947), bk. II, pt. II, Q. 58, a. 11.

11. St. Thomas Aquinas, *On Kingship*, trans. Gerald B. Phelan (Toronto: Pontifical Institute of Mediaeval Studies, 1982), bk. II, ch. IV (I, 15), 120.

12. Friel, *Punishment*, 125.

13. Aquinas, "Theologica," I–II, Q. 87, a. 1.

14. Ibid., I–II, Q. 87, a. 1, ad 2. "Unde ipsa poena non est effectus peccati directe, sed solum dispositive."

15. Ibid., I–II, Q. 87, a. 1, ad 3.

16. Ibid., I–II, Q. 87, a. 3, c. "Sicut supra dictum est, peccatum ex hoc inducit reatum poenae, quod pervertit aliquem ordinem. Manente autem causa, manet effectus: unde quamdiu perversitas ordinis remanet, necesse est quod remaneat reatus poenae."

17. Ibid., I–II, Q. 105, a. 2, ad 9. "Quia majori peccato, caeteris paribus, poena gravior debetur."

18. Brian Calvert, "Aquinas on Punishment and the Death Penalty," *American Journal of Jurisprudence* 37 (1992): 263.

19. Aquinas, "Theologica," I–II, Q. 87, a. 3, ad 2. "Quod poena quae etiam secundum leges humanas infligitur, non semper est medicinalis ei qui

punitur, sed solum aliis sicut cum latro suspenditur, non ut ipse emendetur, sed propter alios, ut saltem metu poenae peccare desistant."

20. Aquinas, *Gentiles*, III–II, ch. 144, 11.

21. Calvert, "Aquinas on Punishment," 268. See Vernon J. Bourke, "The Ethical Justification of Legal Punishment," *American Journal of Jurisprudence* 22 (1977): 4.

22. Aquinas, *Theologica*, vol. 2, II–II, Q. 108, a. 3.

23. Aquinas, *Gentiles*, III–II, ch. 145, 4.

24. Aquinas, *Theologica*, vol. 2, II–II, Q. 65, a. 1, c. "Si vero membrum propter putredinem sit totius corporis corruptivum, tunc licitum est de voluntate ejus cujus est membrum, putridum membrum praescindere propter salutem totius corporis; quia unicuique commissa est cura propriae salutis."

25. Ibid., II–II, Q. 65, a. 1, ad 1. "Et similiter mutilare aliquem membro, etsi sit contra naturam particularem corporis ejus qui mutilatur, est tamen secundum naturalem rationem in comparatione ad bonum commune."

26. Ibid., II–II, Q. 108, a. 3, c.

27. Ibid., II–II, Q. 65, a. 2, ad 1.

28. Ibid., II–II, Q. 65, a. 3, obj. 1.

29. Ibid., II–II, Q. 65, a. 3, ad 1. "Et ideo homo qui peccando abusus est libero usu suorum membrorum, conveniens est incarcerationis materia."

30. Ibid., II–II, Q. 65, a. 3, c.

31. Ibid. "Nisi fiat secundum ordinem justitiae, aut in poenam, aut ad cautelam alicujus mali vitandi."

32. Aquinas, "Theologica," I–II, Q. 96, arts. 3, 4. See James F. Ross, "Justice Is Reasonableness: Aquinas on Human Law and Morality" *The Thomist* 58 (1974): 86–103.

33. See Ross, "Justice Is Reasonableness," 100.

34. Aquinas, *Theologica*, vol. 2, II–II, Q. 64, a. 2.

35. St. Thomas Aquinas, *Commentary on the Nicomachean Ethics*, trans. C. I. Litzinger (Chicago: Henry Regnery, 1964), X. L.XIV:C 2151.

36. Aquinas, *Theologica*, vol. 2, II–II, Q. 64, a. 2, c.

37. Ibid., II–II, Q. 64, a. 2, ad 1. "Quando vero ex occisione malorum non imminet periculum bonis, sed magis tutela et salus, tunc licite possunt mali occidi."

38. Ibid., II–II, Q. 64, a. 2, ad 2.

39. Ibid., II–II, Q. 64, a. 2, c. "Et propter hoc videmus quod si saluti totius corporis humani expediat praecisio alicujus membri, puta cum est putridum vel corruptivum aliorum membrorum, laudabiliter et salubriter abscinditur."

40. Ibid., II–II, Q. 64, a. 4, ad 2.

41. Ibid., II–II, Q. 64, a. 3.

42. Aquinas, *Gentiles*, III–II, ch. 140, 2.

43. Aquinas, *Theologica*, vol. 2, II–II, Q. 64, a. 7.

44. Ibid., II–II, Q. 64, a. 8.

45. Ibid., II–II, Q. 64, a. 8, c. "Et ideo ea quae casualia sunt, simpliciter loquendo, non sunt intenta neque voluntaria. Et quia omne peccatum est voluntarium, secundum Augustinum (lib. De vera relig. cap. 14, in princ.), consequens est quod casualia, inquantum hujusmodi, non sunt peccata."

46. Ibid., II–II, Q. 61, a. 4, ad 1.

47. Ibid., II–II, Q. 64, a. 6, ad 2.

48. Ibid., II–II, Q. 64, a. 6, ad 3. "Quod judex, si scit aliquem innocentem esse, qui falsis testibus convincitur, debet diligentius examinare testes, ut inveniat occasionem liberandi innoxium, sicut Daniel fecit. Si autem hoc non potest, debet eum superiori relinquere judicandum."

49. Ibid., II–II, Q. 64, a. 6, ad 3.

50. Calvert, "Aquinas on Punishment," 277.

51. Aquinas, *Theologica*, vol. 2, II–II, Q. 64, a. 2, ad 3.

52. Ibid. "Et ideo decidit a dignitate humana, prout scilicet homo est naturaliter liber, et propter seipsum existens; et indicit quodammodo in servitutem bestiarum, ut scilicet de ipso ordinetur, secundum quod est utile aliis. . . . Pejor enim est malus homo quam bestia et plus nocet, ut Philosophus dicit (Polit. lib. I, cap. 2, et Ethic. lib. VII, cap. 6, in fine)."

53. Ibid., II–II, Q. 62, a. 2, c; a. 2, ad 2.

54. Ibid., II–II, Q. 62, a. 3, c.

55. Ibid.

56. See Randy E. Barnett, "The Justice of Restitution," *American Journal of Jurisprudence* 25 (1980): 117–132.

57. Aquinas, *Theologica*, vol. 2, II–II, Q. 62, a. 6, sed contra. "Ille qui peccavit, tenetur satisfacere. Sed restitutio ad satisfactionem pertinet. Ergo ille qui abstulit, tenetur restituere."

58. Ibid., II–II, Q. 62, a. 8.

59. Aquinas, *Gentiles*, III–II, ch. 144, 2.

60. Ibid., III–II, ch. 141, 3.

61. Aquinas, *Theologica*, vol. 2, II–II, Q. 62, a. 2, c. "Cum ergo conservare justitiam sit de necessitate salutis, consequens est quod restituere id quod injuste ablatum est alicui, sit de necessitate salutis."

CHAPTER 11

The Relevance of Thomistic Jurisprudence

As these ruminations on Thomistic jurisprudence near closure, the reader is urged to treasure its relevance to a beleaguered justice system and exhorted to apply its content and philosophical approach to the pressing problems so rampant in contemporary judicial process. Thomistic jurisprudence is offered as a last clear chance for a crumbling and malfunctioning legal machine. Thomistic jurisprudence affords the justice system a perennial model for justice and truth, a dependable and unchangeable series of parameters for judicial conduct and legal advocacy, and an unassailable foundation upon which any system of justice can flourish. Even today, judges and lawyers, by and through various ethical codes, such as the *Code of Judicial Conduct* (*CJC*) and the *Model Rules of Professional Conduct* (*MPR*), are governed by professional boundaries, but these will prove unavoidably inadequate. However, hope glimmers on the horizon, for the debate on the relevancy and utility of natural-law reasoning, as evident in the judicial confirmation processes for appellate courts and in select case law, proves that neither the natural law nor its advocacy can be blotted out from the hearts of men.

THOMISTIC JURISPRUDENCE
AND THE INADEQUACY OF POSITIVISM

Is a legal philosophy that encompasses virtue, truth, and the good realistic? Is a jurisprudence reliant upon the imminent instruction of the natural law, that integrates the human player into the plan

of a creative God, plausible in a modern legal setting? Or is a jurisprudence addressing simple human needs and wants more attractive? In the latter case, the law serves as remedy and rectifier,
correcting real or perceived injustices to people and things, and at
all costs elevating personalized, individualized rights as the law's
primary aim. Commonly, lawyers, judges, and advocates perceive
law as primarily aiding the human condition. In addition, the public demands "action" from its legislative bodies and elected officials
and measures their effectiveness by the depth and breadth of their
lawmaking. Inactivity is perceived as political weakness, while promulgation, even at a frenetic pace, is admirably viewed. At every
corner of the legislative halls, laws are promulgated to ameliorate
harm. Laws medicinally prescribe and cure injustices like racism,
sexism, poverty, and inequality. Laws are looked to in order to stave
off illegal immigration, prevent criminality, insure employment
protections, and prevent sexual harassment and other confronta-
tions. Law, as an agent of change, as a prescriptive antidote for
tragedy and injustice, is impossibly ambitious. Law certainly tends
to harms and imbalances in political and social life, but the impact
and influence of the law should not be exaggerated. Yet the culture's
willingness and almost inordinate affection for laws signifies an
exaggerated expectation.

This disproportionate reliance trickles throughout the most general aspects of daily existence. The simple example of home sales
illustrates the overdependence on law. For generations, isolated
pockets of this nation drafted neither deed nor document to represent the transfer of real estate. In their place, the conveyers and
conveyees orally promised their intentions. Since a promise binds
a person in conscience, it was inconceivable that a party might withdraw from an obligation to buy or sell realty. Handshakes and oral
promises were enough, because these acts mirrored each party's
soul. Paperwork, the formal documentation that serves as
memorialization and evidentiary anchor in the event of dispute, is
today the exclusive method of realty transfer. Historically, lawyers
spent the bulk of their time abstracting the chain of title, not litigating promissory disputes. The promise was deeply burned into
the conscience of the promisor. Granted, this portrayal is simplis-
tic, but it edifies a world in which contracting parties were not adjudged separately from personal and spiritual character.

Today, the lawmaker's identity is tied tightly to enacting, making, and promulgating laws. The public measures the political scene
by levels of legislative activity. Laws, the designers allege in the
majority of cases, better the lot of the human race. Is this so? Do
welfare laws eradicate poverty? Will damages or fines in sexual

harassment cases make the harasser temperate? Will employment quotas in an affirmative action plan eliminate racism and hatred? Will the incarceration of "deadbeat dads" or abusive spouses halt the misery so repetitively inflicted? If law facilitates the virtuous life, how does it account for the dearth of virtue in modern life? Surely we have laws—an endless sea of them. When people proclaim "rights," what type of rights are they? How permanent are these rights? Upon what rests their foundation? Are they metaphysical or moral rights, derived directly from God or nature? Do these rights attach their legitimacy to the promulgative quality of the law itself?[1] Positivism starts and ends with enactment, and then, when the law no longer "fits," the process starts over again. Just as transiently, "rights," the by-product of the enactment, evolve and dissipate until another right is conceived.[2] Thomas's jurisprudence avoids the metamorphosis because its pilings are teleological and its foundation perennial. If the judges and lawyers ground their decision making on human arguments alone, which argument prevails and for how long? The traditional theory of legal *precedent* cannot be comfortable with this changeability, since it assumes continuity of legal principles and stability in legal decision making. Precedent solely based on human whims is a changeable phenomenon that jurists cannot rely upon. A windswept positivism whose moral dependability and steadfastness is as loose as a tumbleweed fosters chaos in legal analysis. Positivism will not and cannot supply a jurisprudence of permanency. In the temporary landscape of legal verbiage, legal words are not a "phenomenon exhaustively explicable in its own terms."[3] If not universal truth, ordination of reason, nature, and the good, are laws accurately described as that "which are enacted by its lawmaking agency?"[4] If not to morality, where does the law anchor itself? Is it better to hack away the moral limbs from the law's trunk so that it is purified of judgment and rational determination? A jurisprudence based on positivism has little choice but to divide and separate law and morality, "because in some way or another the validity and the content of law depend upon social practices or usages."[5]

A legal system bound to mores and cultural conditions for its base lacks permanency and immutability, since social and cultural practices are either fixed or fluid. Change will also come to the rulers of a nation, to kings and princes; power bases will shift, constitutions will be amended, and ethical canons and professional codes will be modified and even repealed. Individuals and communities are in dire need of a jurisprudence better than this. Opinion polls, the wind gauge of political sentiments, are an equally inadequate foundation on which to erect a jurisprudence.[6]

Positivists, utilitarians, fundamentalists, and realists are incapable of constructing a legal system that is predictable and good. Their formula for professionalism, for judges and lawyers, is as flawed as its foundational support.[7] Comparatively, positivism and Thomism are continents apart, for the former owes its existence to human agency alone while the latter emphasizes holistic teleology. One can be certain that man "is not infallible and with the best will in the world people fall into subjective error in working out the details of right and wrong."[8] Thomas's jurisprudence conceives law, lawyers and judges, and legislators and lawmakers in both ontological and theological terms. In other words, the positivist interpreter of a law, typically a judge, wears only one hat, that of a legal decision maker. For St. Thomas, this is a serious flaw in understanding. The judicial interpreter is undoubtedly an occupation, but a man and moral agent as well. Thomas withstands any effort to compartmentalize the functions of the jurist from the trappings of human identity. At the same time, Thomas never denigrates the promulgative side of law and finds positive, human law indispensable and "most necessary for mankind."[9] Thomas's entire approach is both idealized and integrated, for reason, person, and practice are inseparable. Alasdair MacIntyre believes Thomas's worldview is an integrated order, where everything "has its due place in the order of things."[10] From various angles, St. Thomas's legal thinking is confident in the power and magnificence of human beings. Personhood does not entail the imposition of law without proaction or reaction, as if dull-witted beings waited for the law's lashing. Human beings are the central architects of law, and live not as stark, wayward creatures but as "an autonomous human nature [in] the image of God ordered to union with his infinite Creator though sensitive, intellectual and volitional activity."[11]

THOMISTIC JURISPRUDENCE IS
UNIVERSAL AND IMMUTABLE

Compared to the fluidity of positivism, Thomistic jurisprudence is fundamentally fixed, not in excessive rigidity but as a mirror to human operations. It charitably coerces and cajoles human persons to discern their natures, to reflect on their inclinations and dispositions, to identify appropriate goods, and to evaluate how civilizations flourish or fail in light of both individual and communal activity. Reason, nature, and the imprint of the eternal law, by and through the natural law, instructs and educates the human agent. Within the preservative domain of the natural law, a human agency procreates, socially interacts, loves its offspring, avoids evil, seeks good, desires truth and virtue, and yearns for the supreme perfection of God. Lawyers and judges, as human players, are disposed identically and to act contrary to these inherencies is bound to produce ineffective and unjust practitioners. Both the justice system and its chief participants, lawyers and judges, desperately need a legal foundation that comports with this universal and unchangeable perspective. Positive law will not serve this end, because positive law should be in service to the universal and immutable laws of our nature and of God. Positive law cannot be at odds with this permanent, ontological framework, but should be nothing more than an "ordering toward the general ends expressed in the general principles of natural law."[12] Positive law stands below yet side by side with the natural law, for its legitimacy depends upon its compatibility with the natural law. Natural law, that extremely limited series of precepts, serves as a generalized guide and a globalized map of human activities. The positive law embellishes and vivifies the natural law by determining and specifying the general tenets of the natural law. Positive law "is related to the natural law not by way of conclusion, but by way of determination."[13]

Herein a dilemma emerges. If human law is ephemeral and changeable, how can a legal system be other than changeable? Why can't a judge on the U.S. Supreme Court disregard the natural law when ruling on abortion or euthanasia? Isn't the legal advocate on sound ethical grounds advocating a position known to be antagonistic to natural-law principles? Isn't it the job of a lawyer to represent a client vigorously, at any cost and in any manner? None of these scenarios fulfill the premise advanced by St. Thomas.

A few recent cases from the U.S. Supreme Court offer minor glints of the natural-law tradition. In the right-to-die (physician-assisted suicide) case, *Washington, et al. v. Harold Glucksberg, et al.*, the court unanimously upheld a Washington state statute that criminalized the activity and simultaneously rejected the constitutional assertion that citizens possess a "right" to die.[14] Chief Justice William Rehnquist, author of the opinion, meticulously traces the ethical thicket such a case causes and indicates a preference for moral as well as legal inquiry. The Court recognized that any reasoned debate encompasses morality, legality, and practicality of this novel practice.[15] Said examination, to be rational in any context, accepts that our "Anglo American common law tradition has punished or otherwise disapproved of both suicide and assisting suicide."[16] This precedential awareness and analysis of tradition is painstakingly part of Rehnquist's analysis. Citing Sir Edward Coke, Henry Bracton, and the "ecclesiastical prohibition on suicide," Rehnquist displays a taste for permanency and universality in his legal message.[17] He even refers to a sixteenth-century legal decision, *Hales v. Petit*,[18] in which suicide was typed an "offence against nature, against God, and against the king."[19] Any form of self-destruction is "contrary to nature and a thing most horrible."[20] When compared to the positive constitutionalism of the abortion decision, *Roe v. Wade*, there are subtle signs of natural-law reasoning in *Glucksberg*.[21] Indeed, Rehnquist's opinion insists that any decision on the matter of physician-assisted suicide will travel first to the human agent's foundations. Once there, the results become self-evident.[22]

Positivists, relativists, and utilitarians can easily accommodate transient circumstances because they cannot hitch their horses to a post that stays in the ground long enough. Is it any wonder that same-sex marriage, partial birth abortion, and animal rights activism find support in these legal schools. By contrast, Thomas's ship stays in port because his natural-law jurisprudence is perennial, and while there are varied levels of personal knowledge and intuition as to its content, every human being, including the judge to don a robe and a lawyer a suit, knows it too. Permanency, universality, and commonality is what distinguishes Thomas from his positivist counterparts.[23] Remember that Thomas distinguishes this type of immutability from the descending and particularized quality and content of positive laws. Differences can and do arise at the more particularized contingent level. He writes, "The practical reason, on the other hand, is concerned with contingent matters, which is the domain of human actions; and, consequently, although there is necessity in the common principles, the more we descend towards the particular, the more frequently we encounter defects."[24]

It is the common, indisputable precepts of the natural law that never change. As a result, this form of jurisprudence resolves legal dilemmas uniformly, it endows man with rights compatible with nature, it simultaneously proscribes conduct and behavior universally, and it tolerates minor disturbances to individual and community. It creates rights only when those rights are metaphysically and morally grounded. More exacting, it elucidates to lawyers and judges what activities are in complete and foreboding opposition to Thomas's natural-law jurisprudence. Laws disconnected to life and human goods are far from permanent or universal.[25] Thomistic jurisprudence "refers to a way of life, to a quest for right living."[26] It is this toughness that begs the conscience of lawyer, jurist, and lawmaker. From Thomas's mind, right answers to moral and legal dilemmas come forth. Neither yielding nor bending to pressure, the Thomist legal thinker nullifies any law that is contrary to this plan, labels any law opposite the tenets of the natural law a perversion that does violence to the law itself.[27] An unjust law garners no obedience nor can it demand recognition. If anything, St. Thomas insists that legal practitioners engage in the type of inquiry consistent with individual and communal perfections, not exclusively attendant to legal verbiage and its mastery. In a sense, the security and comfort Thomism supplies the legal player arises from the fundamental presumptions and presuppositions, as MacIntyre indicates, of "truth, rationality and intentionality . . . independent of the inquirer, founded on something other than social agreement."[28]

Changeability and relativity in moral terms cannot survive in the Thomistic forest. Thomas's law "is written in men's hearts and cannot be blotted out."[29] Nature images the immutability and unchangeability of the Creator. How else could the Creator be? Certainly, God can only author creatures with proper ends, engineer beings who desire, from the first minutes of existence, their own preservation, or manufacture beings who marry, procreate by sexual intercourse, and prefer community to isolation. Man, as a creature, has unchangeable components manifested precisely in the natural law. Thomas's jurisprudence, so often caricatured as morally impositional, is generously honest, open to only consistency and rationality, and driven by goods that allow the human agent to develop and flourish.[30] Judges and lawyers acting in contravention to these purposes or, minimally, without a reasoned inquiry into these principles, are outside Thomas's way of thinking. Judges are "moral legislators."[31]

Certainty and truth go a long way toward assuring a just legal system and the cadre of professionals working within it. Legal practice and reasoning are more than "flipping coins."[32] They are a *summa ratio*.[33] "For all legislation derives from some vision of the 'good.' All men are attracted by the good in general and Natural Law is generated when this attraction expresses itself regulatively, as a rule laid on the whole domain of human activity directing it towards the good."[34]

Changeability and its perverse attraction to all that is relative squashes moral objectivity. Instead, the legal positivist searches for meaning, not in immutable principles, but in those that shift. St. Thomas perceives the inherent insubstantiality and insufficiency of human law and human happiness without a tie to a higher, metaphysical order. Thomas's *On Kingship*, when dealing with the government structure most conducive to happiness, zeroes in on this question: "Now it is manifest that all earthly things are beneath the human mind. But happiness is the last perfection and the perfect good of man, which all men desire to reach. Therefore there is no earthly thing which could make man happy, nor is any earthly thing a sufficient reward for a king."[35] Thomas's jurisprudence, so affectionately dependent on rationality, the hierarchical construct that cascades from the divine exemplar, the blending of law, goods, and ends, provides, as John Finnis argues, a "backbone" to any proposed legal order.[36]

Any other proposition drifts according to the winds of change, not permanency and immutability. Lawmaking for the positivist is in a chasm away from morality and is solely legitimate by its en- actment, "sociologically defined," and free of "moral and other evalu- ative judgment."[37] Trudging through the changeable, third world of positivism, the legal practitioner is impoverished by a lack of standards, waiting in expectancy and misery for the next right or protection, which lasts only as long as its legislative life. In the domain of positivism, man, devoid of every sense of objective truth, inhabits, as Raymond Dennehy terms it, an "intellectual darkness in an age of metaphysical blindness."[38] Hiding behind innocuous and saccharine descriptors like the "dignity of man," "human rights," "self-esteem," and "personal respect," positivism provides little so- lace for the legal system and its practitioners. In contrast to Thomas's perspective, positivism inspires "to persuade modern man that the intellect, far from having the capacity to know what things are, is confined to a knowledge of their sensible properties or, at least, to a knowledge of our measurements of them."[39] Failing to discern an objective, material world and rejecting the intelligibil- ity of objective reality itself, the positivist, the utilitarian, and the realist resist anything incorruptible. In the end, the positivist, the functionalist, and the legal realist offer up the gas chamber and abortion clinic, the suicide machine and the lynch mob, as poten- tially lawful practices, or designates them unlawful, not knowing why. The positive, utilitarian, relative person is an empty crea- ture, aimlessly meandering through an existence sure to change. Today's dignity will be tomorrow's scourge.

THOMISTIC JURISPRUDENCE AND CONTEMPORARY CODES OF CONDUCT

By now, it is obvious that Thomistic thinking about law is largely at odds with the majoritarian view. The assaults are launched from diverse fronts: a lack of moral or factual objectivity and cultural and moral relativism contrary to pluralism and incompatible with democracy and the folly of exaggerating law beyond its function. In this "Who are you to tell me what to do!" environment, one wonders if it is possible for Thomas's jurisprudence to be relevant at all. The times illustrate the dilemma.

At the 1991 U.S. Senate Judiciary Committee confirmation hearings involving the nomination of Supreme Court Justice Clarence Thomas, the tension between the positivist and the natural-law jurist was soon apparent. It was a charged and contentious environment for more than jurisprudential reasons.[40] During the early phase of the hearings, Justice Thomas was aggressively confronted by Delaware Senator Joseph Biden, the Judiciary Committee chairman, on his view of the natural law in judicial decision making. Biden was troubled by Judge Thomas's firm belief that there is such a thing as the natural-law and a higher-law jurisprudence.[41] Biden acknowledged the teleological emphasis inherent in natural-law jurisprudence but cringed at the thought of relating such a philosophy to actual lawmaking and legal practice. Biden, the positivist, could not envision the relevancy of natural-law reasoning in constitutional or other adjudication. Judge Thomas, surely feeling the pressures and pitfalls of the confirmation process, moderately defended his jurisprudence with talk of natural rights, an accommodation that humanists can live with. What was clear was Judge Thomas's unshakable understanding of law beyond promulgation. Indeed, Clarence Thomas told Senator Biden that natural-law jurisprudence would have abolished slavery, a slavery the positivists unhesitatingly allowed.[42] It is arguable whether the founders of the nation conceived the natural law in an identical context as Thomas, but it is undeniable that the Framers believed in a higher law, a metaphysical order that leapt beyond the temporal.[43]

Clarence Thomas's natural-law reasoning, despite his best political efforts, could and would have no other purpose than a jurisprudence grander than positivism. Biden tagged Justice Thomas's jurisprudence as one containing objective truth. Arguing supportively of the natural law, Clarence Thomas did what was necessary for confirmation: He assured the committee chair that the natural law has a minimal, if not nonexistent, role in constitutional analysis. The Biden–Clarence Thomas debate simultaneously represents the depths to which this perennial theory has fallen and the impact such a jurisprudence still has on the political and legal scene. Select members of the Judiciary Committee, acting as attack dogs, wanted desperately to keep Justice Clarence Thomas at bay, hoping to block his confirmation to avoid a return to "antiquated" legal thinking. Others believed, in good faith or bad, the allegations of harassment or conservative tokenism.

Ironically, both the Judiciary Committee and the legal system, to ensure survival and to advance justice in both individual and communities, are in urgent need of the Thomist ideal. Jean Porter's well-received treatise, *The Recovery of Virtue: The Relevance of Aquinas for Christian Ethics*, announces Thomas Aquinas as "permanently significant" for the legal system and every other facet of human existence.[44] For the lawyers and judges who hope to carry out their professional responsibilities, Thomas offers a jurisprudence of rationality, goodness, and happiness, a jurisprudence that fosters that "natural rectitude in human acts is not dependent on things accidentally possible in the case of one individual, but, rather, on those conditions which accompany the entire species."[45]

Clarence Thomas's gauntlet of confirmation was intense partially because of his jurisprudential leanings. His colleague on the Court, Antonin Scalia, escaped such a litmus test, but has long been typecast as sympathetic to natural-law reasoning, though the evidence is largely more rumor than fact. During a 1997 question-and-answer session with students of Thomas Aquinas College, Scalia appeared to deny the place of natural-law reasoning in his legal method. Textualism and limited judicial power are part of his regular pitch. The natural law may interfere with judicial reasoning, Scalia fears.[46] In his zeal to be a textualist, Scalia balks at being labeled any more than a judge of a law's language. This narrow self-perception belies the language of his opinions, especially those pertinent to abortion. In *Planned Parenthood v. Casey*, Scalia's moral tendencies are evident.[47] It is the very activism and social engineering so manifest in *Roe v. Wade* that makes moral discourse an impossibility. Because of *Roe v. Wade*, abortion is now a political and social matter that detaches itself from moral and ethical inquiry. Scalia's opinion in *Casey* is often provocative.[48]

Scalia's ruminations on homosexuality offer inferential proof of his Thomistic sympathies. Denying such legal inclinations in public does not eradicate the power of his legal insight. In *Roy Romer, et al. v. Richard G. Evans, et al.*, Scalia tackles the idea of homosexual rights.[49] If he was merely a textualist, any claim for constitutional protections would be dismissed without much argument. His opinion ventures further than the literalist and affords the disputants a deeper rationale for his conclusion. Homosexuality, Scalia argues, is adjudged in the fullness of reason and reasonableness. It is reasonable, given our traditions and our moral underpinnings, to disapprove and even condemn the activity. Moral heritage and centuries of disapproval mean something in legal decision making. Scalia often displays an affection for historical tradition as a sign of dependability in his opinions.[50] Prohibiting sodomy and denying special rights or privileges to homosexuals are not the promulgations of the moral dictator or tyrant, but a practice "making homosexual conduct a crime."[51] Scalia draws upon the court's own historical condemnation of bigamy and polygamy to support the prohibition and criminalization of a nonconstitutionalized homosexuality. Intentionally, Scalia relies on an 1885 decision crafted by Justices Harlan and Bradley (condemning the bigamist and polygamist) to buttress his view:

Certainly no legislation can be supposed more wholesome and necessary in the founding of a free, self governing commonwealth, fit to take rank as one of the co- ordinate States of the Union, than that which seeks to establish it on the basis of the idea of the family, as consisting in and springing from the union for life of one man and one woman in the holy estate of matrimony; the sure foundation of all that is stable and noble in our civilization; the best guaranty of that reverent morality which is the source of all beneficent progress in social and political improvement.[52]

Morality, family, matrimony, and the common good leap way beyond the pages of the textualist, and though denying advocacy in the "culture war," Scalia's words mirror his incessant yearning for tradition.[53] As is apparent from this discussion, Justices Thomas and Scalia signify a reserved and equivocal alignment with Thomistic jurisprudence.

Echoes of the Thomistic vision are evident in the professional codes that govern judges and lawyers. The *Code of Judicial Conduct*, which defines the role and functions of the judiciary, and the *Model Code of Professional Responsibility*, which sets out ethical expectations for lawyers, are attempts to impose more than professional competencies. They are an ethical and moral framework to carry out these proficiencies. A brief overview of both as applicable to St. Thomas's theory of law follows.

Judges, the *Code of Judicial Conduct*, and Thomistic Jurisprudence

In its preamble, the *Code of Judicial Conduct* proclaims that its canons and sections are "rules of reason," an expression of rationality that Thomas would be honored by.[54] Judges are "public officials" who "must respect and honor the judicial office as a public trust and strive to enhance and maintain confidence in our legal system."[55] A judge is an arbiter of facts and must resolve legal dilemmas in accordance with legal principles, a judging quality Thomas would wholeheartedly agree with.[56] In Canon 1 of the *CJC*, judges must be honorable, possess integrity, and act compatibly with the "high standards of judicial conduct."[57] Just as Thomas mandates justice as a virtue in judges and lawyers (doing just rather than unjust things), the *CJC* demands judges that are virtuous, and they "should respect and comply with the law and should act at all times in a manner that promotes public confidence in the integrity and impartiality of the judiciary."[58]

On a more functional front, the *CJC* and St. Thomas agree that judges should perform their duties and tasks conscientiously, avoiding rumor and suspicion and being attentive to due process and evidentiary requirements.[59] The *CJC*'s Canon 3 (A), "Adjudicative Responsibilities," contains nothing adverse to Thomistic jurisprudence, calling upon jurists to be competent, impartial, professional, and dignified.[60]

The remainder of the *CJC* is dedicated to other secular topics, such as judicial disqualification, conflicts, holding political office, investments, and other extrajudicial activities. The bulk of the *CJC* is positivist muddle, praising the judiciary while primarily cataloging roles and functions. At the end of the *CJC*, one is left with the same emptiness that all positive law brings to the bar. Being a good judge is certainly a more complicated matter than acting the part. Where the *CJC* parts ways with St. Thomas is in its strictly secular view of what the law is. Not surprising, there is an abject absence of discussion about goods and ultimate ends, and only a smattering of references to respect, courtesy, and patience for all.[61] Strikingly missing is Thomas's regular and predictable exhortation that judge and man are composed of both corporeal and spiritual components: "The spiritual man, by reason of the habit of charity, has an inclination to judge aright of all things according to the Divine rules; and it is in conformity with these that he pronounces judgment through the gift of wisdom: even as the just man pronounces judgment through the virtue of prudence conformably with the ruling of the law."[62]

Lawyers, the *Model Rules of Professional Conduct*, and Thomistic Jurisprudence

The *Model Rules of Professional Conduct*, in laying out the ethical responsibility of lawyers, generally adopts the same philosophical approach as the *CJC*.[63] Commencing with the flowery portrayal of a lawyer, the *MPR* states, "A lawyer is a representative of clients, an officer of the legal system and a public citizen having special responsibility for the quality of justice."[64] Further on in its preamble, professional and personal expectations are delineated: "A lawyer's conduct should conform to the requirements of the law, both in professional service and in the lawyer's business and personal affairs."[65]

On what basis are these expectations measured? Or is the promulgation of the standard sufficient alone? The current state of American lawyering leads to the conclusion that morality, an ethic, a justice for lawyers, demands something more than words. In the final analysis, how does the *MPR* enforce its high-minded professional ethos without an immutable legal philosophy? If the *MPR* asks the advocates not "to engage in conduct" disruptive to the tribunal, by what authority does its command bind?[66]

Throughout most of the *MPR*'s content we witness the typical justifications for fees, the elastic interpretation of conflicts in cases and clients, and caveats about confidences and evidentiary privilege. Only when the discussion turns toward lawyers as advocates do we deduce slight signs of Thomistic jurisprudence. In Rule 3.1, for example, the lawyer as advocate is obliged to advocate only "meritorious claims and contentions."[67] Frivolous cases, those lacking factual or legal merit, are not to be advocated. The frivolousness in the *MPR* and Thomas's critique of those advocating unjust accusations, falsity in claim, or advocating by calumny, collusion, or evasion are partially synonymous.[68] For St. Thomas, the advocate's use of reason, concern with virtue (especially justice), God, and an understanding of proper ends transforms the issue of merit into something far more complex than an assessment of simple facts or law. Thomas thrusts the lawyer–advocate into the soul's mirror and critiques those who advocate unjustly in undiplomatic terms: "For though he may seem to deserve praise for showing skill in his art, nevertheless he sins by reason of injustice in his will, since he abuses his art for an evil end."[69]

The *MPR* employs the standard of "candor" when addressing the legal profession, and it extends to the "tribunal," as well as "opposing counsel."[70] Making false statements, failing "to describe a material fact to a tribunal when disclosure is necessary to avoid assisting a criminal or fraudulent act by the client," comports with Thomas's general admonitions to the advocates.[71] Rule 3.4 insists that fairness be the guide and measure of the advocate dealing with client and counsel, including that of the opposition. The *MPR*'s Rule 3.4 forbids manipulation and destruction of evidence, falsification of evidentiary form, conflicts of interest deleterious to the client, and frivolous tactics in each phase of litigation.[72] The *MPR* authors an *ad seriatim* list of professional misconducts, all of which touch the issues of candor in dealings. Conducts that are criminal, untrustworthy, and involve every form of dishonesty, deceit, and fraud are roundly condemned as inconsistent with the legal profession. Inducing others to engage in these chicaneries is just as intoler-

able. Undue influence is never proper.[73] The *MPR* employs language
that condemns knowing falsehoods, and requires "truthfulness in
statements to others."[74] St. Thomas could only concur, since the
lawyer is bound and obliged by reason to act for justice, to advocate
just cause for the profession at large, to advocate in accordance
with the law and evidence, to counsel defendants and witnesses on
the importance of truthfulness in the judicial process, to offer sufficient evidence, to meet burdens and presumptions, and to ferret
out those who by personal character or incompetence should be
"debarred" from the office of the advocate.[75] Prosecutorial responsibilities are special to Thomas and the *MPR*, since both authorities
mandate a standard of proof, provision for representation, resistance to falsehood and guile, confrontation and accusation, and recognition of defense and mitigation.[76] Care for the poor is also a
shared concern for St. Thomas and the *MPR*.[77] Both suggest the
contribution of time and the forbearance of fees. *MPR* Rule 6.1 lays
out detailed criteria for pro bono activities.[78]

The similarities of purposes and ends are not mere coincidences,
but a reflection of a tradition originating in Plato and Aristotle and
journeying to the present. Each phase of human history gazes to
the horizon for justice. In Plato, justice is the ideal, the form itself
that we participate imperfectly in.[79] For Aristotle, justice is not a
form like bedness, but a virtue, an ordered disposition consistent
with reason, giving each his due. Thomas continues this thread,
but, more elaborately, ties it to the ultimate truth, the final end of
the human species, God. The *MPR* offers no such blueprint for lawyers, but predictably speaks of professional competency in humanistic and occupational terminology. The *MPR* is riddled with
high-sounding, ethical verbiage that cautions lawyers to act appropriately. To be sure, there are glints and squints of Thomas's teleological insight, but mostly the *MPR* is a self-contained employment
contract, setting out a series of do's and don'ts without knowing the
foundation it rests on.

THOMISTIC JURISPRUDENCE:
THE LAST CLEAR CHANCE

Will the *Model Rules of Professional Conduct* or the *Code of Judicial Conduct* embrace Thomas's holistic system, in which laws,
judges, lawyers, virtues, ends, and ultimate purposes pool together?
How would a modern advocate reconcile this Thomistic warning:
"Now an advocate by defending an unjust cause, helps the ungodly.
Therefore he sins and deserves the wrath of the Lord"?[80] Or is it too
medieval, too archaic to entertain this type of professional inquiry?

The legal theory of St. Thomas is not couched in apologies or political compromise. A natural-law jurisprudence beckons for the abolition of grave immorality so prevalent in the land of the positivists. Consistency, uniformity, and predictability are the seeds of Thomistic jurisprudence.

If not Thomism, then what? The transformative, evolving legal idea that Antonin Scalia describes as "growing and bending"?[81] Indeed, why is there a gnawing need to abandon tradition, that genealogical framework that supports a credible jurisprudence? Too many contemporary thinkers seem duty bound to reject the past and invent a new and improved version of truth or a progression of some sort. Thomism anchors itself in truth and rationality, while select schools of modern thought see philosophical thinking in evolutionary or deevolutionary terms. Alasdair MacIntyre finds this type of rejection unfortunate:

And in this perspective the accounts which they have given of truth, rationality and intentionality are to be understood as culminating achievements in a history of such progress. Where the Thomist sees stages in a movement away from adequate conceptions of truth and rationality, stages in a decline, the protagonists of the dominant standpoints in contemporary philosophy, so it will be said, will see stages in an ascent, a movement towards—but the problem is: towards what?[82]

Those who balk at Thomistic jurisprudence, labeling it a restrictive, regimented, and intractable series of orders and mandates, understand it the least. Thomas's theory of law is elementary, and amazingly, if followed, will lead to happiness, tranquility, and prosperity in individual and state. It will, says St. Thomas, "order men in regard to each other that each man may keep his order . . . for men to be at peace with each other."[83] Governance under its model is the best alternative in an imperfect world, for it first, guarantees respect for all human life: old, young, fetal, deformed, and decrepit. First, life, as a good, seeks its own preservation at any cost. Second, human life is social, stressing a communal, familial structure over isolation. Family, marriage, and children are the bulwarks of a thriving nation. Third, the human species desires to propagate, to procreate, not to abort and artificially control. Children are the centerpieces of marriage and country. Children are desired, loved, and expected, never seen in burdensome terms or as troublesome interruptions. Thomas's theory of law advances cultures, elevates individuals, promotes virtue, assures happiness, and constructs a theory of rights in a higher law rather than in the transient human dimension. Rights are eternally ensured, not subject to modification, alteration, or destruction by a temporal power. Kings, politicians, and judges should be aligned to a life of virtue, to teach "the law of God" so that "the multitude subject to him may live well."[84] Finally, Thomistic jurisprudence ponders the imponderable and places at its apex, at its superlative height and perfection, God, whose exemplar for all creation imprints a law of operations in us. This natural law cannot be extinguished from the human agent and its composition is unchangeable, as its author, for all eternity. A state that adduces any effort to alter these foundational precepts of the natural law is an unjust one, and those who advance and foster a natural-law jurisprudence are rightly labeled just.

NOTES

1. For a cogent examination of this formalistic debate, see Iredell Jenkins, "The Concept of Rights and the Competence of Courts," *American Journal of Jurisprudence* 18 (1973): 2.

2. U.S. Supreme Court Justice Antonin Scalia, reputed for his obsessive textualism, the interpretive school rigorously dependent on the language of the law, foretells the circuitous route inevitably chosen by the pure positivist: "It sounds wonderful until you to think, 'now, wait a minute. Do these people, who want to chuck away the old original, constitution, is it flexibility they're looking for?' What was the situation in *Roe vs. Wade*? If you wanted a right to an abortion, create that right the way a democratic society creates most rights. Pass a law. If you don't want it, pass a law against it." Justice Antonin Scalia, "A Theory of Constitutional Interpretation" (speech delivered at the Catholic University of America, Washington, D.C., 18 October 1996). Available at <http://www.courttv.com/library/rights/scalia.html>, visited 31 August 1998.

3. Igor Grazin, "Natural Law as a Form of Legal Studies," *American Journal of Jurisprudence* 37 (1992): 13.

4. Martin P. Golding, "Aquinas and Some Contemporary Natural Law Theories," *Proceedings of the American Catholic Philosophical Association* 48 (1974): 239.

5. Neil MacCormick, "Natural Law and the Separation of Law and Morals," in *Natural Law Theory*, ed. Robert P. George (Oxford: Clarendon Press, 1992), 107.

6. See Henry Mather, "Natural Law and Right Answers," *American Journal of Jurisprudence* 38 (1993): 317.

7. Heinrich A. Rommen, *The Natural Law*, trans. T. Hanley (St. Louis: B. Herder, 1948), 127, concludes that positivism and other non-Thomistic schools are unpredictable and undependable:

This boundary is continually shifting; a common body of ethical and legal ideas is wanting. Here the law of the stronger holds sway. Callicles had spoken of this long before, and he as well as Spinoza had identified it with the natural law because they regarded nature as the antithesis of mind. Consequently there is no eternal justice, nor is there an unalterable moral law. The state is the creator of morality and law, but the state in turn is merely a product of the struggle of social classes and servant of the class that rules at any given time.

8. Noel Dermot O'Donoghue, "The Law Beyond the Law," *American Journal of Jurisprudence* 18 (1973): 158.

9. St. Thomas Aquinas, "Summa Theologica," in *Basic Writings of St. Thomas Aquinas*, ed. Anton C. Pegis, vol. 2 (New York: Random House, 1945), I–II, Q. 95, a. 1. Igor Grazin, "Natural Law," 14, wisely narrates this symbiotic dependency:

I do not want to underestimate the importance of positive laws and legal positivism here. Both natural law and positive law need each other. Natural law without actual legal authorities, legislatures and policemen, judges and law professors, is helpless. But it is the other way also. In spite of all its powerful machinery the positive law lacking its natural legal foundation appears to be inefficient.

10. Alasdair MacIntyre, *After Virtue*, 2d ed. (Notre Dame: University of Notre Dame Press, 1981, 1984), 176–177.

11. Gerald A. McCool, "Is Thomas's Way of Philosophizing Still Viable Today?" in *The Future of Thomism*, ed. Deal W. Hudson and Dennis W. Moran (Notre Dame: University of Notre Dame Press, 1992), 59–60.

12. Daniel J. Degnan, Jr., "Two Models of Positive Law in Aquinas: A Study of the Relationship of Positive Law and Natural Law," *The Thomist* 46 (1982): 12.

13. Ibid., 2.

14. *Washington, et al. v. Harold Glucksberg, et al.*, 521 U.S. 702 (1997).

15. Ibid., 710.

16. Ibid., 711.

17. Ibid.

18. *Hales v. Petit*, 1 Plowd. Com. 253, 75 Eng. Rep. 387 (1561–1562).

19. Ibid., 1 Plowd. Com. 253, 261, 75 Eng. Rep. 387, 400.

20. Ibid.

21. *Roe v. Wade*, 410 U.S. 113 (1973).

22. Rehnquist articulately comments, "Attitudes toward suicide itself have changed since Bracton, but our laws have consistently condemned, and continue to prohibit, assisting suicide. Despite changes in medical technology and notwithstanding an increased emphasis on the importance of end of life decision-making, we have not retreated from this prohibition." *Washington v. Glucksberg*, 719.

23. Aquinas, "Theologica," I–II, Q. 95, a. 4, c.

24. Ibid., I–II, Q. 94, a. 4, c. "Sed ratio practica negotiatur circa contingentia, in quibus sunt operationes humanae; et ideo, si in communibus sit aliqua necessitas (1), quanto magis ad propria descenditur, tanto magis invenitur defectus."

25. See James V. Schall, "The Natural Law Bibliography," *American Journal of Jurisprudence* 40 (1995): 166–167.

26. Ibid., 168.

27. Aquinas, "Theologica," I–II, Q. 95, a. 2, c.

28. Alasdair MacIntyre, *First Principles, Final Ends and Contemporary Philosophical Issues: The Aquinas Lecture 1990* (Milwaukee: Marquette University Press, 1990), 59.

29. Aquinas, "Theologica," I–II, Q. 94, a. 6.

30. John E. Naus, "The Nature of the Practical Intellect According to Saint Thomas Aquinas," in *Analecta Gregoriana*, vol. 108 (Rome: Libreria Editrice Dell' Universita Gregoriana, 1959), 59. Cornelius Murphy, "Distributive Justice, Modern Significance," *American Journal of Jurisprudence* 17 (1972): 163; M. Gilson, *Moral Values and the Moral Life in the System of St. Thomas*, trans. L. Ward (St. Louis: B. Herder, 1931), 197.

31. Murphy, "Distributive Justice," 163.

32. Barry F. Smith, "Of Truth and Certainty in the Law: Reflections on the Legal Method," *American Journal of Jurisprudence* 30 (1985): 119.

33. J. Stanley McQuade, "Medieval 'Ratio' and Modern Formal Studies: A Reconsideration of Coke's Dictum That Law Is the Perfection of Reason," *American Journal of Jurisprudence* 38 (1993): 368.

34. O'Donoghue, "Law Beyond the Law," 156.

35. St. Thomas Aquinas, *On Kingship*, trans. Gerald B. Phelan (Toronto: Pontifical Institute of Mediaeval Studies, 1982), bk. I, ch. 8, 64.

36. John Finnis, "Natural Law and Legal Reasoning," in *Natural Law Theory*, ed. Robert P. George (Oxford: Clarendon Press, 1992), 148, compellingly argues,

The moral absolutes give legal reasoning its backbone: the exclusion of intentional killing, of intentional injury to the person and even the economic interests of the person, of deliberate deception for the sake of securing desired results, of enslavement which treats a human person as an object of a lower rank of being than the autonomous human subject. These moral absolutes, which *are* rationally determined and essentially determinate, constitute the most basic human rights, and the foundations of the criminal law and the law of intentional torts of delicts, not to mention all the rules, principles, and doctrines which penalize intentional deception, withdraw from it all direct legal support, and exclude it from the legal process.

37. Jeremy Waldron, "The Irrelevance of Moral Objectivity," in *Natural Law Theory*, ed. Robert P. George (Oxford: Clarendon Press, 1992), 160.

38. Raymond Dennehy, "The Ontological Basis of Human Rights," *The Thomist* 42 (1978): 461.

39. Ibid.

40. Judge Thomas had been accused of sexual harassment by Anita Hill in events and circumstances more than a decade old. The fact that Judge Thomas was a black conservative added to the tumultuous tone of the confirmation hearings.

41. Senator Biden queried Justice Thomas,

Just let me read some of your quotes in a speech before the *Federalist Society* at the University of Virginia, in a variation of that speech that you published in the *Harvard Journal of Law and Policy*, you praised the first justice [John] Harlan's opinion in *Plessy v. Ferguson*, and you said: "Implicit reliance on political first principles was implicit rather than explicit, as is generally appropriate for the Court's opinions. He gives us a foundation for interpreting not only cases involving race, but the entire Constitution in the scheme of protecting rights." You went on to say, "Harlan's opinion provides one of our best examples of natural law and higher law jurisprudence." Then you say, "The higher law background of the American government, whether explicitly appealed to or not, provides the only firm basis for a just and wise constitutional decision." Judge, what I would like to know is, I find it hard to understand how you can say what you are now saying, that natural law was only a—you were only talking about the philosophy in a general philosophic sense, and not how it informed or impacted upon constitutional interpretation. *Congressional Quarterly*, vol. 47, 102nd Cong., 1st sess., 1991, 18-E

42. Judge Thomas responded,

My purpose was this, in looking at this entire area: The question for me was from a political theory standpoint. You and I are sitting here in Washington, D.C., with Abraham Lincoln or with Frederick Douglass, and from a theory, how do we get out of slavery? There is no constitutional amendment. There is no provision in the Constitution. But by what theory? Repeatedly Lincoln referred to the notion that all men are created equal. And that was my attraction to, or beginning of my attraction to, this approach. But I did not—I would maintain that I did not feel that natural rights or natural law has a basis or has a use in constitutional adjudication. My interest in this area started with the notion, with a simple question: How do you end slavery? By what theory do you end slavery? After you end slavery, by what theory do you protect the right of someone who was a former slave or someone like my grandfather, for example, to enjoy to fruits of his or her labor? Ibid.

43. Suzanna Sherry, "Natural Law in the States," *University of Cincinnati Law Review* 61 (1992): 173, argues that our natural law heritage is not the express pronouncement of our Founding Fathers, but the laws that emerged from their deliberations: "The best evidence in support of a natural law heritage, then, is not what the founders (or the philosophers who influenced them) *said*, but what courts *did*."

44. Jean Porter, *The Recovery of Virtue* (Louisville, Ky.: Westminster/John Knox Press, 1990), 172.

45. St. Thomas Aquinas, *Summa Contra Gentiles*, trans. Vernon J. Bourke, vol. 4 (Notre Dame: University of Notre Dame Press, 1975), bk. III, pt. II, ch. 122, 7.

46. Justice Antonin Scalia, "Remarks at Thomas Aquinas College," 24 January 1997. Available at <http://johnh.wheaton.edu/~jonmitch/tac.html>, visited 31 August 1998, responded to a query on the role of natural law as follows:

I don't deal in natural law. I'm an American judge interpreting American laws. I mean, I have my notions of what is moral and immoral, and at the point where American law requires me to do something I believe immoral, I will resign. But I will not alter the meaning of a law that's been enacted, on the basis of my notions of natural law. How can I do that? The only power I derive is from the Constitution. I can't bite the hand that's feeding me.

47. *Planned Parenthood v. Casey*, 505 U.S. 833 (1992).

48. Justice Scalia's dislike for the progeny of *Roe v. Wade* is well known:

Roe's mandate for abortion on demand destroyed the compromises of the past, rendered compromise impossible for the future, and required the entire issue to be resolved uniformly, at the national level. At the same time, *Roe* created a vast new class of abortion consumers and abortion proponents by eliminating the moral opprobrium that had attached to the act. ("If the Constitution *guarantees* abortion, how can it be bad?"—not an accurate line of thought, but a natural one.) Many favor all of those developments, and it is not for me to say that they are wrong. But to portray *Roe* as the statesmanlike "settlement" of a divisive issue, a jurisprudential peace of Westphalia that is worth preserving, is nothing less than Orwellian. *Roe* fanned into life an issue that has inflamed our national politics in general, and has obscured with its smoke the selection of Justices to this Court, in particular, ever since. And by keeping us in the abortion-umpiring business, it is the perpetuation of that disruption, rather than of any *Pax Roeana* that the Court's new majority decrees. Ibid., 995–996.

49. *Roy Romer, et al. v. Richard G. Evans, et al.*, 517 U.S. 620 (1996).
50. As an example:

Of course it is our moral heritage that one should not hate any human being or class of human beings. But I had thought that one could consider certain conduct reprehensible—murder, for example, or polygamy, or cruelty to animals—and could exhibit even "animus" toward such conduct. Surely that is the only sort of "animus" at issue here: moral disapproval of homosexual conduct, the same sort of moral disapproval that produced the centuries old criminal laws that we held constitutional in *Bowers*. Ibid., 645.

51. Ibid. *Bowers v. Hardwick*, 478 U.S. 186 (1986).
52. *Murphy v. Ramsey*, 114, U.S. 15, 45 (1885).
53. *Romer v. Evans*, 646–649.
54. See the *Code of Judicial Conduct* (hereafter *CJC*), adopted by the Supreme Court, 9 October 1995.
55. St. Thomas Aquinas, *Summa Theologica*, trans. English Dominican Friars, vol. 2 (New York: Benziger, 1947), II–II, Q. 67; *CJC*, Preamble.
56. Aquinas, *Theologica*, vol. 2, II–II, Q. 67, a. 2.
57. *CJC*, 4.
58. Aquinas, *Theologica*, vol. 2, II–II, Q. 59, a. 2; *CJC*, Canon 2(A).
59. Aquinas, *Theologica*, vol. 2, II–II, Q. 68.
60. See *CJC*, Canon 3(A):

a. Judges should be faithful to the law and maintain professional competence in it.
b. Judges should be unswayed by partisan interests, public clamor or fear of criticism.
c. Judges should maintain order and decorum in proceedings before them.
d. Judges should be patient, dignified and courteous to litigants, jurors, witnesses, lawyers and others with whom judges deal in their official capacity, and should require similar conduct of lawyers, and of the staff, court officials and other subject to their direction and control.

61. Ibid., 5.
62. Aquinas, *Theologica*, vol. 2, II–II, Q. 60, a. 1, ad 2. "Quod homo spiritualis ex habitu charitatis habet inclinationem ad recte judicandum de omnibus secundum regulas divinas, ex quibus judicium per donum sapientiae pronuntiat; sicut justus per virtutem prudentiae pronuntiat judicium ex regulis juris."
63. American Bar Association, *Model Rules of Professional Conduct* (hereafter *MPR*) (1995).
64. Ibid., Preamble.
65. Ibid.
66. Ibid., Rule 3.5.

67. Ibid., Rule 3.1.

68. Aquinas, *Theologica*, vol. 2, II–II, Q. 68, a. 3; Q. 69, a. 1; Q. 69, a. 3, 4.

69. Ibid., II–II, Q. 71, a. 3, ad 1. "Quamvis enim laudabilis videatur quantum ad peritiam artis, tamen peccat quantum ad injustitiam voluntatis, quia abutitur arte ad malum."

70. *MPR*, Rule 3.3; Rule 3.4.

71. Ibid., Rule 3.3(2).

72. Thomas could only agree wholeheartedly with the language of ibid., Rule 3.4.

A lawyer shall not:

(a) unlawfully obstruct another party's access to evidence or unlawfully alter, destroy or conceal a document or other material having potential evidentiary value. A lawyer shall not counsel or assist another person to do any such act;

(b) falsify evidence, counsel or assist a witness to testify falsely, or offer an inducement to a witness that is prohibited by law;

(c) knowingly disobey an obligation under the rule of a tribunal except for an open refusal based on an assertion that no valid obligation exists;

(d) in pretrial procedure, make a frivolous discovery request or fail to make reasonably diligent effort to comply with a legally proper discovery request by an opposing party;

(e) in trial, allude to any matter that the lawyer does not reasonably believe is relevant or that will not be supported by admissible evidence, assert personal knowledge of facts in issue except when testifying as a witness, or state a personal opinion as to the justness of a cause, the credibility of a witness, the culpability of a civil litigant or the guilt or innocence of an accused; or

(f) request a person other than a client to refrain from voluntarily giving relevant information to another party unless:

(1) the person is a relative or an employee or other agent of a client; and

(2) the lawyer reasonably believes that the person's interests will not be adversely affected by refraining from giving such information.

73. Ibid., Rule 8.4, includes the following description of misconduct:

It is professional misconduct for a lawyer to:

(a) violate or attempt to violate the rules of professional conduct, knowingly assist or induce another to do so, or do so through the acts of another;

(b) commit a criminal act that reflects adversely on the lawyer's honesty, trustworthiness or fitness as a lawyer in other respects;

(c) engage in conduct involving dishonesty, fraud, deceit or misrepresentation

(d) engage in conduct that is prejudicial to the administration of justice;

(e) state or imply an ability to influence improperly a government agency or official; or

(f) knowingly assist a judge or judicial officer in conduct that is a violation of applicable rules of judicial conduct or other law.

74. Ibid., Rule 4.1.

75. Aquinas, *Theologica*, vol. 2, II–II, Q. 71, a. 3; Q. 68, a. 3; Q. 69, a. 1, 2; Q. 70, a. 4; Q. 70, a. 2; Q. 71, a. 2.

76. *MPR*, Rule 3.8.

77. Ibid., Rule 6.1.

78. Ibid.,

A lawyer should aspire to render at least (50) hours of pro bono publico legal services per year. In fulfilling this responsibility, the lawyer should:

(a) provide a substantial majority of the (50) hours of legal services without fee or expectation of fee to:

(1) persons of limited means or

(2) charitable, religious, civic, community, governmental and educational organizations in matters which are designed primarily to address the needs of persons of limited means; and

(b) provide any additional services through:

(1) delivery of legal services at no fee or substantially reduced fee to individuals, groups or organizations seeking to secure or protect civil rights, civil liberties or public rights, or charitable, religious, civil, community, governmental and educational organizations in matters in furtherance of their organizational purposes, where the payment of standard legal fees would significantly deplete the organizations's economic resources or would be otherwise inappropriate;

(2) delivery of legal services at a substantially reduced fee to persons of limited means; or

(3) participation in activities for improving the law, the legal system or the legal profession.

In addition, a lawyer should voluntarily contribute financial support to organizations that provide legal services to persons of limited means.

79. Plato, *The Laws of Plato*, ed. Thomas L. Pangle (New York: Basic Books, 1980).

80. Aquinas, *Theologica*, vol. 2, II–II, Q. 71, a. 3, sed contra. "Sed advocatus defendens causam injustam, impio praebet auxilium. Ergo peccando iram Domini meretur."

81. Scalia, "Interpretation," 3.

82. MacIntyre, *First Principles*, 66.

83. Aquinas, *Gentiles*, III–II, ch. 128, 3.

84. Aquinas, *Kingship*, II, ch. IV (I,15), 116.

Bibliography

WORKS OF ST. THOMAS AQUINAS

An Apology for the Religious Orders. Ed. John Procter. St. Louis: B. Herder, 1902.

Basic Writings of St. Thomas Aquinas. Ed. Anton C. Pegis. New York: Random House, 1945.

Commentary on the Nicomachean Ethics. Trans. C. I. Litzinger. Chicago: Henry Regnery, 1964.

De Regimine Principum. Trans. G. B. Phelan. Toronto: St. Michael's College, 1935.

"De regno ad regem Cypri (De regimine prinicpum)." In *Opuscula Omnia necnon Opera Minora*, edited by J. Perrier. Paris: Lethielleux, 1947.

La Notion de la Loi. Trans. Andre Stang. Paris: Editions et Publications Contemporaines, 1926.

On Aristotle's Love and Friendship. Trans. Pierre Conway. Providence: Providence College Press, 1951.

On Kingship. Trans. Gerald B. Phelan. Toronto: Pontifical Institute of Mediaeval Studies, 1982.

Scriptum super libros Sententiarium (Commentary on the Sentences). 4 vols. Ed. P. Mandonnet and M. F. Moos. Paris: P. Lethielleux, 1929, 1933, 1947.

Sententia libri Ethicorum. Leonine ed. Vol. 47. Roma: Polyglotta, 1969.

Summa Contra Gentiles. Trans. Vernon J. Bourke. Notre Dame: University of Notre Dame Press, 1975.

Summa Theologica. Vols. 2–4. Paris: Bloud et Barral, Bibliopolas, 1882.

Summa Theologica. Trans. English Dominican Friars. 22 vols. London: Burns, Oates, and Washbourne, 1912–1936.

Summa Theologica. Trans. English Dominican Friars. 3 vols. New York: Benziger, 1947.

Treatise on Law. Ed. R. J. Henle. Notre Dame: University of Notre Dame Press, 1993.

Treatise on the Virtues. Trans. John A. Oesterle. Notre Dame: University of Notre Dame Press, 1966.

"Quaestiones de malo." In *Quaestiones disputatae*, Marietti edition. Vol. 2. 8th ed. Turin: Editio Tourini, 1949.

Quaestiones de veritate. Ed. A. Dondaine. Vol. 22. Roma: Polyglotta, 1970–1974.

OTHER PRIMARY SOURCES

Abaelardus, Petrus. *Opera.* Trans. Victor Cousin. New York: Georg Olms Verlag, 1970.

Abailard, Peter. *Sic Et Non: A Critical Edition.* Trans. Blanche E. Boyer and Richard McKeon. Chicago: University of Chicago Press, 1976–1977.

Abelard, Peter. *Collationes.*

———. *Ethics.* Trans. David Luscombe. Oxford: Clarendon Press, 1971.

———. *Letters IX–XIV.* Ed. L. J. Engels. Rotterdam: Groningen, 1983.

Alberti Magni. *De Bono.* Adeibus Aschendorff: Monasterii Westfalorum, 1951.

———. *De Intellectu et Intelligibili.* Adeibus Aschendorff: Monasterii Westfalorum, 1951.

———. *Opera Omnia.* Adeibus Aschendorff: Monasterii Westfalorum, 1968.

———. *Summa de creaturis.* Borgnet edition. Paris: Apud Ludovicum Vives, 1890–1895.

———. *Super Ethica.* Adeibus Aschendorff: Monasterii Westfalorum, 1987.

Albertus, Magnus. *Opera Omnia.* Borgnet edition. Paris: Apud Ludovicum Vives, 1890–1895.

Albertus, Magnus. *Summa Universae Theologica.* Florentiam: Ex Typographia Collegiis Bonaventurae, 1948.

Anselm. *Cur Deus Homo.* In *Opera Omnia.* Trans. Franciscus Salesius Schmitt. Stuttgaart: Friedrich Frommann Verlag, 1940.

———. *De Conceptu Virginali et de Originali Peccato.* In *Opera Omnia.* Trans. Franciscus Salesius Schmitt. Stuttgaart: Friedrich Frommann Verlag, 1940.

———. *De Veritate.* In *Opera Omnia.* Trans. Franciscus Salesius Schmitt. Stuttgaart: Friedrich Frommann Verlag, 1940.

———. *St. Anselm's Treatise on Free Will.* Kent, Ohio: Toucan Press, 1977.

Anselmi, S. *Opera Omnia.* Trans. Franciscus Salesius Schmitt. Stuttgaart: Friedrich Frommann Verlag, 1940.

Aristotle. "Metaphysics." In *The Basic Works of Aristotle*, edited by Richard McKeon. New York: Random House, 1941.

———. *Nicomachean Ethics.* Trans. Martin Ostwald. New York: Bobbs-Merrill, 1962.

———. "Nicomachean Ethics." In *The Basic Works of Aristotle*, edited by Richard McKeon. New York: Random House, 1941.

Augustine, St. *The Confessions of St. Augustine.* Trans. John K. Ryan. New York: Doubleday, 1960.

———. *On Free Choice of the Will.* Trans. Anna S. Benjamin and L. H. Hackstaff. New York: Macmillan, 1964.

Averroes. *Averroes on Plato's Republic.* Trans. Ralph Lerner. Ithaca, N.Y.: Cornell University Press, 1974.

Avicenna. *Remarks and Admonitions: Part One, Logic.* Trans. Shams Constantine Inati. Toronto: Pontifical Institute of Medieval Studies, 1984.

Bellarmini, Roberti. *Opera Omnia, De Summo Pontefice, Tomus Primus.* Naples, 1872.

Boethius. *In Ciceronis Topica.* Trans. Eleonore Stump. Ithaca, N.Y.: Cornell University Press, 1988.

Bonaventure, St. *Breviloquium.* Venetiis, 1894.

Cicero. "On the Laws: Book One." In *Selected Works of Cicero*, translated by Harry M. Hubbett. New York: Walter J. Black, 1948.

Duns Scotus, John. *Duns Scotus on the Will and Morality.* Ed. William A. Frank. Trans. Allan Wolter. Washington, D.C.: Catholic University of America Press, 1986.

Gratian. *The Treatise on Laws (Decretum DD. 1–20).* Trans. James Gordley. Washington, D.C.: Catholic University of America Press, 1993.

Isidore of Seville, St. *Isidori Hispalensis Episcopi Etymologiarum sive Originum Libri.* Ed. W. Lindsay. London: Oxford University Press, 1962.

———. *The Letters of St. Isidore of Seville.* Trans. Gordon B. Ford, Jr. 2d ed. Amsterdam: Adolf M. Hakkert, 1970.

John of St. Thomas. *Cursus Philosophicus Thomisticus.* 3 vols. Paris: Vives, 1883.

Merkelbach, Benedictus, O.P. "De judiciis publicis." In *Summa Theologiae Moralis.* Paris: Desclee, 1932.

Plato. *The Laws of Plato.* Ed. Thomas L. Pangle. New York: Basic Books, 1980.

Tully. *Three Books of Offices.* Trans. T. Cockman. London, 1732.

William of Ockham. *Philosophical Writings: A Selection.* Trans. Philotheus Boehner. Indianapolis, Ind.: Hackett, 1989.

William of Ockham. *Quodlibetal Questions.* Trans. Alfred J. Freddoso and Francis E. Kelley. New Haven: Yale University Press, 1991.

SECONDARY SOURCES

American Bar Association. *Model Rules of Professional Conduct.*

American Jurisprudence, Natural Law, and Clarence Thomas. Available at <http:aaps.kiz.mi.us/~smitha/ct1.html>.

Araujo, R. J. "Thomas Aquinas: Prudence, Justice, and the Law." *Loyola Law Review* 40 (1995): 897–922.

Armstrong, R. A. *Primary and Secondary Precepts in Thomistic Natural Law Teaching.* The Hague: Martinus Nijhoff, 1966.

Aubert, Jean-Marie. *Le Droit Romain Dans L'oeuvre De Saint Thomas.* Paris: Librairie Philosophique J. Virn, 1955.

Barnett, Randy E. "The Justice of Restitution." *American Journal of Jurisprudence* 25 (1980): 117–132.

Benedictis, Matthew M. *The Social Thought of St. Bonaventure.* Westport, Conn.: Greenwood Press, 1972.

Bentham, Jeremy. *The Principles of Morals and Legislation.* New York: Hafner, 1948.

Bettoni, Efrem. *Duns Scotus: The Basic Principles of His Philosophy.* Trans. Bernadine Bonansea. Washington, D.C.: Catholic University of America Press, 1961.

Biden, Joseph R., Jr. "Law and Natural Law: Questions for Judge Thomas." *The Washington Post,* 8 September 1991.

Binyon, Millard Pierce. *The Virtues: A Methodological Study in Thomistic Ethics.* Chicago: University of Chicago Press, 1948.

Boedder, Bernard. *Natural Theology.* New York: Longmans-Green, 1927.

Bourke, Vernon J. "The Ethical Justification of Legal Punishment." *American Journal of Jurisprudence* 22 (1977): 1–18.

———. "Justice as Equitable Reciprocity: Aquinas Updated." *American Journal of Jurisprudence* 27 (1982): 17–31.

———. "The Nicomachean Ethics and Thomas Aquinas." In *St. Thomas Aquinas 1274–1974,* edited by Arman D. Maurer. Toronto: Pontifical Institute of Mediaeval Studies, 1974.

———. "Right Reason in Contemporary Ethics." *The Thomist* 38 (1974): 106–124.

———. "Thomistic Bibliography: 1920–1940." *Modern Schoolman* 21 (1945): entire supp.

Brennan, Rose E. *The Intellectual Virtues According to the Philosophy of St. Thomas.* Washington, D.C.: Catholic University of America Press, 1941.

Brown, Louis M., and Thomas L. Shaffer. "Toward a Jurisprudence for the Law Office." *American Journal of Jurisprudence* 17 (1972): 125–152.

Brumbaugh, Robert S. "Aristotle's Outline of the Problems of First Philosophy." *Review of Metaphysics* 7 (1954).

Buijs, Joseph A., ed. *Maimonides: A Collection of Critical Essays.* Notre Dame: University of Notre Dame Press, 1988.

Buytaert, E. M., ed., *Peter Abelard: Proceedings of the International Conference, Louvain, May 10–12, 1971.* Louvain: Leuven University Press, 1974.

Callahan, Thomas G. *William Ockham and Natural Law.* Ann Arbor: Xerox University Microfilms, 1975.

Calvert, Brian. "Aquinas on Punishment and the Death Penalty." *American Journal of Jurisprudence* 37 (1992): 259–281.

Centore, F. F. "Aquinas on Inner Space." *Canadian Journal of Philosophy* 4 (1974): 351–363.

Cessario, Romanus. *The Moral Virtues and Theological Ethics.* Notre Dame: University of Notre Dame Press, 1991.

Chroust, Anton-Hermann. "The Fundamental Ideas in St. Augustine's Philosophy of Law." *American Journal of Jurisprudence* 18 (1973): 57–79.

———. "The Philosophy of Law from St. Augustine to St. Thomas Aquinas." *New Scholasticism* 20 (1946): 26–71.

————. "The Philosophy of Law of St. Thomas Aquinas: His Fundamental Ideas and Some of His Historical Precursors." *American Journal of Jurisprudence* 19 (1974): 1–38.

Clancy, Patrick M. J. "St. Thomas on Law." In *The Summa Theologica* translated by English Dominican Friars. Vol. 3. New York: Benziger Brothers, 1947.

Clark, Ralph W. "Aquinas on Intentions." *The Thomist* 40 (1976): 303–310.

Clarke, Francis Palmer. *The Intellect in the Philosophy of St. Thomas.* Philadelphia: St. Michael's College, 1928.

Connell, Fr. Francis J. *Morals in Politics and Professions: A Guide for Catholics in Public Life.* Westminster, Md.: Newman Bookshop, 1946.

Crowe, Michael Bertram. *The Changing Profile of the Natural Law.* The Hague: Martinus Nijhoff, 1977.

————. "Natural Law Terminology in the Late 12th and Early 13th Centuries." *Tijdschrift voor Filosofie* 39 (1977): 409–420.

————. "Natural Law Theory Today: Some Materials for Re-Assessment." *Irish Ecclesiastical Review* 109 (1968): 353.

————. "Synderesis and the Notion of Law in St. Thomas." In *Actes du Premier Congres International de Philosophie Medievale.* Paris: Louvain, 1958.

————. "The Term *Synderesis* and the Scholastics." *Irish Theological Quarterly* 23 (1956): 151–164, 228–245.

Cunningham, Stanley B. "Albertus Magnus and the Problem of Moral Virtue." *Vivarium* 7 (1969): 81–119.

Damich, Edward J. "The Essence of Law According to Thomas Aquinas." *American Journal of Jurisprudence* 30 (1985): 79–96.

Davitt, Thomas E. *The Nature of Law.* St. Louis: B. Herder, 1951.

De Koninck, Charles. "In Defense of Saint Thomas." *Laval Theologique et Philosophique* 2 (1945).

De Wulf, Maurice. *A History of Mediaeval Philosophy.* Trans. Ernest C. Messenger. 3d ed. New York: Longmans-Green, 1935.

Deferrari, Roy J. *A Complete Index of the Summa Theologica of St. Thomas Aquinas.* Baltimore: s.n., 1956.

————. *Lexicon of St. Thomas Aquinas.* Washington, D.C.: Catholic University of America Press, 1948–1953.

Degnan, Daniel A., Jr. "Two Models of Positive Law in Aquinas: A Study of the Relationship of Positive Law and Natural Law." *The Thomist* 46 (1982): 1–32.

Dennehy, Raymond. "The Case for Natural Law Re-Examined." *Natural Law Forum* 1 (1956): 5–52.

————. "The Ontological Basis of Human Rights." *The Thomist* 42 (1978): 434–463.

Dolan, Joseph V. "Natural Law and Modern Jurisprudence." *Laval Theologique et Philosophique* 16 (1960): 32–63.

————. "Natural Law and the Judicial Function." *Laval Theologique et Philosophique* 16 (1960): 94–141.

Donnelly, P. T. "St. Thomas and the Ultimate Purpose of Creation." *Theological Studies* 2 (1941): 53–83.

Eisgruber, Christopher. "Justice Story, Slavery, and Natural Law Foundations of American Constitutionalism." *University of Chicago Law Review* 55 (1988): 273–327.

Eschmann, Ignatius T. *The Ethics of St. Thomas Aquinas.* Toronto: Pontifical Institute of Mediaeval Studies, 1997.

———. "Studies on the Notion of Society in St. Thomas Aquinas." *Mediaeval Studies* 9 (1947): 19–55.

Farrell, Walter. *The Natural Moral Law According to St. Thomas and Suarez.* Ditchling: St. Dominic's Press, 1930.

Finnis, John. "Natural Law and Legal Reasoning." In *Natural Law Theory*, edited by Robert P. George. Oxford: Clarendon Press, 1992.

———. "Object and Intention in Moral Judgments According to Aquinas." *The Thomist* 55 (1991): 1–27.

Friel, George Quentin. *Punishment in the Philosophy of Saint Thomas Aquinas and among Some Primitive Peoples.* Washington, D.C.: Catholic University of America Press, 1939.

Froelich, Gregory. "Ultimate End and Common Good in Summa Theologiae, Secunda Pars." *The Thomist* 57 (1993): 609.

Garrigou-Lagrange, R. "La prudence et la vie interieure." *Vie Spirit* 51 (1937): 24–41.

Gelinas, E. T. "Right and Law in Thomas Aquinas." In *Myth and Philosophy*, edited by George F. McLean. Vol. 45. Washington, D.C.: American Catholic Philosophical Association, 1971.

George, Robert P., ed. *Natural Law Theory.* Oxford: Clarendon Press, 1992.

Gilson, Etienne. *The Christian Philosophy of St. Thomas Aquinas.* Trans. L. K. Shook. New York: Random House, 1956.

———. *The Philosophy of St. Bonaventure.* New York: Sheed & Ward, 1938.

———. *The Philosophy of St. Thomas Aquinas.* Trans. Edward Bullough. 2d ed. St. Louis: B. Herder, 1929.

Gilson, M. *Moral Values and the Moral Life in the System of St. Thomas.* Trans. L. Ward. St. Louis: B. Herder, 1931.

Golding, Martin P. "Aquinas and Some Contemporary Natural Law Theories." *Proceedings of the American Catholic Philosophical Association* 48 (1974): 238–247.

Grazin, Igor. "Natural Law as a Form of Legal Studies." *American Journal of Jurisprudence* 37 (1992): 1–16.

Grisez, Germane, Dennis Boyle, and John Finnis. "Practical Principles, Moral Truth, and Ultimate Ends." *American Journal of Jurisprudence* 32 (1987): 122–125.

Gustafson, Gustaf J. *The Theory of Natural Appetency in the Philosophy of St. Thomas.* Washington, D.C.: Catholic University of America Press, 1944.

Haine, Antoine J.J.F. *Theologiae Moralis Elementa.* 3d ed. Lovanii: C. Fonteyn, 1894.

Hall, Jerome. "Plato's Legal Philosophy." *Indiana Law Journal* 31 (1955–1956).

Hallett, Garth. *Christian Moral Reasoning.* Notre Dame: Notre Dame University Press, 1983.

Harding, Michael. "True Justice in Courts of Law." In St. Thomas Aquinas, *Summa Theologica*, translated by the English Dominican Friars. Vol. 3. New York: Benziger, 1947.

Hegel, G.W.F. *Science of Logic*. Trans. Miller. London: Allen, 1969.

Henle, Robert John. "Saint Thomas Aquinas and American Law." In *Thomistic Papers II*, edited by Leonard A. Kennedy and Jack C. Marler. Houston: Center for Thomistic Studies, 1986.

The Holmes–Pollock Letters. Vol. 2. Cambridge, 1941.

Jaffa, Harry V. *Thomism and Aristotelianism: A Study of the Commentary by Thomas Aquinas on the Nicomachean Ethics*. Chicago: University of Chicago Press, 1952.

Jenkins, Iredell. "The Concept of Rights and the Competence of Courts." *American Journal of Jurisprudence* 18 (1973): 1–17.

Kendzierski, Lottie. "Object and Intention in the Moral Act." *Proceedings of the American Catholic Philosophical Association* 24 (1950): 102–110.

Kors, J. B. *La Justice Primitive et Le Péché Originel*. Paris: Librairie Philosophique J. Vrin, 1930.

Kraut, Richard. "Are There Natural Rights in Aristotle?" *Review of Metaphysics* 49 (1996): 755–774.

Kreilkamp, K. *The Metaphysical Foundations of Thomistic Jurisprudence*. Washington, D.C.: Catholic University of America Press, 1939.

Kreyche, Robert J. "Virtue and Law in Aquinas: Some Modern Implications." *Southwestern Journal of Philosophy* 5 (1974): 111–140.

Leclercq, Jacques. "Natural Law the Unknown." *Natural Law Forum* 1 (1962).

———. "Note sur la justice." *R N P* 28 (1926): 269–283.

Lerner, Max, ed. *The Mind and Faith of Justice Holmes*. New York: Modern Library, 1954.

Lewis, C. S. *Studies in Words*. Cambridge: Cambridge University Press, 1961.

Luscombe, D. E. *Peter Abelard's Ethics*. Oxford: Oxford University Press, 1971.

MacCormick, Neil. "Natural Law and the Separation of Law and Morals." In *Natural Law Theory*, edited by Robert P. George. Oxford: Clarendon Press, 1992.

MacGuigan, Mark R. "The Problem of Law and Morals in Contemporary Jurisprudence." *Catholic Lawyer* 8 (1962): 293.

MacIntyre, Alasdair. *After Virtue*. 2d ed. Notre Dame: University of Notre Dame Press, 1984.

———. *First Principles, Final Ends and Contemporary Philosophical Issues: The Aquinas Lecture 1990*. Milwaukee, Wisc.: Marquette University Press, 1990.

———. *Whose Justice? Which Rationality?* Notre Dame: University of Notre Dame Press, 1988.

Madden, Marie R. *Political Theory and Law in Medieval Spain*. New York: Fordham University Press, 1930.

Marenbon, John. *The Philosophy of Peter Abelard*. Cambridge: Cambridge University Press, 1997.

Mather, Henry. "Natural Law and Right Answers." *American Journal of Jurisprudence* 38 (1993): 297–334.

McCool, Gerald A. "History, Insight and Judgment in Thomism." *International Philosophical Quarterly* 27 (1987): 299–313.

———. "Is Thomas's Way of Philosophizing Still Viable Today?" In *The Future of Thomism*, edited by Deal W. Hudson and Dennis W. Moran. Notre Dame: University of Notre Dame Press, 1992.

McDonnell, Kevin. "William of Ockham and Situation Ethics." *American Journal of Jurisprudence* 16 (1971): 25–35.

McInerny, Ralph. *Ethica Thomistica: The Moral Philosophy of Thomas Aquinas.* Washington, D.C.: Catholic University of America Press, 1982.

———. "Prudence and Conscience." *The Thomist* 38 (1974): 291–305.

McNabb, Vincent. *St. Thomas Aquinas and the Law.* London: Blackfriars, 1955.

McQuade, J. Stanley. "Medieval 'Ratio' and Modern Formal Studies a Reconsideration of Coke's Dictum That Law Is the Perfection of Reason." *American Journal of Jurisprudence* 38 (1993): 359–389.

Messner, J. *Social Ethics: Natural Law in the Modern World.* Trans. J. J. Doherty. St. Louis: B. Herder, 1952.

Miethe, Terry L., and Vernon J. Bourke. *Thomistic Bibliography, 1940–1978.* Westport, Conn.: Greenwood Press, 1980.

Miller, Eugene F. "Prudence and the Rule of Law." *American Journal of Jurisprudence* 24 (1979): 181–206.

Mirhady, David C. "Aristotle on the Rhetoric of Law." *Greek, Roman and Byzantine Studies* 31 (1990): 393–410.

Morrow, Glenn R. "Plato and the Rule of Law." *Philosophical Review* 10 (1941): 105–126.

Mullady, Brian T. "The Meaning of the Term 'Moral' in St. Thomas Aquinas." In *Studi Tomistica.* Vol. 27. Vatican City: Libreria Editric Vaticana, 1986.

Mulligan, Robert W. "Ratio Inferior and Ratio Superior in St. Albert and St. Thomas." *The Thomist* 19 (1956): 339–367.

———. "Ratio Superior and Ratio Inferior: The Historical Background." *New Scholasticism* 29 (1955): 1–32.

Murphy, Cornelius. "Distributive Justice, Modern Significance." *American Journal of Jurisprudence* 17 (1972): 153–165.

Naus, John E. "The Nature of the Practical Intellect According to Saint Thomas Aquinas." In *Analecta Gregoriana.* Vol. 108. Rome: Libreria Editrice Dell' Universita Gregoriana, 1959.

Nelson, Daniel Mark. *The Priority of Prudence: Virtue and Natural Law in Thomas Aquinas and the Implications for Modern Ethics.* University Park: Pennsylvania State University Press, 1992.

Nemeth, Charles P. *Law and Evidence: A Primer for Criminal Justice, Criminology, Law and Legal Studies.* Upper Saddle River, N.J.: Prentice Hall, 2001.

———. *Litigation, Pleadings and Arbitration.* 2d ed. Cincinnati: Anderson, 1997.

———. *The Paralegal Resource Manual.* 2d ed. 2 vols. Cincinnati: Anderson, 1995.

Newman, Jeremiah. *Foundations of Justice*. Cork: Cork University Press, 1954.

Oakley, F. "Medieval Theories of Natural Law: William of Ockham and the Significance of the Voluntarist Tradition." *Natural Law Forum* 6 (1961): 65–83.

O'Donoghue, Noel Dermot. "The Law Beyond the Law." *American Journal of Jurisprudence* 18 (1973): 150–164.

O'Mahony. *Man's Ultimate End: Moral Principles and Practice*. Cambridge: Sheed and Ward, 1932.

O'Meara, Joseph. "Natural Law and Everyday Law." *Natural Law Forum* 83 (1960).

O'Neil, Charles. "Prudence, the Incommunicable Wisdom." In *Essays in Thomism*, edited by R. E. Brennan. New York: Sheed and Ward, 1942.

O'Neill, Onora. "Justice and the Virtues." *American Journal of Jurisprudence* 34 (1989).

O'Toole, G. B. "Truth Is in the Judgement." *New Scholasticism* 27 (1943): 1–15.

Owens, Joseph. "Judgment and Truth in Aquinas." *Mediaeval Studies* 32: 1138–1158.

Pace, E. A. "Order in the Philosophy of St. Thomas." *New Scholasticism* 2 (1928): 51–72.

———. "The Teleology of St. Thomas." *New Scholasticism* 1 (1927): 213–231.

Panagiotou, Spiro, ed. *Justice, Law and Method in Plato and Aristotle*. Edmonton, Alberta: Academic, 1987.

Pegis, Anton C. "Nature and Spirit: Some Reflections on the Problem of the End of Man." *Proceedings of the American Catholic Philosophical Association* 23 (1949–1950): 3–20.

———. "St. Thomas and the *Nicomachean Ethics*: Some Reflections on *Summa Contra Gentiles* III, 44, 5." *Mediaeval Studies* 25 (1963): 1–25.

Porter, Jean. *The Recovery of Virtue*. Louisville, Ky.: Westminster/John Knox Press, 1990.

Postema, Gerald J. *Bentham and the Common Law Tradition*. Oxford: Clarendon Press, 1986.

Quinn, John F. *The Historical Constitution of St. Bonaventure's Philosophy*. Toronto: Pontifical Institute of Medieval Studies, 1973.

Rand, E. K. *Cicero in the Courtroom of St. Thomas Aquinas*. Milwaukee, Wisc.: Marquette University Press, 1946.

Regan, George M. "The Need for Renewal in Natural Law." *Catholic Lawyer* 135 (1966).

Reilly, George C. *The Psychology of Saint Albert the Great Compared with That of Saint Thomas*. Washington, D.C.: Catholic University of America Press, 1934.

Reinhard de Liechty, L'Abbe. *Albert Le Grand et Saint Thomas D'Aquin ou La Science Au Moyen Age*. Paris: Societe Generale de Librairie Catholique, 1880.

Roberts, Lawrence David. *John Duns Scotus and the Concept of Human Freedom*. Ann Arbor, Mich.: Xerox University Microfilms, 1969.

Rommen, Heinrich A. *The Natural Law*. Trans. T. Hanley. St. Louis: B. Herder, 1948.

Rooney, Miriam Theresa. "Justice, Law and Juridical Decision-Making." *Log Anal* 14 (1971): 375–386.

Ross, James F. "Justice Is Reasonableness: Aquinas on Human Law and Morality." *The Thomist* 58 (1974): 86–103.

Rousselot, Pierre. *The Intellectualism of St. Thomas.* Trans. James E. O'Mahony. New York: Sheed and Ward, 1935.

Scalia, Justice Antonin. "Remarks at Holocaust Remembrance Ceremony." Washington, D.C., 8 May 1997.

———. "Remarks at Thomas Aquinas College." Thomas Aquinas College, New York, 24 January 1997.

———. "A Theory of Constitutional Interpretation." Speech delivered at Catholic University of America, Washington, D.C., 18 October 1996.

Schall, James V. "The Natural Law Bibliography." *American Journal of Jurisprudence* 40 (1995): 157–198.

Schram, Glenn. "Pluralism and the Common Good." *American Journal of Jurisprudence* 36 (1991): 119–124.

Sertillanges, A. D. *Foundations of Thomistic Philosophy.* St. Louis: B. Herder, 1931.

———. "Les Principes de la nature selon Saint Thomas d'Aquin." *Revue Thomiste* 17 (1909): 538–561.

———. *S. Thomas d'Aquin.* 2 vols. Paris: Felix Alcan, 1910.

Shahan, Robert W., and Francis J. Kovach, eds. *Bonaventure and Aquinas: Enduring Philosophers.* Norman: University of Oklahoma Press, 1976.

Sherry, Suzanna. "Natural Law in the States." *University of Cincinnati Law Review* 61 (1992): 1–222.

Sherwin, Michael. "St. Thomas and the Common Good. The Theological Perspective: An Invitation to Dialogue." *Angelicum* 70 (1993): 307–328.

Simon, Yves R. *A General Theory of Authority.* Notre Dame: University of Notre Dame Press, 1962, 1980, 1991.

———. *Nature and Functions of Authority.* Milwaukee, Wisc.: Marquette University Press, 1940.

Skok, Charles D. *Prudent Civil Legislation According to St. Thomas and Some Controversial American Law.* Rome: Catholic Book Agency, 1967.

Smith, Barry F. "Of Truth and Certainty in the Law: Reflections on the Legal Method." *American Journal of Jurisprudence* 30 (1985): 97–119.

Staley, Kevin M. "Happiness: The Natural End of Man?" *The Thomist* 53 (1989): 215–234.

Sternburg, William P. "Natural Law in American Jurisprudence." *Notre Dame Lawyer* 13 (1938): 89–100.

Strauss, Leo. *The Argument and the Action of Plato's Laws.* Chicago: University of Chicago Press, 1975.

Sullivan, Daniel J. *An Introduction to Philosophy: The Perennial Principles of Classical Realist Tradition.* Rockford, Ill.: Jan Books, 1992.

"Symposium in Honor of St. Thomas and St. Bonaventure: 1274–1974." *International Philosophical Quarterly* 14 (1974).

"Thomas and Bonaventure: A Septicentenary Commemoration." *Proceedings of the American Catholic Philosophical Association* 48 (1974).

Tierney, Brian. *The Idea of Natural Rights: Studies on Natural Rights, Natural Law and Church Law*. Atlanta, Ga.: Scholars Press, 1998.

Tonneau, J. "La vertu cardinale de justice," *R S P T* 28 (1939): 71–73.

———. "The Teaching of the Thomist Tract on Law." *The Thomist* 34 (1970): 13–83.

Torrell, Jean-Pierre. *Saint Thomas Aquinas: The Person and His Work*. Trans. Robert Royal. Washington, D.C.: Catholic University of America Press, 1996.

Tremblay, Bruno. "Pourquoi la Prudence, Vertu Intellictuelle de L'agir, est-elle Pour Thomas D'Aquin une Sorte de Sagesse?" *Angelicum* 69 (1992): 37–53.

Tugwell, Simon, ed. and trans. *Albert and Thomas: Selected Writings*. New York: Paulist Press, 1988.

Tyrrell, Francis M. "Concerning the Nature and Function of the Act of Judgement." *New Scholasticism* 26 (1952).

———. *The Role of Assent in Judgment*. Washington, D.C.: Catholic University of America Press, 1948.

Vann, Gerald. *The Wisdom of Boethius*. London: Blackfriars, 1952.

Velez-Saenz, Jaime. *The Doctrine of the Common Good of Civil Society in the Works of St. Thomas Aquinas*. Notre Dame: University of Notre Dame Press, 1951.

Vier, Peter C. *Evidence and Its Function According to John Duns Scotus*. Franciscan Institute, 1951.

Waldron, Jeremy. "The Irrelevance of Moral Objectivity." In *Natural Law Theory*, edited by Robert P. George. Oxford: Clarendon Press, 1992.

Waluchow, W. J. "Professor Weinrib on Corrective Justice." In *Justice, Law and Method in Plato and Aristotle*, edited by Spiro Panagiotou. Edmonton, Alberta: Academic, 1987.

Weisheipl, James A. *Thomas d'Aquino and Albert His Teacher*. Toronto: Pontifical Institute of Mediaeval Studies, 1980.

Weithman, Paul J. "St. Thomas on the Motives of Unjust Acts." *Proceedings of the Catholic Philosophical Association* (1990): 204–220.

Westberg, Daniel. "Reason, Will and Legalism." *New Blackfriars* 68 (1987): 431–436.

———. *Right Practical Reason Aristotle, Action, and Prudence in Aquinas*. Oxford: Clarendon Press, 1994.

Wild, John. *Plato's Modern Enemies and the Theory of Natural Law*. London: University of Chicago Press, 1953.

Winfield, Richard Dien. "Rethinking the Legal Process." *American Journal of Jurisprudence* 39 (1994): 153–184.

Yartz, Frank "Order and Right Reason in Aquinas' Ethics." *Mediaeval Studies* 37 (1975): 407–418.

———. "Virtue as *Ordo* in Aquinas." *Modern Schoolman* 47 (1970): 305–320.

Zahnd, Eric G. "The Application of Universal Laws to Particular Cases: A Defense of Equity in Aristotelianism and Anglo-American Law." *Law and Contemporary Problems* 56 (1996): 263–295.

OTHER RESOURCES

Code of Judicial Conduct (CJC), 1995.

Congressional Quarterly 47 (1991).

Butchers' Union, ETC., Co. v. Crescent City, ETC., Co., 3 U.S. 652 (1883).

Calder et Wife v. Bull et Wife, U.S. III Dall. 386 (1798).

Cole v. City of La Grange, 5 U.S. 416 (1885).

D'Arcy v. Detchum, U.S. XI How. 165 (1850).

Despotis v. City of Sunset Hills, 619 SW 2d 814 (1981).

Fletcher v. Peck, U.S. VI Cranch 87 (1810).

Griswold v. Connecticut, 381 U.S. 479 (1965).

Hales v. Petit, 1 Plowd. Com. 253, 75 Eng. Rep. 387 (1561–1562).

Hays v. the Pacific Mail Steam-ship Company, U.S. XVII How. 597 (1854).

Murphy v. Ramsey, 114 U.S. 15, 45 (1885).

Pennoyer v. Neff, V U.S. 714 (1877).

Planned Parenthood v. Casey, 505 U.S. 833 (1992).

Roe v. Wade, 410 U.S. 113 (1973).

Roy Romer, et al. v. Richard G. Evans, et al., 517 U.S. 620 (1996).

Smith v. Ginther, 150 N.W. 2d 798 (1967).

St. Louis v. the Ferry Company, U.S. XI Wall. 428 (1871).

Terrett and others v. Taylor and others, U.S. IX Cranch 43 (1815).

United States v. St. Clair, 293 F.Supp. 337 (1968).

Washington, et al. v. Harold Glucksberg, et al., 521 U.S. 702 (1997).

Webster v. Reid, U.S. XI How. 437 (1850).

Index

ABOUT THE AUTHOR

Charles P. Nemeth is a member of the Pennsylvania, New York, and North Carolina Bars and has been active in all facets of criminal and civil practice for more than two decades. Dr. Nemeth has also held academic appointments at Niagara University, University of Baltimore, Rowan University, Waynesburg College, California University of Pennsylvania, and the State University of New York at Brockport, where he is currently Professor of Criminal Justice and Director of International Internships. He has published more than two dozen texts on a wide range of subjects, including criminal law and procedure; evidence, litigation, and appellate practice; canon law; real estate; and wills, estates, and trusts.